DIVINE FOREKNOWLEDGE AND MORAL RESPONSIBILITY (2ND EDITION)

DIVINE FOREKNOWLEDGE AND MORAL RESPONSIBILITY

Richard H. Corrigan

PROGRESSIVE FRONTIERS PRESS

GLOUCESTER

Divine Foreknowledge and Moral Responsibility
Richard H. Corrigan

Progressive Frontiers Press
Gloucester
www.frontierspublications.com

All rights reserved. No part of this publication may be reproduced, stored in a retrival system, or transmitted, in any form or by any means, electronic, photocopying, recording, or otherwise, without the prior written permission of the publisher.

Printed in the USA.

A Catalogue of this title is available from the British Library.

ISBN-13: 978-0-9563288-1-6

Preface

This is the second edition of this book - the first having been published by Prism Academic Publishing in 2007. This revised edition has been expanded to include a glossary and has been modified to allow for greater ease of reference.

The project that eventually resulted in this book was begun in 2003 as my doctoral dissertation at University College Dublin, under the supervision of the late Dr. Gerry Hanratty. Subsequently it benefitted from the input of Dr. Brendan Purcell and Dr. Rowland Stout.

Various parts of the text have been previously published in academic journals. The issues that are discussed in this volume have continued to fascinate me and have made a lasting impact on the direction of my subsequent research.

Richard H. Corrigan
BA, PGCE, MA, PhD

For Mary - my love, muse and inspiration.

Acknowledgements

I would particularly like to thank my mentors: Rowland Stout, Brendan Purcell and the late Gerry Hanratty. I would also like to thank my family, especially my mother whose support, generosity and insight have been boundless and my father who has been a true friend. I would also like to acknowledge my debt to my brother and sister. Peter and Elizabeth Farrell showed unbounded kindness and generosity of spirit to me when it was most needed. Finally, many thanks to Scruffy, Oscar, Charlie and Jefferson – who were with me through thick and thin.

Contents

Introduction — 1
0.1: Aim and Methodology — 1
0.2: Historical Context of the Problem — 1

Ch1: Morally Responsible Agency — 9
1.1: Introduction to Chapter 1 — 9
1.2: Reflection and the Moral Agent — 10
1.2.1: The Essential Indexical and Moral Responsibility — 10
1.2.2: First-Person Perspectives — 12
1.2.3: Deliberation and Moral Responsibility — 13
1.2.4: Moral Responsibility and the Concepts of Space and Time — 15
1.2.5: Conclusion to Section 1.2 — 15
1.3: Agency, Will, Desire and Moral Responsibility — 16
1.3.1: Ownership and the Will — 16
1.3.2: Ownership and Desire — 17
1.3.3 Conclusion to Section 1.3 — 21
1.4: Evaluation and Morally Responsible Agency — 22
1.4.0: Introduction to Section 1.4 — 22
1.4.1: Benefit and Desire — 22
1.4.2: Benefit and Second-Order Desires — 24
1.4.3: Value and Desire — 24
1.4.4: Evaluation and Motivational Systems — 27
1.4.5: Evaluation, Desire and Moral Responsibility — 29
1.4.6: Conclusion to Section 1.4 — 32
1.5: Conclusion to Chapter 1 — 32

Ch 2: Control and Morally Responsible Agency — 35

2.1: Introduction to Chapter 2 — 35

2.2: The Control Condition — 35

2.2.0: Introduction to Section 2.2 — 35

2.2.1: The Control Condition and Regulative Control — 35

2.2.2: The Principle of Moral Responsibility — 37

2.2.3: Conclusion to Section 2.2 — 37

2.3: Criteria for Responsibility Ascriptions Reconsidered — 38

2.3.0: Introduction to Section 2.3 — 38

2.3.1: Alternative Possibilities and Moral Responsibility Reconsidered — 38

2.3.2: Frankfurt's Principle of Responsibility — 39

2.3.3: Irresistible Desires — 40

2.3.4: Frankfurt's 'Addicts Example' — 44

2.3.5: A Criticism of Frankfurt's 'Addicts Example' — 45

2.3.6: Conclusion to Section 2.3 — 47

2.4: Jones-Style Examples — 48

2.4.0: Introduction to Section 2.4 — 48

2.4.1: An Introduction to Jones-Style Examples — 48

2.4.2: Jones-Style Examples and Irresistible Threat Contexts — 50

2.4.3: Conclusion to Section 2.4 — 51

2.5: The Principle of Possible Action — 52

2.5.0: Introduction to Section 2.5 — 52

2.5.1: An Introduction to the Principle of Possible Action — 52

2.5.2: PPA, FPR and Moral Responsibility — 53

2.5.3: Possible Action and Moral Maxims — 54

2.5.4: Conclusion to Section 2.5 — 57

2.6: Conclusion to Chapter 2	58

Ch 3: God's Essential Attributes and the Power to do Otherwise — 59

3.1: An Introduction to Chapter 3	59
3.2: The Attributes of God	**62**
3.2.0: Introduction to Section 3.2	62
3.2.1: God's Essential Attributes	64
3.3: The Question of the Compatibility of Divine Foreknowledge and the Power to do Otherwise	**67**
3.3.0: Introduction to Section 3.3	67
3.3.1: Pike on Divine Foreknowledge and the Power to do Otherwise	67
3.3.2: Pike's Proposition 1	69
3.3.3: Pike's Proposition 3	70
3.3.4: Pike's Proposition 2	73
3.4: Conclusion to Chapter 3	**74**

Ch 4: Ockhamism — 77

4.1: Introduction to Chapter 4	**77**
4.2: The Ockhamist	**77**
4.3: Necessity	**78**
4.3.0: Introduction to Section 4.3	78
4.3.1: Pike's Use of the Idea of Necessity	78
4.3.2: Accidental Necessity	80
4.3.3: An Ockhamist Response to Pike's Proposition 2	83
4.4: Hard and Soft Facts	**85**
4.4.0: Introduction to Section 4.4	85
4.4.1: Adams's Hard and Soft Fact Distinction	86

4.4.2: A Flaw in Adams's Hard and Soft Fact Distinction	89
4.4.3: Hoffman and Rosenkrantz's Solution to the Flaw in Adams's HSFD	90
4.5: Are God's Beliefs About the Future Hard or a Soft Facts? The First Attempt to Find an Answer	92
4.6: Hard and Soft Facts and Intuitive Plausibility	93
4.7: Fischer on God's Beliefs	95
4.7.0: Introduction to Section 4.7	95
4.7.1: Fischer's Incompatibilist Constraint	95
4.7.2: Fischer's Hard-Core Soft Facts	98
4.7.3: Fischer's Hard-Type Soft Facts	100
4.8: Hasker on God's Beliefs	102
4.8.0: An Introduction to Section 4.8	102
4.8.1: Hasker on Future Indifference	102
4.8.2: Hasker on Conceptual Consistency	105
4.9: More Problems, Zagzebski and Counterfactual Power	109
4.9.0: An Introduction to Section 4.9	109
4.9.1: Counterfactual Power and Plausibility	109
4.9.2: Zagzebski, Lewis and Counterfactual Fixity	116
4.10: Conclusion to Chapter 4	121

Ch 5: Molinism — 125

5.1: Introduction to Chapter 5	125
5.2: The Four Moments of God's Knowledge	126
5.2.0: Introduction to Section 5.2	126
5.2.1: The First Moment: Natural Knowledge	127
5.2.2: The Second Moment: Middle Knowledge	129

5.2.3: The Third Moment: The Creative Act of Will	132
5.2.4: The Fourth Moment: Free Knowledge	133
5.2.5: The Moments Reconsidered	135
5.3: Are There Limits to the Possible Worlds that God can Actualise?	137
5.3.0: Introduction to Section 5.3	137
5.3.2: God and Counterfactual Power	139
5.4: Difficulties for the Molinist	144
5.4.0: Introduction to Section 5.4	144
5.4.1: Molinism and the Law of Conditional Excluded Middle	144
5.4.2: The Grounding Objection	146
5.4.3: Counterfactuals, Truth-Makers and Brute Facts	149
5.4.4: Lewis and Flint on Counterfactuals	151
5.4.5: Lewis on Actuality	156
5.4.6: Subjunctives of Freedom and Agency	157
5.5: CCFs, Creaturely Essences and Brute Facts	158
5.6: Conclusion to Chapter 5	161

Ch 6: Final Discussion and Conclusions   163

References   169

Index   181

Introduction

0.1: Aim and Methodology

The primary aim of this work is to establish whether divine foreknowledge is compatible with morally responsible agency. What I mean by foreknowledge is knowledge that is temporally prior to the state of affairs to which it relates. In order to find a solution to the question I am examining, I will proceed in the following fashion. I will first offer an historical introduction and contextualization of the problem. I will then delineate what is involved in being a morally responsible agent. I will do this by establishing a set of criteria that the agent must be able to satisfy if he is to be capable of moral responsibility. When doing so I will refer to, and critically evaluate, recent literature that can lend insight and terminology.

I will assume a traditional conception of God and will proceed, where appropriate, to describe the divine attributes, powers and abilities that are essential to my discussion. I will then consider what modern philosophers, both compatibilist and incompatibilist, have to say about the particular powers that the agent would require the ability to exercise if he were to be capable of morally responsible action, given the existence of the divine attributes (and principally the existence of infallible foreknowledge).

First, I will test the validity of the claims of the incompatibilist in light of the insights offered by the Ockhamist, who has a sempiternal conception of God (i.e. that God is, in a significant sense, located 'in' time). I will then consider the Molinist conception of God as an atemporal entity whose foreknowledge is logically, rather than temporally, prior to the states of affairs to which it relates.

It is my ultimate intention to offer reasons why we should, or should not, argue for the compatibility of God's anterior knowledge of the agent's particular actions (whether this is understood to be temporal or logical) and morally responsible agency.

0.2: Historical Context of the Problem

I believe it prudent to begin by placing the question of the compatibility of divine foreknowledge and morally responsible agency in its historical context, and to show why it is a question that is still the subject of philosophical enquiry and debate. This will allow for an understanding of the way in which the question has arisen, and the way in which it has developed. It will also provide an understanding of the enduring significance of Medieval thought on the matter, and, more importantly, an understanding of the historical origins of modern Ockhamism and Molinism. These are two schools of thought that have their roots in the Medieval period and which have risen to the fore of modern enquiry into the question of God's infallible foreknowledge. Given their current importance, and the strength of the claims they make, I will consider whether they are capable of offering a means of refuting the incompatibilist thesis that divine foreknowledge is irreconcilable with any agent having the ability to act morally.

When we think of morally significant action we often take it for granted that a particular type of response is appropriate. This response involves the application of the categories of praise and blame. As early as in the Homeric Epics (c. 8 B.C.E.) we have illustrated examples in which individuals are considered to be appropriate candidates for the application of these categories, depending on how they conduct themselves. Generally, it was thought that when one did something that his society considered moral, such as risking his life to save his friend or community, the individual in question was deserving of praise. Conversely, when he did something believed to be morally inferior, he was deserving of blame. I will call the attitudes that accompany the application of these categories 'morally reactive attitudes'. To regard someone as praiseworthy or blameworthy is to implicitly assume that they have particular capacities that they have the power to exercise. Aristotle believed that moral responsibility rested on the capacity for decision making and voluntary action. To be morally responsible the individual had to be in control of his actions in a way that involved the origin of those actions residing in him.

I will use the term 'moral responsibility' to refer to a state of affairs in which an individual is an apt candidate for the justified application of moral categories and morally reactive attitudes. During the course of this work I will attempt to delineate exactly what this justification would involve.

Philosophical reflection on moral responsibility has a long and distinguished history. The questions of what comprises moral responsibility, how it can be characterised, and whether it is even possible given the nature of the world, have long been issues of debate in the philosophical community. This is, in part, because it is generally held that our conception of ourselves as agents is warranted. As agents we believe that we have characteristics that set us apart from non-rational animals. Part of this general conception of agency usually involves the conviction that we alone are capable of moral responsibility.

The problem that the philosopher encounters, when considering whether we are apt candidates for the application of moral categories, is the question of whether possible facts about the world, if proved true, would undermine our conception of ourselves as morally responsible agents. For example, if some factors fatalistically determined the particular actions and internal states of the individual, it may be impossible for us to coherently uphold the view that he is morally responsible for what he does. It is this concern that has given rise to many of the ideas that I will proceed to investigate and which has been the principal motivation of this work. The particular factor that I will focus on is the existence of divine foreknowledge. Thus, I am concerned with the question of whether the existence of God (conceived of as a perfect being), and his ability to foreknow all the particular states of affairs that will occur throughout the entire history of the world, gives sufficient conditions for the occurrence of all future states of affairs – including the particular actions of any individual. If this were the case, it could be argued that if God exists man has no significant power to affect the course of history - everything that occurs in the actual world has been fatalistically determined due to the existence of God, his particular capacity for knowledge, and the content of that knowledge. This idea is what I will call theological fatalism. It appears probable that the idea of theological fatalism developed as a consequence of the shift in Greek and Ancient Mesopotamian religions from polytheism to one sovereign or ultimate God. However, in terms of Christianity, the problem principally emerges from the Epistles of St. Paul.

Since the Stoics, the idea that different characterisations of determinism, if proved correct, would have particular ramifications on the possibility of moral responsibility has been a recurring issue in philosophical works. The Middle Ages saw the emergence of two of the greatest Christian thinkers – Augustine (354-430) and Aquinas (1225-1274) – both of whom addressed the issue of divine foreknowledge and moral responsibility, and attempted to refute the idea of theological fatalism.

Augustine believed that there are two claims that must be shown to be compatible if one is to be capable of validly asserting that divine foreknowledge can be reconciled with human freedom and moral responsibility. The first is that God has infallible foreknowledge of all future events, and the second is that man does not sin of necessity but through the exercise of free will (which he believed to be defective due to the 'Fall'). Thus, Augustine makes a connection between man's volition and his moral responsibility for his actions. As we will see, this is a connection that is still of great significance in the modern debate.

Augustine took the fact that God has infallible foreknowledge as a matter of faith to which the believer should assent. He believed that the question of the incompatibility of this foreknowledge and human responsibility only occurs because individuals approach it in an incorrect fashion - claiming that God's existence makes it impossible for man to be blameworthy for his actions. Augustine insisted that divine foreknowledge of man's future actions does not fatalistically entail its object. Thus, he argues that the way in which God foreknows is not incompatible with the agent's free exercise of his will. Once again, this is an issue that will prove to be of great influence on subsequent thought and the development of the subject. Augustine clearly states 'Though

God foreknows what we will do in the future this does not prove that we do not will anything voluntarily'. In the course of my investigation I will consider whether this position is tenable.

Augustine believed that there was no cause and effect relationship between what God knows will happen and what actually does happen. The basic argument is that the fact that God knows that I will do X does not make me (in the sense of deterministically causing me to) do X – there is no deterministic cause and effect relationship at play. Thus, he believed that the morally reprehensible actions that the agent does are not the necessary product of God's antecedent foreknowledge, they are rather the product of man's deviant exercise of his will and therefore the punishment that they incur from God is justified. We will see that yet again this is an idea that was to enormously influence succeeding thought.

St. Thomas also believed that God's infallible foreknowledge was compatible with free will and moral responsibility. For him, God knows not only the necessary and the actual, but also all possibilities or potentialities. Thus, God knows all things that could be known. Therefore, he argues that God has perfect knowledge of all future contingents. God is thought of as the cause of all things that exist. God has perfect knowledge of himself and all things that from our perspective have existed, do exist, or will exist, are known by him through himself – as he is their cause. For Aquinas, there is a sense in which the future is a possibility that has anterior existence in God as a possibility (before it is actualised through partaking in his causal efficacy). Thus God knows all future contingents, including the way in which the agent will freely exercise his will. Aquinas believed that God's foreknowledge of what an agent will do involves a future contingent and, therefore, it is argued that divine foreknowledge does not eliminate free will and moral responsibility. A contingent action is dependent on the free exercise of the will of the agent and cannot be necessitated by anterior states of affairs. Thus, although God's foreknowledge of future contingents is necessary, it does not necessitate the particular actions to which it relates.

The following are two ways in which necessity can be understood in relation to God's foreknowledge:

1. If God necessarily foreknows that I will do p, then necessarily I will do p.

2. If it is contingently true that I will do p, then God necessarily foreknows that I will do p.

If 1 is true then God's necessary knowledge entails the necessity of p – and this leads to theological fatalism. However, if 2 is true then the contingency of what is known is not affected by the fact that God necessarily foreknows it. I will consider both ways of viewing God's foreknowledge in the course of this book.

The influence of Aquinas was evidenced in the thought of his successors – even those who have not been directly associated with the Thomist School.

The relationship between necessary divine foreknowledge and contingent future occurrences was further developed by the English Franciscan Scholastic Philosopher; William of Ockham (c. 1280 – 1349). It is worth noting, however, that his teachings were firmly rejected by many Thomists who were his contemporaries. His writings, and especially relevant to this investigation his Treatise on Predestination and God's Foreknowledge with Respect to Future Contingents (1321-24), have had an influence that continues to be developed even today.

Ockham believed that there is a significant difference in the way that God knows and the way that the human being knows. He held that it is impossible for the human intellect to offer a demonstration of the truth of a future contingent that involves the exercise of the human will. This is because 'a future contingent fact simply depends on free power and hence is not true in itself'. The best that the fallible agent can achieve is to truly demonstrate 'either X will happen or X will not happen at time t'.

However, Ockham held through faith that it is without any doubt that God knows all future contingent facts evidently and with certainty. Ockham argued that the human intellect can know contingently true propositions through an intuition of their terms as given in experience (for example 'it is raining'). He then extended this line of thought by claiming the divine essence itself is an intuitive cognition by which are known not only necessary and contingent truths about a present fact, but also which side of a future contradiction will prove to be true and which will prove to be false. Thus, God does not only know that I will face a particular choice at some future time, for example that either I will go to work or I will not go to work tomorrow, but he actually knows which contingent fact will prove true and which will prove false. Ockham did not believe that there were any propositions that were not subject to the principle of excluded middle. He did not believe that necessary divine foreknowledge compromised human freedom and moral responsibility, as he was convinced that it was only in virtue of man's exercise of his free power to act in the way that he so chooses that makes it true that he will do a particular act at a particular time.

In the course of my investigations I will consider the thought of modern Ockhamists. Ockhamist thought has been recently revived and rejuvenated by the controversy stimulated by the following influential papers: Nelson Pike's 'Divine Omniscience and Voluntary Action' , John Turk Saunders' 'Of God and Freedom' and Marilyn Adams' 'Is the Existence of God a 'Hard Fact'?' The modern Ockhamist attempts to develop Ockham's claim that the content of God's anterior knowledge of an agent's future contingent actions is dependent on the agent's free exercise of his will at the time of choosing, and does not necessarily entail its object (in the sense suggested by the theological fatalist). The basic claim of the Ockhamist is that, if the agent had chosen other than he did choose in any particular instance, the content of God's foreknowledge would have reflected this fact. Thus, it is contended that a certain class of future contingent facts can have a factual consequent on the past – there is a particular class of facts about the past that are not immutably fixed, in so far as they are subject to a specific type of retro-qualification.

I believe that the modern Ockhamist position is one of the most comprehensive and convincing accounts of the compatibility of the divine foreknowledge and morally responsible agency. Therefore, I will proceed to subject it to further scrutiny and test its assumptions and conclusions.

Luis de Molina (1535-1600) attempted a different approach to that of Ockham. He was intimately acquainted with the work of St. Thomas, having taught on the Summa for over twenty years, and it was to prove influential in his writings. He believed that it was possible to coherently marry foreknowledge, providence, grace and free will.

Molina believed that God's comprehensive knowledge had four logically prioritized 'moments'. He was convinced that it is only through the efficacious contribution of the grace of God that any act could be realized. God offers sufficient grace to concur with morally superior action, but due to the inherent defects of man this grace often remains inefficacious. Thus, even though morally inferior acts require the cooperation of God for their realization, it can be claimed that these acts are permitted rather than intended by him. The deficiency of the act emerges from the deficiency of the agent and not from God's activity.

Molina also believed that the world was the product of divine providence. Nothing occurs that is not in accordance with the will of God – every occurrence is either willed by God or permitted by him.

According to Molina's account, it is due to his prevolitional knowledge and the direction of his will that God can comprehensively foreknow all future states of affairs – including contingent events. God does not have to refer to the external world to see what effects his will has brought about. There are no contingent truths about the world that will be actual until God intends them, or permits them to be true through his act of will.

Molina contended, against the Bañezian Thomists, that God's cooperating grace is neither in itself efficacious or inefficacious. Through prevolitional 'Natural' Knowledge he knows all metaphysically necessary truths, through 'Middle-Knowledge' he knows all metaphysically contingent propositions involving facts about how any undetermined creature would freely act if instantiated in any particular possible state of affairs. He then directs his will such that the possible world that is most in accordance with his desires is actualised. Finally, through his postvolitional 'Free Knowledge' he knows how the creatures he has actualised will in fact proceed to freely act and how he will lend them power through his co-operating grace. Molina believed that this process ensured the freedom and responsibility of man, because God's Middle Knowledge includes knowledge of the contingent free actions that any possible individual would choose to do if he were instantiated in any particular possible state of affairs. God then directs his will such that particular agents are instantiated in specific states of affairs. It can therefore be argued that when acting in morally significant contexts man's actions are contingent (product of an indeterministic secondary cause) and therefore free.

Modern Molinists have taken the insights of Molina and further developed them. They, similar to the Ockhamists, claim that God can have infallible knowledge of future contingent facts about what the agent will do without fatalistically determining the particular actions of that agent. However, they do so in a substantively different fashion. It is because of this fact that I will proceed to consider whether they can offer a viable alternative to the incompatibilist's fatalistic thesis.

Before fully engaging in the question of whether divine foreknowledge is compatible with moral responsibility it is first essential to establish exactly what is meant by a 'morally responsible agent', for it is this type of agent that will be the centre of the majority of my investigations. I will, therefore, proceed to the first chapter.

1

Morally Responsible Agency

1.1: Introduction to Chapter 1

It is my contention that an essential element of the investigation of moral responsibility involves providing an account of a certain kind of agency. This is because the kind of agency in question is specifically that of being a suitable candidate for the application of moral categories. In Chapter 1 I will endeavour to describe this type of agency and to delineate the capacities and abilities that it involves. I will also attempt to justify my account.

However, during the course of my inquiries in this chapter there will be issues that are raised but not adequately resolved. Therefore, it will also serve to establish many of the areas that I will investigate in the following chapters.

In short, the purpose of this Chapter will be to delineate the capabilities and capacities that the individual must possess in order to qualify as a morally responsible agent. It is my contention that an understanding of what I call 'moral agency' is a prerequisite for a comprehensive conception of what it means to be morally responsible.

It is not my intention to provide an account of agency in and of itself, for I will allow that there may be states of agency that do not require moral responsibility. It is rather my objective to provide an account of the traits essential to morally responsible agency. By a 'morally responsible agent' I mean an agent that is a suitable candidate for the justified application of moral categories.[1] Therefore, I will not argue for a strong notion of agency that claims that agency is equivalent to the capacity for moral responsibility (as it is not necessary to do so in order to pursue my guiding hypothesis). I will instead permit the possibility that one can be an agent without being capable of moral responsibility (whilst also acknowledging that the strong notion of agency may be equally valid).

Exactly what my idea of morally responsible agency involves will become apparent through the course of my investigation and will be defined, to the extent made possible by the investigations of Sections 1.2 – 1.4, in the conclusion to this

---

1   To define exactly what constitutes justification in the context of the application of moral categories will be one of the primary aims of this thesis.

chapter. This definition will take the form of criteria that the agent must have the capacity to fulfil, if he is to be capable of moral responsibility. A further criterion will be added at the end of Chapter 2.

1.2: Reflection and the Moral Agent

1.2.1: The Essential Indexical and Moral Responsibility

Non-human animals are capable of action; however, we do not suppose that they are morally responsible for the actions that they perform, as they lack the requisite type of rationality. I will argue that in order to be morally responsible one must be self-aware, and be in possession of certain cognitive capacities including reflective deliberation. I will begin by considering the importance of self-consciousness.

The thought of John Perry will help us to understand the significance of self-awareness to moral responsibility. He asserts that nothing can be successfully substituted for the idea of 'I' and refines this idea into the concept of the 'essential indexical.'[2] The essential indexical relates to one's comprehension of those elements of the self that that one understands as constituting the 'I' that one uses when referring to oneself. What makes the indexical essential is that it grounds any specification by the agent of his actions and intentions. Perry believes that the ability to utilise the essential indexical is integral to the capacity to understand one's responsibility for one's actions.

Perry undertakes a thought experiment to determine how he can come to a certain conclusion that the person making a mess in a store is in fact himself. He argues that without some knowledge of himself as himself, it would be impossible to reach the conclusion that it is *he* who is responsible for the action. He needs to be able to make an inferential move from a description of the protagonist making the mess, to the conclusion that part of that description applies to him; if he is to be able to recognise his responsibility (I will differentiate different types of responsibility below). It may even be the case that without this ability he is incapable of being in any way responsible for his actions (I will return to this point in due course).

To recognise his responsibility requires a knowledge of himself, a knowledge of the 'I' that he believes constitutes himself. No matter how complete the description of the events that have transpired, it would be impossible for him

---

2   Perry (1993).

to recognise the person being described as him, or to be aware that he is in fact in the location being alluded to, if he had no knowledge of himself as an 'I'.

One can suggest that while it is true that Perry's hypothetical agent could not know that he is responsible for an act unless he has access to the notion of the essential indexical, it is still possible that he is unknowingly responsible for his actions. In order to address this concern it is necessary to refine our understanding of the different ways in which we use the term 'responsible'.

I will delineate the two usages of the term that are most pertinent to this discussion. These are (i) 'causal responsibility' and (ii) 'moral responsibility'. It is my claim that an individual in Perry's hypothetical situation, who is incapable of using the essential indexical, is an instrumental cause of the actions that he undertakes (that is, making a mess in a store), but is neither causally nor morally responsible for them. One is causally responsible for an action/event if one is responsible for causing the action/event to occur (this may involve causally instigating the action/event or providing an essential causal contribution to the sufficient conditions for the action/event in question. There are certain conditions that are essential to the type of causal contribution that is necessary for causal responsibility – however it is not necessary to delineate them at this stage of the investigation).

An individual who is incapable of recognising and utilising the essential indexical is arguably incapable of intentional action. This brings into question the validity of the claim that he can be causally responsible for his actions. If he does not intend his actions, then it is difficult to uphold the idea that they are *his* in any meaningful way (that he is the cause of them in a significant sense). It is possible that the actions that he performs are nothing more than the product of blind mechanistic causes, and that he acts only in the capacity of a causal instrument. I will make note of this possibility but will not pursue it further, as it is not essential to this enquiry. I will instead return to the question of the necessity of the capacity to use the essential indexical for moral responsibility.

If we are to assert that an individual is morally responsible for his conduct, then it must be possible that he be able to evaluate his actions – that he be capable of identifying those actions as *his own*. If he cannot identify his actions as his own then it appears that it is impossible for him to consider other courses of action with which he should want to identify (that is, in order for his actions to be morally sound).

We can have no expectation of good will from Perry's agent.[3] If the agent cannot understand that an action belongs to him then he cannot learn to take moral responsibility for it, and modify his future actions in light of its moral

---

3   Strawson (1982) believes that the expectation of good will is fundamental to interpersonal relations.

status. He cannot be considered a moral being if he does not understand that his actions are his own. Moral responsibility involves the ability to take ownership of one's actions (even if one does not in fact do so it must be the case that one can do so). I expand upon this claim in Sections 1.3 and 1.4.

I will hypothesise that the form of self-consciousness that the ability to utilise the essential indexical minimally allows is not sufficient for moral responsibility, although it is essential to it. In order to validate this theory I will consider different grades of consciousness and self-consciousness.

1.2.2: First-Person Perspectives

Baker argues that all self-consciousness rests on what she calls the 'first-person perspective.'[4] In order to describe how this perspective operates she divides the way in which creatures have perspectives into two distinct grades – 'weak' and 'strong.'

According to her, all problem-solving animals exhibit 'weak' first person phenomena. This is perspectival in that what is known reflects the animal's ways and means of knowing it. She believes that the non-reflective animal is capable of perspectival thought, it realises that an object is here and not there. It is the origin of the perspective.

Baker argues that because the animal is only capable of a weak first-person perspective, it is not aware of the fact that the perspective that it has is only one of a possible multitude. The animal is thus capable of having a perspective, but is incapable of realising that it is 'his' perspective, as distinct from another conscious creature's perspective (or another possible creature's perspective).[5] Consequently, she believes that only those creatures that exhibit what she terms strong first-person phenomena are capable of perceiving themselves as a first-person entity. I will now ask what is involved in having a strong first-person perspective.

An agent who is capable of strong first-person phenomena (that is, of having a strong first-person perspective) knows that an object is here and not there. He also knows that he has a distinct relation to the object separate from any other creature's perspective. This allows him to situate himself in the world as an agent

---

4   See Baker (2000).
5   I shall conjecture that in order to be able to understand that other creatures have perspectives different to our own, it is necessary that one be able to imagine alternative perspectives (that is, one must be able to imagine the content of alternative perspectives, even if one is not in fact accurate in what one imagines constitutes another creatures perspective). If this is not the case then the argument lacks coherency. This point is discussed in detail in Subsection 1.2.3.

and to realise that the actions that he performs have ramifications for others who do not have a perspective identical to his. This is an ability that Perry's agent, who is capable of utilising the essential indexical, does not necessarily have (I will further clarify this point below). It is my contention that having a strong first-person perspective would allow him to imagine a possible perspective that another agent/creature might be in possession of, and to factor that into his decision making process (the importance of this ability is further discussed below). To this extent, it can be said that the agent with strong first-person phenomena has a certain understanding of, and a possible empathy with, other agents/creatures. I will attempt to show that this capability is essential to morally responsible agency.

Is Baker's conception of strong self-consciousness more than what is necessary for morally responsible agency? It may be possible to achieve a level of deliberation that falls short of Baker's criteria, but still allows for self-consciousness. Consider the following example. Entity B is capable of the following type of deliberation: 'If food is my goal then I cannot have sex now. If sex is my goal then I may go hungry. But my not having sex now is compatible with my having sex later. So food should be my goal now.' This individual is capable of utilising the concept of personal goals and of evaluating individual ends. He has the ability to utilise the essential indexical. He is also capable of projecting his goals into the future and of understanding particular consequences of his actions. This appears to be sufficient for us to credit him with a type of strong self-consciousness,[6] but is it sufficient for moral responsibility?[7]

The above individual does not necessarily have the ability to see his perspective as one of a possible multitude. Why should we therefore insist that he must have this ability if we are to credit him with a level of self-consciousness and reflective deliberation sufficient for moral responsibility? Why is it not enough that he has self-consciousness and is capable of formulating alternative personal goals?

1.2.3: Deliberation and Moral Responsibility

Entity B realises the possibility of pursuing two alternative goals and some of the possible consequences of doing so. The two goals in question are food and sex. But he realises that if he pursues food he will have the possibility of satisfying

---

6   There is no self-apparent reason why an agent must be capable of strong first-person phenomena in order to be capable of this level of deliberation. It may be possible that an agent realise that a goal is *his* goal without also realising that there are others who have goals that are not identical to it. However, I shall not extensively engage with this issue, as my primary concern is that of morally responsible agency.

7   I shall not engage with the question of whether Entity B can be categorised as an agent. I will accept that it is a possibility that he could, but this is not pertinent to my investigation.

his sexual appetite later, whereas if he satisfies the latter first he may go hungry as a consequence. After deliberation he reaches the conclusion that he should avail of the food while he has the opportunity. What I would now like to address is the kind of deliberation that is involved in this decision.

Entity B is capable of what I will call basic prudential deliberation. He is capable of a specific type of analysis that allows him to evaluate what is in his own best interest in certain types of circumstances. But does this capacity allow for moral evaluation? I would conjecture that it does not. To illustrate my point I will make use of another example. Entity B finds himself in a position where he can avail of food that does not belong to him. He is aware that there are certain risks involved in getting it, but because of his deliberative level he is capable of weighing up the risks and decides that he will take the food. He also realises that if he does not then he may go hungry. I will say that it is prudential, from his perspective, in the given circumstances, to take the food (given that he does not realise that his perspective is only one of a possible multitude).

Does his act deserve moral approbation or condemnation? I will say that these categories cannot be justifiably applied for several reasons. Entity B is incapable of empathising with the negative effects that his actions may have on others. He is incapable of stepping outside of his particular perspective, of considering another's perspective, or of even considering an alternative perspective that he himself might have (he is incapable of strong first-person phenomena[8]). He cannot be blamed for not choosing to do other than he does in light of the moral deficiency of his actions, because he is incapable of transcending his personal perspective and objectively analysing the moral worth of his actions. He is incapable of the particular type of evaluative analysis and judgement essential to morally responsible agency.[9] This would require the ability to imagine a perspective other than the one that he actually has.

If one cannot imagine a perspective other than one's own actual perspective, then it is impossible to objectively evaluate the moral status of one's actions.[10] If an individual cannot place himself in the position of another individual who will be affected by his actions, then it appears impossible to blame him for not considering the effects that his actions will have on that other person.[11] It is my

---

8   An individual that does not have strong first-person phenomena may have a perspective and still be incapable of understanding that he could have an alternative perspective. He is caught in the immediacy of his subjectivity – he cannot reflectively divorce himself from the perspective that he actually has. He is incapable of realising that the perspective he has is only one of a possible multitude.
9   The type of evaluative and analysis that is required is given further consideration in Section 1.4.
10 Nagel (1979) discusses the importance of being capable of adopting the 'view from nowhere' – the objective point of view.
11 One could claim that the agent does not need to imagine the perspective of another

claim that this is an essential ability for morally responsible agency.

One may object that it is correct to blame the racist who simply fails to recognise that his perspective is only one of many alternative perspectives. We can respond that until he has made this realisation (for whatever reason or through whatever route) there would be no possibility of him changing. What though if his lack of imagination was wilful or due to laziness? I would argue that in this latter instance the individual can be blamed for his attitude precisely because he has the capacity to imagine other perspectives and yet chooses or neglects to exercise it. If an individual has the capacity to exercise an ability that allows for moral responsibility he has the duty to employ it.

1.2.4: Moral Responsibility and the Concepts of Space and Time

Moral responsibility is not a purely internal phenomenon, it also incorporates man's interactions with those things that are situated outside of him and which have a discrete existence. Therefore, one must be capable of utilising the concepts of space and time. It is my claim that one must be able to recognise oneself as existing in an objective world (so as to be able to avail of the concept of discrete spatial locations) and know when a specific time is alluded to. This is essential if one is to recognise that one was/is/will be accountable for a specific action that occurred/is occurring/will occur in a specific location at a specific time.

If the agent cannot recognise that his actions will have immediate and/or future consequences that affect other discrete individuals then it is difficult to imagine how he could be morally responsible for his actions. This point has been implicitly assumed in much of the preceding discussion.

1.2.5: Conclusion to Section 1.2

In conclusion to this section I will begin to list the various attributes that one can now insist the agent must possess if he is to be capable of moral responsibility. I believe that the analysis that I have undertaken in this section is sufficient to justify the following criteria.

The morally responsible agent must:

   (i)   Be capable of utilising the essential indexical.

---

creature but only needs to be able to imagine what his perspective would be if he were placed in the circumstances in question. However, this does not alleviate the problem as it still requires the ability to imagine multiple perspectives and this requires strong first-person phenomena.

(ii) Exhibit strong first-person phenomena.

(iii) Be capable of a specific type of deliberation that incorporates the ability to imagine other possible perspectives.

(iv) Be capable of recognising that he exists in an objective world and understand the concepts of space and time.

1.3: Agency, Will, Desire and Moral Responsibility

In this section I attempt to show why the ability to act in accordance with a will with which he identifies (in a particular way) is crucial to the agent's capacity to take ownership of his actions, which itself is necessary for morally responsible agency.

1.3.1: Ownership and the Will

We have so far seen that, in order to be morally responsible for what he does, the agent must be able to utilise the essential indexical. We have seen that this capacity involves a comprehension of the concept of an 'I' that he understands as constituting him. This is a part of what ultimately allows him to appreciate that a particular action is his.[12] However, this is not all that is involved in the ability to take ownership of an action. To be morally responsible for an act requires that the agent have the capacity to identify the action for which he is to be blamed or praised as his in a particular way. This has not been adequately dealt with in my discussion of the essential indexical and strong first-person phenomena. I will now proceed to ask what this means, and what further capacities it involves. I will primarily focus on the issue of ownership first, and then progress to the matter of its relationship to moral responsibility.

It is important to be aware that my current enterprise is to delineate the capacities and abilities that the agent must be *capable* of exercising if he is to be morally responsible, irrespective of whether he does in fact choose to exercise them. This is because there is a significant difference between being able to do something and actually doing it – and I maintain that in many instances the former is all that is required for morally responsible agency. This will be made apparent through examples, arguments and illustrations.

---

12 Recall the example I have discussed regarding the agent's ability to identify the fact that the person making a mess in a store is in fact him.

What are the conditions that allow an agent to take ownership of a specific action? Firstly, the agent must be able to act such that what he does is in accordance with his will. He must also intuitively understand that this is the case – he must be capable of knowing that his action is something that he willed to occur – something that he desired to happen (in a particular sense), and something that he made happen (this presupposes a knowledge of the essential indexical and is part of strong first-person phenomena).

What do we mean when we refer to the agent's 'will'? Frankfurt offers us the following characterization:

> To identify the agent's will is either to identify the desire (or desires) by which he is motivated in some action he performs or to identify the desire (or desires) by which he will or would be motivated when or if he acts… it is the notion of an effective desire, one that moves (or will or would move) a person all the way to action.[13]

The agent's will is not just what he desires to do, but what he desires to do enough to move him to actually do it. The effective desire is thus the agent's will – even if (in some sense) he would like to have done a different action to X, but actually performs X, we can still say that he was moved by the desire to X, and that this was what effected his will (assuming that he was not compelled by external factors). This is the definition that I will adopt, and it is this characterisation that I will mean when referring to the will from this point onwards.

If the agent is not aware that the actions that he performs are the product of his will (either implicitly or explicitly), then it is difficult to imagine a way in which we could assert that those actions are his in any significant sense (this would be like the case of a non-rational animal – we would say that it is capable of acting, but not capable of taking ownership of what it does) – he might have a will, but it would be *his* will in a very weak sense (as he would not identify it as his – he would not be capable of strong first-person phenomena).

1.3.2: Ownership and Desire

My definition of the agent's will involves an understanding of his desire, but what do I mean when I say that an agent has a 'desire'? My general definition of a desire is: a particular type of feeling that accompanies an unsatisfied state; a want for something to obtain – but, as I am currently investigating ownership of action,

---

13   Frankfurt (1971), p. 8.

desires may also be understood as a disposition or tendency act in a particular way that is felt with varying degrees of intensity. It is my contention that there are different orders of desires, and I will now attempt to give an account of them.

To say that a creature wants something, or desires something, can be confusing, as there are different ways in which this assertion may be interpreted.[14] This is shown to be true when we consider that (a) a creature may simply desire to X in a way that does not involve, or require, any reflective analysis of whether it wants to have that desire (this form of desire does not require rationality) or, (b) it may, upon reflection, want it's desire to X – I will call this identifying with a desire (that is, identifying with a particular desire of type (a) is synonymous with wanting to have that particular desire of type (a)). For the remainder of this discussion, unless otherwise stipulated, the terms 'want' and 'desire' are to be understood as synonymous.

These forms of wanting or desiring, although related, are significantly different. All conscious creatures are capable of (a) but only creatures with the capacity for reflective thought are capable of (b) (it is my claim that this is therefore a part of what constitutes strong first-person phenomena). Frankfurt calls (a) a first-order desire and (b) a second-order desire. Second-order desires require that the agent be able to offer some reason/s for his identification with a first-order desire – I will show below that the reasons that can be provided are reflective of the way in which that identification occurs and the factors that are involved.[15]

Desire ascriptions are key components of rationalisations of intentional action – and I have already argued that the ability to act intentionally is a prerequisite for moral responsibility (if one is incapable of intending what it is that one does then one cannot be held responsible for it, as one can exercise no control over it. The issue of control is dealt with in Chapter 2).[16]

A first-order desire causes the agent to feel some discomfort that he wants to alleviate by bringing about a particular state of affairs – by acting in a particular fashion.[17] This is what I mean when I say that first-order desires give rise to propensities, dispositions or tendencies to act. Desire is essentially related to pleasure (or satisfaction) and pain (or dissatisfaction), although identical to neither.[18]

The fact that an agent has a desire offers some reason as to why he acts in a

---

14 Ibid, p. 7.
15 For a discussion of the relation between reason and desire see Stampe (1987) and Schueler, (1995), esp. pp. 33-35.
16 Platts (1986), p. 143.
17 See Schiffer (1976), pp. 351-352 for a discussion of the ways in which desires can be reason-providing.
18 See Bradley (1888), pp. 16 ff.

certain fashion, irrespective of whether there are other 'strong' reasons or not.[19] What I mean is that the agent can rationalise his act to the extent that he can offer his desire to act in a particular way as a reason for his actually doing so. What I mean by 'strong' reasons for acting are reasons that appeal to more than just first-order desires in the rationalisation of an action (I do not mean to imply that in the sense I am proposing a 'strong' reason is necessarily an objectively valid reason).

Let us consider the following: Jones wants to strike Black (first-order desire) and proceeds to act on that desire. We can say that Jones' first-order desire was reason providing, to the extent that, if questioned, Jones can offer his desire as a rationalisation of his action – 'I struck Black because I desired (or wanted) to do so'. However, this is not what I have referred to as a strong reason; a strong reason would involve further justification. One does not automatically have such further justification for one's action each time one acts in accordance with a first-order desire. Further justification might include the fact that by acting in a particular fashion one believed oneself to be acting morally, to be acting in a way that is reflective of the sort of person that one wants to be, because one believes that certain goals and ends will be promoted or satisfied, and so forth.

One can, of course, have conflicting first-order desires – and this can give rise to the agent feeling torn between alternative desires.[20] Thus, often in satisfying one desire the agent frustrates another. We will see that this is especially significant when considering the agent's responsibility for what he does. In future subsections I will speak of desires as having different strengths and of them effecting the agent's will (that is, constituting it).

The agent is capable of taking ownership of his actions when he can act in accordance with a desire with which he identifies. Part of what I mean by this is that an agent has ownership of his action if it issued from a desire that he wanted to be his will. This is because he did exactly what he wanted to do without external interference (for future reference, I will include pathological conditions that determine an individual's will as an external interference) and he wanted to have the desire that effected his will. That is not to say that second-order desires are necessarily reflective of

> ...what [the agent] would want himself to want... were he to contemplate his present situation from a standpoint fully and vividly informed about himself and his circumstances, and entirely free of cognitive error or lapses of instrumental rationality.[21]

Second-order desires are reflective of what the agent actually wants to desire

---

19 Stampe (1987), pp. 342-343.
20 For a discussion of this issue see Neely (1974), p. 39.
21 Railton (1986), p. 16.

given the conditions in which he finds himself placed (including such factors as his psychological constitution, beliefs[22] and the information that he is taking into account).

Because it is possible to gain a new perspective at any time, the agent's second-order desires can change. Once he identifies with a particular desire he is not then bound such that he cannot cease in that identification. Any number of things could give the impetus for such a change. Just because the agent once identified with a desire does not mean that he will always do so – this is evidenced in the everyday world where people often change their minds about what it is that they really want (when I refer to an agent 'really' wanting something, I mean that he has a second-order desire for it).

Does an agent have no ownership of an act if it issued from a first-order desire with which he would not want to identify? This does not necessarily follow. One may point out that people often do not take ownership of the questionable things that they do, but that this does not mean that they have no ownership of those acts. It may be possible that an agent can ignore his ability to reflect on whether he wants to act in accordance with an immediate (first-order) desire. Let us return the example of Jones' assault on Black. We will assume that Jones does not want to have the desire to assault others because he is angry – but that does not mean, in itself, that he has no ownership of his action. He still did exactly what he wanted to do, and could have done otherwise if he had so chosen (this is assuming that it was not a reflex action).

It is the capacity to make a desire with which he identifies his will that allows us (assuming the fulfilment of the other conditions that I am extrapolating) to assert that Jones has ownership of what he has done – he could have taken the time to consider whether or not he really wanted the desire to strike Black. If he found that he did not have that second-order desire, then in virtue of this fact he could have made some other desire his will, and thereby not acted such that an unwanted desire became his will. This sounds very complicated, but in practice it could be accomplished by Jones asking himself the simple question 'Do I really want to strike Black?' and then acting, or not acting, so as to be in accord with the answer.

Jones has ownership of the action he performed precisely because it resulted from his choice to act in accordance with a desire with which he would not want to identify, or, because he negligently abdicated his ability to judge whether he 'really' wanted to do something else, and then act on that judgement. To say that, at the time of acting, he never even considered whether he would identify with the desire that gave rise to his act is no excuse.

If the agent does not consider whether he really wants to do something before

---

22 See Price (1989), Broome (1991) and MacKay, (1982).

he does it, then this is due to either negligence or intention on his part, and either way this does not mitigate his ownership of what he does. The agent may own an action that he does not want to own, or denies owning. Jones has ownership of what he has done because he had the capacity to act in accordance with one of his second-order desires or, alternatively, not to act at all. In refusing to question the status of the desire upon which he acts, there is a sense in which he is implicitly aware that there is a chance that the act that he performs is something that he will regret. Therefore, not exercising the capacity to consider whether an act is accordance with a second-order desire is no excuse when it comes to the agent's ownership of the action that ensues and the states of affairs that it gives rise to. Jones may not willingly take ownership of his action, but that does not mean that he has no ownership of it.

If Jones did not have the capacity to take ownership of his actions, through acting in accordance with his second-order desires (that is, the capacity to have a will with which he identifies), then he could not have responsibility for anything he does, as he would never have any control over the content of his will (in the sense of ensuring that a desire that he wants effects it) – he would merely unreflectively respond to the strongest first-order desire that arose. He could not act intentionally. He would be incapable of taking ownership of his actions in an apposite way. The morally responsible agent must be able to understand (implicitly) that the will with which he acts is his will, and that the acts that come about are the product of his desires. Furthermore, he must be able to identify with the will that he has – he must be able to exercise control over the content of his will, in the sense of ensuring that a desire that he wants to have effects it (once again, irrespective of whether he actually does so).

Conclusion to Section 1.3

In conclusion, it is my claim that the ability to take ownership of his actions isessential to the agent's moral responsibility for them. In order to assert that an agent is morally responsible for an act X it must be possible to ascribe ownership of that action to him. He must be able to understand why it is he who is to be praised or blamed for an action or state of affairs – he must understand that the action is his in a particular way. Part of any such understanding will rely on the agent being able to act in accordance with his will, and his having the capacity to have a will with which he identifies (this is of course accepting that the desire in question can be fulfilled. Not all desires can be fulfilled – for instance, one may desire to never die.[23] One can do nothing to make the desired state of affairs obtain). It also assumes that he does not have to act in accordance with a desire

---

23   Platts (1986), p. 143.

with which he does not identify.[24] This is part of what constitutes strong first-person phenomena.

My investigation of the agent's will and desires will now allow the addition of a further condition to the criteria of morally responsible agency.

The morally responsible agent must:

> (v) Be capable of having ownership of his actions in an apposite way – this requires being able to act in accordance with a will with which he identifies (which involves the ability to form second-order desires and act in conformity with them).

In the next section I will consider the role of judgement in morally responsible agency. I will also investigate why it is that an agent comes to identify with one desire (second-order desire) as opposed to another and how this has significance for morally responsible agency.

1.4: Evaluation and Morally Responsible Agency

1.4.0: Introduction to Section 1.4

This Section explores the areas of desire, value, and motivation and their relationship to morally responsible agency. I set down further requirements that must be fulfilled if the agent is to have the capacity for moral responsibility.

1.4.1: Benefit and Desire

We have already seen that the ability to act intentionally is essential to moral responsibility. I will now argue that the agent must believe that the action that he intends to do is in some way beneficial, if he is to intentionally perform it.[25] Davidson believes that this has 'an air of self-evidence' as 'in so far as a person acts

---

24   Although here I should make clear that it may be possible to hold an agent morally responsible for the actions that he now performs, even if he can no longer act such that he identifies with his will, in special circumstances. For example, if someone intentionally started taking drugs, in full knowledge that it could lead to addiction, then later acts of drug-taking may still be in some sense deemed morally reprehensible due to the fact that the agent negligently placed himself in such a position at a time when he still could have acted in accordance with a will with which he would identify.
25   See Kenny (1968), p. 154 and Miller (1982), pp. 106-108.

intentionally he acts, as Aquinas put it, in the light of some imagined good'.[26] In this context 'imagined good' is to be understood as identical to 'expected benefit'.[27]

It is the expected benefit that provides the stimulus for the agent to act on a particular desire – it is what lends motivational strength to a desire (I make a distinction between the 'strength' and 'intensity' of a desire below). In order for a specific desire to become the agent's will, the expected benefit of fulfilling it must have a sufficient degree of motivational efficacy. By motivational efficacy I mean sufficient motivational power to make the desire his will. Thus, I am claiming that there is a relationship between expected benefit and effective desire – only if there is an expected benefit in satisfying a desire will the agent be moved to act on it. As doing something of benefit involves the fulfilment of a desire, there is an element of satisfaction in making it obtain (see Section 1.3). This satisfaction will always be part of the expected benefit. I will proceed to argue that motivational strength is proportional to expected benefit and will attempt to provide reasons why this is the case.

What the agent believes it is most beneficial for him to do in a particular circumstance will include his belief as to what is accomplishable.[28] It will also reflect his system of values, and his general dispositions and tendencies.[29] This conception is not necessarily synonymous with what would be actually (or objectively) most beneficial - it may be the case that what he imagines to be beneficial will actually have a negative consequence, or would not be thought of as beneficial if he had more information or insight.[30] It is rather that he believes that performing a particular action (satisfying a particular desire) has the greatest potential to be of benefit at the time of acting (this will obviously reflect how much consideration he has given the issue and his hierarchy of values).[31]

The agent will not always judge the act that he performs to be of greater benefit than any other act; he may just act in accordance with his most intense first-order

---

26 Davidson (1980), p. 22. See also Anscombe (1958), esp. p. 37, who makes a similar observance when speaking of 'desirability characteristics'.
27 'Expected benefit' is to be understood as a blanket term. For example, one may insist that when one is acting from duty one is not necessarily acting in order to achieve a particular 'benefit'. However, all that I mean is that the agent must in such cases take it for granted that there is some sense in which it is beneficial to act according to duty – for example that it is beneficial in the sense of bringing some kind of satisfaction to the agent.
28 Even in cases where the agent does not believe what he is about to do is accomplishable he still believes that the attempt is beneficial. He can perform the attempt even if he cannot fulfil it – therefore one can state that the attempt itself is accomplishable (even if it does not succeed).
29 See Geiger (1925), p. 636.
30 For a discussion of desires and the agent's best interests see Murphy (1999).
31 See Parfitt (1984), p. 247.

desire without deliberation (see Section 1.3). This operates in the same fashion as the agent's abdication of his capacity to act in accordance with a desire with which he identifies. However, even then he would be acting in order to gain a benefit (though not necessarily what he would judge to be the greatest benefit were he to take the time to consider) – the sense of promotion of pleasure and avoidance of pain that manifests itself as the result of fulfilling a desire.

1.4.2: Benefit and Second-Order Desires

If second-order desires are to have any explanatory efficacy it must be possible to provide an account of why the agent wants to have one desire above another. If an agent identifies with a desire he must be able to explain why. There must be reasons for his doing so – there must be reasons that he can offer by way of justification for his identification (these reasons may be 'good' or 'bad' – in the sense of actually being valid or not – nevertheless, the agent must be convinced that they serve to justify).[32] If there were not, we would be left with the puerile and uninformative claim that the agent wants a desire for no further reason.

We have seen that second-order desires are desires that the agent wants to have – they are therefore desires that he believes to be of benefit. The capacity for evaluative judgement is essential to the ability to form effective second-order desires. The agent must be able to want to have a particular desire more than some other conflicting desire. In order to be able to do so, he must be able to judge that a particular desire is more beneficial than one or more others.

The agent wants to have the desires that he judges to be of greatest benefit, or which lead to states of affairs that he judges to be so – this will inherently be part of any justification for his identification with them (that is not to say that he does not think there would be any benefit in identifying with those desires that he does not actually want – it is rather that the degree or type of benefit is not sufficient for his identifying with it – I have already suggested that the idea of benefit that has motivational efficacy is dependent on the particular system of values that moves the agent to action – see Subsection 1.4.1). He can therefore account for his identification with a desire in terms of the benefits that he judges it will yield.

In conclusion to this subsection, my claim is that the capacity for evaluative judgement is essential to morally responsible agency.

1.4.3: Value and Desire

Watson draws a distinction, in the Platonic tradition, between valuing and

---

32 See Aaronovitch (1979), esp. pp. 173-176.

desiring.³³ Thus, he believes that when the agent refers to what he wants most, he is not necessarily confined to dealing exclusively with those things that he *desires* the most; he can also be referring to what he *values* the most. Is this merely a clever semantic turn? Watson would insist that there is a definite and substantial difference in drawing this distinction. He believes that one can have a hierarchy of values that, while related to one's desires, is not dependent on them. Thus, one can be moved to pursue that which one does not desire the most because one is moved by one's value system to attempt to realise an alternative state of affairs to that which one desires.

But, we may ask, is the question of desire misconstrued by Watson? Perhaps it is not the case that the agent is not moved to realise what he desires most, but rather what he desires most is to see his hierarchy of values reflected in his actions? He identifies with this desire because what he values most is what he believes to be of greatest benefit (I am referring to the agent's actual values and not values that he might like to have or believes are worth having).³⁴

He responds to this criticism by insisting that there are (i) "instances in which that which is desired is not valued to any degree and is not held to be worthwhile, or thought good [beneficial]".³⁵ It is also possible that (ii) "the strength of one's desire may not properly reflect the degree to which one values its object; that is, although the object of desire is valuable, it may not be deemed the most valuable in the situation and yet one's desire for it may be stronger than the want for what is most valued".³⁶ I will now test the validity of these claims.

Watson's argument relies on a specific characterisation of the concepts of 'wanting' and 'desiring'. In the previous discussion I have taken the two terms to be interchangeable. What exactly then is the substance of Watson's distinction? The agent's desire differs from his want, in so far as his desire may be construed as a hindrance whereas his want may not. The agent will not wish to eradicate his want but may wish to eradicate or ignore his desire if it falls short of a certain level in his hierarchy of values.

There are objections that can be levelled against such a model. I could, by simple turn of phrase, insist that the agent's want to implement a course of action alternative to his first-order desire, because he deems it to be of greater value, is in itself a particular type of desire. It is the desire to perform an act that he believes is of the greatest value (in terms of benefit – he believes the greatest

---

33 Watson (1982a), p. 100.
34 It is also possible to argue that the appreciation of value is dependent on reason, and reason is incapable of providing sufficient motivational efficacy for action without desire – but this is merely a suggestion and not something that I will attempt to defend – see for example Hume ([1739] 2000), Sect. II. Part III.
35 Watson (1982a), p. 100.
36 Ibid, p. 100.

benefit is to be had by acting in accordance with his hierarchy of values). That is to say, (a) The agent does not perform X (an act that would satisfy his first-order desire d) because he believes that performing Y will conform to a standard that has greater value. But I can now insist that (b) his decision to perform Y is a consequence of his greater desire n, where n is his desire to perform an act that has the greatest benefit.

With regard to Watson's first assertion, I would reply that of course the agent can view certain first-order desires as a hindrance. He will inevitably have first-order desires that he does not want to act upon. However, he will not feel that his second-order desires are a hindrance in any meaningful way, as he identifies with them.

The intensity with which the agent feels a desire is not necessarily reflective of the strength of the desire. In the example we have been considering, Jones wants to strike Black for a perceived insult – he feels this desire intensely – it gives rise to an immediate feeling of discomfort that inclines him to act in accordance with it, so that it may be alleviated (it has a degree of strength proportional to the expected benefit – in terms of the understanding of benefit that the agent identifies with, and which has motivational efficacy for him. This is what I will mean by 'benefit' from here onwards). However, Jones also has the desire to see his value system implemented (which includes the value of not striking in anger), he identifies with this desire, and it has sufficient strength to prevent his succumbing to the lure of his first-order desire to lash out (it is of greater strength because it is closer to the understanding of greatest benefit with which he identifies).[37]

I would therefore argue that Watson makes the mistake of conflating the *strength* of a desire and the *intensity* with which it is felt in (ii). It is not that the *strength* of the agent's desire may not properly reflect the degree to which its object is valued; it is rather that the *intensity* of the desire is not proportional to the degree to which its object is judged beneficial. It is the strength of the desire that is essential to its effecting the will and not its intensity (although the most intense desire may also be the strongest).

If the agent acts in accordance with an intense first-order desire without considering whether or not he judges it to be of greatest benefit, then he does not allow any other second-order desire, which may potentially be stronger, to effect his will. It is up to the agent whether he allows weaker but more intense first-order desires to become his will, or whether he allows stronger but less intense second-order desires to do so. The strongest second-order desire is the

---

[37] This is somewhat akin to the distinction Hume made between 'strong' and 'calm' passions – where a calm passion has significant motivational strength even though it is not felt as an incompatible strong passion. Hume ([1739] 2000).

desire that the agent judges to be most beneficial.

What I am suggesting is that we can model what is occurring in the following fashion: the agent has two desires X and Y, where X is a pre-reflective desire (first-order) and Y is the reflective second-order desire/want to act in a way that has, what he perceives to be, the greatest benefit. If he yields to the reflective desire he does so because he has made an evaluative judgement and has elected to pursue the course that he perceives to have most benefit. This is obviously not a particular reason for him to yield to the reflective desire to Y; it is rather an explanation of how he comes to do so. He can do so because his reflective (second-order) desire is stronger than his first-order desire, as it is thought to be of greater benefit. If he yields to the pre-reflective desire, without evaluative consideration, he chooses to ignore his ability to evaluate where the desire or ensuing act falls in terms of expected benefit. A particular reason for his acting in accordance with Y is that he deems it to be of greatest benefit to do so.

1.4.4: Evaluation and Motivational Systems

As we have seen, to be able to judge one choice to be more beneficial than another, the agent must be able to attribute a degree of value (in terms of expected benefit) to each of the options. After Watson, I will call the sum of the factors and capacities that allow him to do so the agent's *evaluation system*.[38] This system is reflective of the agent's hierarchy of values – the values that have motivational efficacy for the agent, as they are judged to be of benefit by him.[39]

The agent's reasons for having a particular hierarchy of values will reflect the benefits that he believes are to be gained from acting in accordance with them. However, his particular hierarchy of values will also reflect the degree of cost that he is willing to bear in order to live in accordance with the values that it embodies. For example, the agent believes that there are benefits to living according to Christian values – for instance, the feeling of satisfaction gained from piety, righteousness, the possibility of eternal salvation and so forth. However, he also realises that in order to live according to Christianity he must give up the pleasures of living as a hedonist. He judges the cost of doing so to outweigh the gain – he thereby more strongly identifies with hedonism and allows its continued integration in his evaluation system (the cost of modifying value systems may also be seen in terms of feelings of dislocation from community, betrayal of culture and so forth – basically anything that contributes to the agent's

---

38   See Watson (1982a), I am not suggesting that Watson would endorse the account of the agent's evaluation system that I am developing.
39   It should be noted that, for the agent, a certain action's/desire's value may be context specific (that is, what is judged to be most valuable in one specific set of circumstances may be judged to be of diminished value in another).

belief that it is better to retain his current hierarchy of values).

Is there a set of values that the agent should adopt purely in virtue of his participation in a given culture? The evaluation system of a culture is not a completely closed and consistent system in the logical sense.[40] However, there must be some common values, as this is in part what constitutes a culture. Yet it is obvious that different groups within a culture have different values. Therefore, the individual in society is caught in what I will call a 'state of compromise'; he is caught between competing values.[41] I am not necessarily refuting the suggestion that society strives for a harmonious integration of evaluation systems; I am rather suggesting that this is very difficult to accomplish when there is not complete consensus. Personal evaluation systems are perspectival[42] – they reflect the individual's interpretation of, and reaction to, his society, culture and personal experiences.

Because of the existence of the state of compromise, evaluation systems are not fixed constants. They have a plasticity that allows development and change over time. I am not defending the idea that the agent can modify his hierarchy of values on a whim – values may be deeply ingrained. I am rather suggesting that particular states of affairs may cause the agent to reassess his hierarchy of values or to modify them. These may be social or personal but must provide sufficient stimulus for the individual to reconsider his personal evaluation system. However, when I argue that the agent must have the ability to make evaluative judgements in order to have the capacity for moral responsibility, and that the ability to do so is dependent on his having an evaluation system, I mean that at the time of judging how to act he must be capable of evaluative analysis on the basis of his *current* evaluation system.

This is distinct from his *motivational system*.[43] A motivational system is a set of factors that moves an agent to action (I shall not attempt to give an account of each of these factors). It will include his desires and may include his evaluation system (unless he is abdicating his ability to evaluate his actions and/or desires). The agent's motivational system does not necessarily coincide with his evaluation system each time he chooses to act. As we have seen, when he acts according to a first-order desire with which he would not identify, he is not acting according to his evaluation system. Nevertheless, he still has a motivational system (part of which is constituted by his first-order desire).

There are inevitably grey areas where the merit of a particular action/desire/

---

40 See Koivisto (1955), p. 55.
41 See Myrdal (1944), App. 1, 2 and 3.
42 See Mannheim (1946), p. 266.
43 This term is taken from Watson (1982a). I am not suggesting that Watson would endorse the account of the agent's motivational system that I am developing, although I will draw on his account.

goal has not been clearly established – and these may only be evaluated as they arise. There are areas in which the agent's initial evaluation may be subject to revision or in which special circumstances require him to suspend a general conviction – but all of this can be accommodated by his evaluation system. It is only in light of evaluation that a second-order desire becomes the agent's will - when he wants to have a particular desire there is reflective consideration involved – there are reasons why he believes the desire to be of greatest benefit.

In order for an agent to have the capacity for moral responsibility, it must be possible for his evaluation system and motivational system to completely coincide. If this does not occur then the individual would be incapable of performing the actions that he believes, upon reflection, are of the greatest moral value. In the following subsection I will consider why this must be the case and attempt to show the relevance of the preceding investigation to morally responsible agency.

1.4.5: Evaluation, Desire and Moral Responsibility

In order to accurately judge what desire or action has the greatest moral value, the agent must have an understanding of the correct moral standard against which it should be assessed (I shall assume that there is such a thing as a correct moral standard and that morality is not purely subjective – this is because in later chapters I will be assuming the existence of God – and it is usually thought that this in itself entails the falsity of ethical subjectivism).[44] When referring to 'the moral standard' from here onwards I mean the correct moral standard unless otherwise stated. It is in light of the moral standard that an agent's acts can be accurately morally assessed. It is a gauge that allows accurate assessment of the moral value of an act, desire, intention and so forth.

If the agent does not have the capacity to reach an understanding of the moral standard (through whatever route, possible candidates for which being habituation, revelation, intuition, reflective consideration, inherent knowledge, and so forth), then there is no way that he can consistently assess the moral worth of different desires/actions and accurately judge them to be morally superior or deficient (we have already seen that an agent's hierarchy of values reflects what action/desire he believes is of greatest benefit – in terms of the moral standard what is of greatest benefit will be that which has the greatest moral worth).

This understanding does not have to be explicit – the agent does not have to be able to give an exact account of the structure of the moral standard. An implicit understanding of it is sufficient for moral responsibility (he does however have to be capable of using it when making moral judgements).

---

44 For a discussion of the possibility of a universal moral standard see Sharp (1921).

To be able to conform to a moral standard, the agent must be sensitive to the normative requirements that it entails. The moral standard helps to establish moral norms for those who adopt it as part of their evaluation system.[45] Moral norms are rules and prescriptions, either general or specific, for what it is morally correct to do.[46] In light of the moral standard it is rational to adopt the moral norms that it entails. In order to justify blaming someone for not conforming to a moral norm it must be possible to rationalise one's moral censure – there must be a reason why one feels morally indignant.

Moral norms are what allow the formation of 'ought' and 'ought-not' type moral imperatives (for example, 'you ought to be generous', 'you ought not to steal'). These imperatives are, in part, justified by appeal to the values embodied in the moral standard. One of the reasons that one can provide for blaming someone for doing something that one believes morally deficient, is that they should have known what they were doing was wrong and this should have supplied sufficient motivation for them not to do it. In other words, the moral norm was something that they should have complied with, as it was possible and rational to do so.

The ability to adopt the moral standard, and live according to it, does not necessarily mean that the agent can harmonize all of his first-order desires with that standard, it is rather that he is capable of accepting the hierarchy of values that it embodies and forming second-order desires that are in accordance with it.[47] The ability to live according to it requires the capacity to make the desire to conform to the moral norm one's will and to act accordingly. In order to have the capacity to become the agent's will his desire to conform to the moral standard must be the desire with the greatest latent strength (the desire that can be stronger than all other desires and thereby become the agent's will, if he chooses to identify with it). In order for the desire to act morally to become his will, the agent must believe that there is greater benefit in acting in accordance with moral norms than acting contrary to them. This is what will give the desire effective strength and make it the agent's will.

Making the desire to conform to the moral norm one's will is not necessarily synonymous with being moral – the agent could act in accordance with the moral standard without believing in the moral values that it embodies (for example, he could do so from fear). Thus, for the agent to be moral, as opposed to just having the ability to act in accordance with moral norms, requires that he have the desire to be moral (and not just the desire to act in a way that will most likely be perceived by others to be moral), to want that desire, and be able to make it his will. This will involve the capacity to make the moral standard the dominant hierarchy of values in his evaluation system – and to identify with the values

---

45 See Copp (1995), esp. pp. 21, 82 and 103.
46 See Gibbard (1985), esp. p. 12.
47 For a discussion of this issue see Pettit and Smith (1996), p. 443.

that constitute it. It is not sufficient that the agent be aware that there is such a thing as a moral standard, and that it can be used as the yardstick against which the value of individual actions and desires can be measured. He must have the actual capacity to use it as such a measure. He must be able to come to the belief that being moral is of greatest benefit.

I will now return to the example of Jones' desire to strike Black (first-order desire). I will assume that Jones has identified with and adopted the moral standard. He knows that he has two options – he can either act in accordance with his first-order desire, or he can choose not to do so. He judges it to be morally superior not to strike Black. This conclusion is reached due to the fact that the moral standard is part of his evaluation system and his knowledge of it informs him that it is morally deficient (there is no moral value) to strike people because of a trivial affront. He does not want to have the desire to strike others, as he recognises that harbouring it leads to morally deficient thoughts/actions/and so forth, which do not conform to the moral norm. Because of his identification with the moral standard, he believes it to be of greatest benefit not to strike Black. He therefore does not form the second-order desire to do so. His first-order desire is thereby held in check (it lacks strength because it is not judged to be most beneficial). In this case, his evaluation and motivational systems coincide.

If he had acted according to his first-order desire then not only would he have had to take ownership of both his desire and action, he would also have had to accept moral responsibility for them (as he had knowledge of the moral standard, it formed part of his evaluation system and could have been an effective part of his motivational system if he had so chosen).

Certain first-order desires may have moral content in themselves, but all first-order desires are pre-reflective. Therefore, the agent does not necessarily have any control over whether they arise or not (although it may be possible for him to avoid circumstances in which he knows that a certain desire could, or would, emerge). The agent cannot be morally responsible for having a desire that he is powerless to avoid. Therefore, it is at the level of identification with those desires that the agent's moral responsibility begins to manifest itself. Negligent or intentional failure to integrate the moral standard into one's evaluation system is no excuse for failing to act morally, providing one could do so (and that it was rational for one to do so). The failure to make a judgement about the moral status of one's desires or actions is morally reprehensible in itself, providing one can do so.

It is possible to be morally responsible for having a morally deficient second-order desire that one does not act on because of a lack of courage or determination. For example, one may be a racist, desire to inflict harm on different ethnic groups, want to have this desire and yet act on the stronger desire to stay out of trouble. Given that racist violence is morally deficient, it is my claim that identifying with the desire to engage in it is also morally deficient (this is assuming that racism and racist violence is judged/known to be morally deficient in light of the moral standard, and that the racist has access to the moral standard and can adopt it).

1.4.6: Conclusion to Section 1.4

I have argued in this section that evaluative judgement plays a role in the agent's ability to take moral ownership of the actions that he performs and the desires with which he identifies. I have contended that if the agent is capable of making such judgements and fails to do so, intentionally or due to negligence, he is still responsible for the actions that issue from the unevaluated desires, and must assume responsibility for leaving them unevaluated. However, I have also attempted to show that the capacity for evaluative judgement, in itself, is not sufficient for moral responsibility. The ability to make moral judgements is not synonymous with the ability to act morally. The agent must also be able to identify with the desire to be moral and to make that desire his will.

In light of the investigations undertaken in this Section, it is my conclusion that the morally responsible agent must:

(vi) Be capable of making judgements based on evaluative comparison (this involves having an evaluation system that embodies a hierarchy of values).

(vii) Be capable of doing that which he judges to be of greatest benefit (given what is accomplishable).

(viii) Be capable of having evaluative and motivational systems that completely coincide.

(ix) Have the capacity to adopt the correct moral standard against which his actions and/or desires should be measured (even if he does not do so intentionally or negligently).

(x) Have the capacity to act in accordance with the moral norms that follow from the moral standard.

(xi) Be capable of forming the second-order desire to be moral and be capable of making it his will.

1.5: Conclusion to Chapter 1

In this chapter I have attempted to provide the foundation for a coherent theory of the conditions that are essential to morally responsible agency. I have provided arguments for the validity of each of the eleven criteria that I have proposed the agent must be capable of satisfying if he is to be capable of moral responsibility. However, my account is still not complete, as I have not yet adequately addressed the issue of the type of control that is necessary for morally responsible agency. This shall, therefore, be the topic of the next chapter.

2

Control and Morally Responsible Agency

2.1: Introduction to Chapter 2

Chapter 2 is an investigation into the issue of the type of control that the agent must possess, and be capable of exercising, if he is to have moral responsibility for his actions. Finding an adequate formulation of the type of control that is essential to moral responsibility will allow for the addition of the final capacity that the individual must be in possession of in order to be capable of morally responsible agency.

2.2: The Control Condition

2.2.0: Introduction to Section 2.2

In this section I present an incompatibilist understanding of moral responsibility that relies on a particular conception of the agent's control over his actions, and the principles upon which it is based.

2.2.1: The Control Condition and Regulative Control

> Control Condition: An agent is morally responsible for an action if, and only if, he had control over that action.[48]

This principle, or something closely akin to it, is generally explicitly or implicitly accepted as true by those who engage with the question of moral responsibility (irrespective of whether or not they believe that the agent is in fact morally responsible for his actions).[49] However, it is the definition of

---

48 See McKenna (2001), p. 38.
49 See, for example, Frankfurt (1969 and 1975), Greenspan (1978), van Inwagen (1978 and 1983), Fischer (1982), Zimmerman (1988), Fischer and Ravizza (1991 and

the type of control that is involved that causes divergence and debate.[50]

I will call 'Moral Control' the type of control that is essential to moral responsibility. The incompatibilist believes that Moral Control is synonymous with what I will call 'Regulative Control'.[51]

One of the minimal conditions of being an incompatibilist is having the conviction that the agent must have multiple actualisable alternatives available to him at the time of acting if he is to be free in relation to his actions, and morally responsible for what he does.[52] What this means is that he believes that the agent must have the power to X, and have the power to not X, at *t* (the time of choosing to act), irrespective of the state of affairs that constitutes the actual world at t, if he is to be responsible for the action that he actually performs. I will call this the 'forking-paths' model of freedom and moral responsibility. This forking-paths model is reflected in the incompatibilist understanding of what it means for the agent to be in control of his actions.

I will now attempt to define this concept:

P is a particular action/state/event. *t* represents any particular instant of time in the past (relative to the agent's action).

> Regulative Control: An agent has Regulative Control over *P* if, and only if, the agent has the power to choose to act, and can act, at *t* such that he can cause or allow *P*, and such that he can cause or allow *not P*, to obtain irrespective of the state of the world at *t*.

I will say that an agent has 'multiple actualisable alternatives' with respect to *P* if he has Regulative Control over *P*.

I will proceed in the following subsection to apply this understanding of Regulative Control to the Control Condition. I will assume that the Control Condition must be accepted by anyone engaging in the debate about moral responsibility. I am claiming that an agent, who has no control (for whatever

---

1998), Glannon (1995), Speak (2002), and Haji (2003).
50 For a discussion of the necessity of control for freedom and responsibility that does not rely on the structures essential to compatibilism and determinism see Greenspan (1978), pp. 225-240. She makes an interesting example of the type of behaviour control exercised on Alex in *A Clockwork Orange*.
51 The term 'Regulative Control' is taken from Fischer and Ravizza (1998), and although the characterisation of it that I propose is not identical to theirs it is fundamentally similar. See chapters 1-2 for a discussion of Regulative Control and Guidance Control.
52 For further definitions and discussions of incompatibilism see, for example, Lamb (1977), Nathan (1984), Kane (1989), Honderich (1996) and Otsuka (1998). Many compatibilists would also agree with this position. Therefore, in the course of my investigation, I will make apparent the distinguishing features of incompatibilism.

reason) over his action, is incapable of being morally responsible for that action. This assumption will be justified in the course of this chapter. The question that still needs to be addressed though is whether the control in question must be Regulative or not.

2.2.2: The Principle of Moral Responsibility

From the above investigations and observations I will now assert that the incompatibilist is committed to the claim that:

> Incompatibilist Principle of Moral Responsibility (PMR): the agent is morally responsible for P (an action/event/state) only if he had Regulative Control over P.

This Principle merges the Control Condition with the incompatibilist's insistence that Regulative Control is synonymous with Moral Control. The principle is also implicitly committed to the claim that moral responsibility is integrally connected to the incompatibilist understanding of the ability to do otherwise (that is, the forking paths model). This development goes further than the Control Condition and does not necessarily follow from it. It is therefore in need of further investigation and justification.

If we were to accept that the agent must have Regulative Control in order to be morally responsible for his actions, we would also have to accept that there is a sense in which he must be the ultimate source of those actions. What I mean by this is that it must be the agent's choice to do X or fail to do X, and his acting upon that choice, that fulfils the set of sufficient conditions for causing X to obtain or not X to obtain.[53] It is further argued by the incompatibilist that the outcome of that choice cannot be entailed by any determining factors, for, if it was, then we could extrapolate that these factors would be the ultimate source of the action (that is, the sufficient power that gives rise to it is not the agent). At this stage I am merely highlighting this possibility and am not critically evaluating it. At a later stage this possibility will be dealt with in much greater detail.

I will call the type of incompatibilist who believes that there can be no exceptions to PMR a 'strong incompatibilist'.

2.2.3: Conclusion to Section 2.2

So far in this Section I have introduced the Control Condition and the Incompatibilist Principle of Moral Responsibility. However, I have not justified

---

53   For a discussion of agent causation see, for example, Bishop (1983), and Rowe (1991).

the validity of insisting that Regulative Control constitutes Moral Control – as it not the sole possible candidate for the type of control that is essential to Moral Control. It is also possible that Guidance Control is appropriate. What is Guidance Control?

> Guidance Control: An agent has Guidance Control when he can act in accordance with the second-order desire that he wants to be his will, and is responsive to reason in an apposite way.[54]

Guidance Control obviously does not necessitate Regulative Control. In the next Section I will consider the possibility that it is not necessary to have Regulative Control in order to have morally responsible agency.

2.3: Criteria for Responsibility Ascriptions Reconsidered

2.3.0: Introduction to Section 2.3

In this section I investigate an alternative conception of moral responsibility to that characterised by the Incompatibilist Principle of Moral Responsibility. This alternative conception involves the idea that the agent can be morally responsible for his actions even if it is true that he could not exercise Regulative Control over them.

2.3.1: Alternative Possibilities and Moral Responsibility Reconsidered

Dennett insists in *Elbow Room* that the incompatibilist's insistence that the agent must have multiple actualisable alternatives in order to have moral responsibility is of little interest, as it is not the deciding criterion for distinguishing whether the agent is responsible for the acts that he performs.[55] This assertion includes, by implication, that Regulative Control is not synonymous with Moral Control.

He draws our attention to the example of Luther when he said, here I stand, I can do no other. In saying this he was justifying his position with regard to his break with the Roman Church. Dennett maintains, quite validly, that Luther is in no way suggesting that he is not responsible for the position that he upholds,

---

54 Once again this term is borrowed from Fischer and Ravizza (1998), Chapters 1-2. This is not the definition that they offer of Guidance Control, and I am not claiming that they would endorse it.
55 Dennett (1986), p. 133.

even though he feels bound by his conscience to such an extent that he cannot do other than hold steady in his opposition. Accordingly, Dennett states, 'we simply do not exempt someone from praise or blame for an act because we think he could do no other.'[56]

The question that I will proceed to ask is whether Luther is justified in his assumption that he is in fact responsible for his position, even if there really is no way that that he can do anything else. If we adopt the use of PMR as our criterion for assessing the validity of ascribing morally reactive attitudes to actions and their instigators, then it appears that Luther's conviction that he should be held accountable for his beliefs is a self-delusion (assuming that he has no actualisable alternatives in this regard). However, the compatibilist may be able to formulate an alternative principle that is sufficient for moral responsibility.

Colmpatibilism is the thesis that it is possible to reconcile free will and moral responsibility with determinism. This requires a specific characterisation of the word 'free'. Compatibilists believe that, once there is no external force (or forces) that compel the agent, either physically or psychologically, to do an action, the action in question qualifies as free and morally significant. Freedom and responsibility are thus reliant on the independence from certain kinds of constraints. I will examine what this idea involves in the following subsection.

If it is possible to construct a coherent compatibilist theory of the criteria for moral responsibility, it may be possible to undermine the incompatibilist assertion that Regulative Control is essential to Moral Control.

What argument can the compatibilist offer to counter the strong incompatibilist's claims – for it must be admitted that for many people the latter's claims have intuitive appeal?

2.3.2: Frankfurt's Principle of Responsibility

Frankfurt believes that Regulative Control is not necessary for moral responsibility. He believes that there is an alternative principle to PMR that is capable of reconciling moral responsibility with determinism. I will call this principle 'Frankfurt's Principle of Responsibility' (FPR):

> FPR[57]: An agent is not morally responsible for what he has done if, and only if, he did it because he could not have done otherwise.[58]

---

56   Ibid p. 133.
57   From here on called FPR. This is my label and not Frankfurt's.
58   See Frankfurt (1969), p. 838. It should be noted that Frankfurt does not give this exact formulation – this principle is intended to reflect the most cogent aspects of his argument.

Frankfurt argues that it follows from FPR that the agent can be held morally responsible for his actions irrespective of determinism, as long as he is free from particular constraints. I will initially presume that FPR is valid, in order to appreciate the way in which it functions. Once I have done so, I will then subject its validity to closer scrutiny.

It follows from FPR that an agent is responsible for his actions if he would have chosen to do them anyway, irrespective of whether he was compelled or not.[59] The claim is that if, and only if, an agent 'genuinely' desired to do otherwise (that is, if his strongest second-order desire was to do something else),[60] but was in some way externally prevented from doing so (that is, was forced to act contrary to the desire that he most strongly wanted to be his will), can we truly say that he was not responsible for the actions that he performed.[61] What is involved in this contention is in need of greater explanation. I will attempt to justify and clarify this argument in the remainder of this chapter.

2.3.3: Irresistible Desires

In order to consider the conditions of FPR, and the principle's validity, it will be beneficial to have first established an understanding of 'irresistible desire', as this concept is integral to many of the ideas that I will examine.[62] If the force of an agent's desire is irresistible, it may be the case that he acts in virtue of the fact that he is compelled to do so by it. The question that this raises for this inquiry is whether it can be claimed that the agent's responsibility for a specific action would be nullified if there was an irresistible desire at play in the conditions that gave rise to his act. In other words, one must ask if irresistible desires lead to a lack of responsibility under the criterion of FPR. I will therefore test FPR to see if it can incorporate irresistible desire, and, if it can, delineate the specific conditions under which it may do so.

What I mean by an 'irresistible desire' is a desire that inevitably becomes an agent's efficient motivator, irrespective of whether he would prefer an alternative desire to play that role (that is, in the case of being subject to an irresistible desire,

---

59 The relevance of this distinction will become apparent when I reconsider Luther's freedom with respect to his position.
60 By 'genuinely wanted to do otherwise' I mean that an agent actually wanted a desire to become his will in a strong sense. There is a sense in which there may be several conflicting second-order desires that we want to become our will, but only one of them can actually do so. I have already argued a weighted system of desires in Chapter 1 and explained the way in which a desire becomes the agent's will.
61 In Chapter 1 I have discussed at length what it means for a person to do what he really desires to do. This included an explanation of Frankfurt's idea of higher-order desires.
62 For a discussion of 'irresistible desires' see Neely (1974), and Mele (1990).

his other desires (first or second order) cannot provide sufficient causal efficacy to affect the action that he actually undertakes). In other words, it is the only desire upon which an agent can act – it is impossible for him to form an alternative desire with sufficient force to allow him to undertake an alternative action. The agent is powerless to act contrary to an irresistible desire. Thus, irresistible desire is not just an abdication of the moral responsibility involved in choosing to act in accordance with a specific desire (for instance, for the agent to allow himself to be governed by his strongest desire without considering whether or not he is being morally responsible in doing so); it is rather a desire that becomes the principal efficient motivator irrespective of whether the agent identifies with it or not. If an agent is subject to an irresistible desire, with respect to an action, he cannot have actualisable alternatives.

The force of an irresistible desire is such that the agent cannot exercise sufficient control (of any kind) to resist it, even if that is what he really wants to do. I would emphasise that I am not suggesting that the agent will not form the complimentary second-order desire and want the irresistible desire to be his will.

It may be the case, if we are determined, that all of our actions are due to irresistible desires (that is, it may be that certain determining factors give rise to desires that we cannot resist and thereby causally determine what we do). It may also be the case that the identification, or failure to identify, with particular first-order desires is also determined by these factors. Thus, we may only have Guidance Control over the second-order desires that we want to be our will.

I will define an Irresistible Desire as follows:

> A desire is irresistible if, and only if, the agent is powerless to prevent it from becoming effective due to some determining factor, or set of determining factors, F, which the agent is powerless to affect.

One might ask though, what of an example such as Odysseus having himself tied to the mast of his ship so that he would not join the sirens?[63] He knows in advance that if he hears the sirens song he will be irresistibly lured by them, and he knows that they lie in wait for him. He therefore takes measures before encountering them to ensure that he will not be able to act in accordance with what would otherwise be an irresistible desire to join them. Here, the desire to join with the sirens would be irresistible but is not effective due to the fact that Odysseus is tied to the mast. I would point out that Odysseus was not determined by some factor/s F, such that he could not prevent the desire to join with the sirens from becoming effective. His ability to have himself tied to the mast meant that he had sufficient control (power), in advance of the occurrence of a desire that would have become irresistible if not countered before its manifestation, to take measures to ensure that the desire, when it occurred, could not become

---

63 See Homer's *Odyssey* for an account of this mythic occurrence.

effective. Thus, this shows that Odysseus desire to join with the sirens was not truly irresistible (according to my characterisation) due to the fact that Odysseus was not determined such that it was beyond his power to take measures to ensure that the desire did not become effective.

This sort of example can be expanded to incorporate other similar scenarios. For instance, the man who knows that he will inevitably become violent when drunk cannot claim that he acted on an irresistible desire when inebriated if it was within his power at some earlier time to ensure that he would not become drunk.

It should be noted that owing to the above characterisation of irresistible desire there is no reason to assume that the agent will actually want to prevent an irresistible desire from becoming effective. It may very well be the case that every desire that he acts upon is irresistible according to my characterisation, and yet he still may want each of the irresistible desires to effect his will (assuming that they are compatible). The irresistible desires may not be in conflict with his conception of benefit. In fact, although the irresistibility of the desire forms part of his motivational system it may be that it is still in perfect cohesion with his evaluative system. He may still be able to make what he most desires, and considers to be of greatest benefit, his will.

If the irresistibility of the desire is the crucial factor that determines that an individual act in a certain fashion, then can the agent be held morally responsible for the actions that ensue? We have not yet encountered anything that runs contrary to the criterion of morally responsible agency that I have so far established. If we accept FPR, it is possible that there are certain instances in which the agent can act in accordance with an irresistible desire and still be morally responsible for the ensuing action. This is another strategy for arguing that if 'hard-determinism' obtains it does not necessarily lead to a lack of moral responsibility.

In the following discussion I will use the term 'hard-determined' to refer to a state of affairs where an agent is determined by some factor/s F such that he does not have the power to do other than one particular action (and/or to form one particular desire, intention and so forth). This means that when an agent is hard-determined he does not have multiple actualisable alternatives available to him – there is no sense in which he has the power to do otherwise; he is compelled by factor/s F to do X.[64]

I have already claimed that just because a desire exerts an irresistible influence on an agent, it does not consequently entail that the agent will not identify with the irresistible desire in question. I will now attempt to illustrate how this is possible by returning to the example of Luther.

---

64   This does not necessarily mean that he will not also have the desire to do X.

Let us suppose that Luther believes that the reason he cannot do other than break with the Church is because he is bound by his conscience. He believes that his conscience has determined him to be the sort of person who stands up for what he believes is right. For the purpose of this example, we will accept that he is correct in this belief and will assume that his conscience is a determining factor that he is powerless to change (that is, he cannot act so that he has a different conscience). He is convinced that, under the circumstances, breaking with the Church is right. He is happy with the conscience that he has. He does not want it to change it. He identifies with his conscience and desires to do those actions that are in accordance with it.[65]

He believes that actions that are in accordance with his conscience are of greatest benefit and he wants them to be his will. It may be the case that this is an irresistible desire (in so far as he cannot form an alternative desire that would motivate him to do otherwise – there is some determining factor F; his conscience, that prevents him from doing so), but that does not necessarily mean that he is not responsible for acting in accordance with it (under FPR). This is because Luther is not only breaking with the Church because he cannot do otherwise; he is also doing so because he wants to act in accordance with his conscience. He can exert Guidance Control over the action that he does – he can perform the action that is in accordance with his strongest second-order desire and it may be claimed that he has appropriate reasons for doing so.

Thus, the compatibilist would insist that Luther identifies with his irresistible desire in an apposite way (the importance of this point will be shown in the discussion of addiction below) and that this is sufficient for moral responsibility, as long as he had Guidance Control over what he actually proceeded to do. One may propose that this is sufficient to undermine the incompatibilist insistence that Regulative Control over an action is necessary for Moral Control.

This is a fact that can be exploited by the compatibilist who wants to make use of FPR to justify the compatibility between determinism and moral responsibility. Under the criterion of responsibility stated in FPR, the only way that Luther would not be morally responsible for his action would be if, and only if, he broke with the Church because he could not have done otherwise. This is clearly not the case. This argument allegedly undermines PMR, as it supposedly shows that multiple actualisable alternatives (which are fundamental to Regulative Control) are not necessary for moral responsibility. I will test the validity of this assumption.

---

65 The actions that he performs that are in accordance with his conscience are also in accordance with his will, and conform to the second-order desires with which he identifies.

2.3.4: Frankfurt's 'Addicts Example'

Frankfurt attempts to illustrate some of the ramifications of FPR by way of an example involving two addicts and their respective responsibilities with regard to their drug addictions.[66] According to Frankfurt, due to their addiction, both act from irresistible desires. They are powerless to act contrary to their addiction. Frankfurt allows that addiction is a sufficient cause of its object – being addicted entails that one must feed one's addiction – addiction hard-determines the fact that both addicts must take drugs. I will not contest this fact as it serves as a general exemplar for compelled action. The question is; do both addicts act without moral responsibility, irrespective of their attitude to their addiction?

In the example, one addict is willing in his addiction, in so far as he desires to take drugs, and the other is unwilling, in so far as he does not desire to do so.[67] Both addicts are powerless to stop themselves from continuing to feed their addiction. It is argued that the difference in their moral status lies in the level of responsibility that each has due to the nature of the desires with which he identifies.[68]

The willing addict, like Luther (this is assuming that he is hard-determined), has no choice in his actions but, nevertheless, identifies with them – they are what he desires to do, and he has no wish to do otherwise (he believes his continuing to take drugs to be of greatest benefit – his motivational and evaluative systems coincide). The unwilling addict, however, does not identify with his desire to take drugs (he believes that there is greater benefit in ceasing to do so and has formed the complimentary second-order desire that he wants to be his will). He would much rather to be free of his addiction, but he is compelled by an irresistible desire and cannot make his second-order desire his will.

One can argue that this is an unsuitable example, as it does not account for the fact that neither of the addicts may be deemed appropriate candidates for illustrating the way that morality should be understood in the actions of responsible subjects. This is because, under Frankfurt's own insistence, they are both suffering from pathological conditions. One can therefore question whether they have formed their second-order desires in apposite ways.

I will not pursue the above objection however, as the addicts in the example are used to illustrate the general area of compelled action and irresistible desire. The addicts are not free in the libertarian (forking paths-model) sense because they cannot do other than they do (that is, they do not have Regulative Control over their actions with respect to feeding their addictions). The formation of

---

66   Frankfurt (1975).
67   Ibid, p. 118.
68   Ibid, p. 118.

their second-order desires may be within their control (understood as either Guidance or Regulative – the consequences of accepting either definition is not yet important, but will be shown to be of significance before this investigation has concluded), but are ineffective as sufficient motivators of action (the addicts may be able to desire that they cease to take drugs, or desire that they continue to do so – but irrespective of this fact they will still continue to feed their addiction because it has given rise to an irresistible desire). With respect to their addiction, they are determined in a hard sense.

The addicts' desire to take drugs is irresistible under my characterisation, as they are 'powerless to prevent it from becoming effective due to some determining factor, or set of determining factors, F [where F is their addiction]'.

Neither of the addicts are responsive to reason (with respect to their addiction) – no matter what reasons are presented to them to stop taking drugs they cannot be motivated to alternative action as a consequence. In this sense, they are not merely weak-willed, as they cannot discontinue their actions because of a set of sufficient reasons to do so.[69]

It is therefore difficult to see how one could insist that the unwilling addict has responsibility for the actions that occur as a consequence of his irresistible desire (unless, perhaps, one can show that he made a morally responsible choice that led to the situation where he now finds himself). This is of course assuming that the *only* reason that he continues to feed his addiction is because he cannot do otherwise (that is, as asserted in FPR).

We are more likely to portion moral disapprobation on the willing addict rather than his counterpart, because of the way that he views his addiction. Why is this so? It can be argued that in the case of the willing addict the compulsive nature of the irresistible desire is of no significance to the moral status of the actions undertaken. For this reason, even though he could not have done otherwise, the willing addict can still be deemed morally responsible for his actions. He would have chosen to take drugs anyway, even if it was possible for him not to (that is, even if he were able to exercise Regulative Control over his narcotics use). It is not the case that the only reason that he takes drugs is because he cannot do otherwise. Therefore, he is responsible under FPR. This line of argument avoids any appeal to actualisable alternative possibilities, as it denies the validity of PMR by insisting that Regulative Control is not essential to moral responsibility.

2.3.5: A Criticism of Frankfurt's 'Addicts Example'

There is much food for thought in Frankfurt's example. However, when we

---

69 Fischer and Ravizza (1998), esp. pp. 43- 48.

scrutinise it further we begin to see that it may not be an apt example of how we should understand responsibility in relation to morally responsible agents. It is true that we may be more likely to portion blame on the willing addict as he identifies with his addiction and does not wish to change it. However, it is in the justification of such an attitude that we encounter difficulty.

The reason that we generally hold subjects accountable for their actions is precisely because we believe that they have a choice as to what they will do in the situations where they find themselves, as well as the fact that they do that which they wish to do. One of the appealing things about FPR (for those who lean towards compatibilism) is that it distances libertarian accounts of free action from moral responsibility, such that identifying with a desire in a specific way is sufficient for moral responsibility, even if the agent cannot do other than he does. In so doing, it arguably shows that PMR is a false account of the criterion of moral responsibility. Thus FPR may undermine our everyday view of the grounding of moral responsibility (assuming that I am correct in my assumption about the everyday view of the moral world).

I will now ask whether holding an addict accountable for his current actions, despite the fact that we freely acknowledge that he could not do otherwise, is to transgress the very criteria under which our moral reactive attitudes can be justifiably upheld.

Irrespective of whether the addict is willing or not, we cannot credit him with any sense of 'could do otherwise' – he is hard-determined in all that he does with respect to his addiction. It is not that *if* he decides not to be addicted then he *could* stop his addiction; he simply cannot act contrary to his addiction (this is assuming that his addiction ensures that he is hard-determined by irresistible desires). Given that he is an addict, there is no sense in which he *could* cease taking drugs *if* he so chose. Part of the sufficient conditions for his ceasing to take drugs would rely on his not being addicted to them (that is, if left to his own devices – as I will assume he is for the purposes of the example). Thus, all possible worlds in which he can cease to take drugs would necessarily require that he is not an addict in those worlds. Thus, to say that he could cease his addiction if he so chose has little power to convince (at best one could assert that 'if he were not an addict then he could cease to take drugs' – and this is an obviously puerile claim).

It may be possible to justifiably blame the addicts for the initial act of taking drugs, which led to their compulsion, prior to their actual addiction – because at this time they may still have been appropriate candidates for reactive attitudes (as they were not suffering from a pathological condition). But now that they are addicts, we can no longer blame them for continuing to take drugs, as, irrespective of their former actions, they can no longer reform of their own accord. They have a complete loss of control in relation to the specific action of taking drugs. However, if an addict is free at the level of intention formation, we may blame him for not forming a morally appropriate intention even if he is powerless to act in accordance with it.[70] This is part of the reason that we are more likely to portion blame on the willing addict.

It is my claim that blaming someone for what they want to do is significantly different from blaming them for not doing something that they cannot do. In the example of the addicts, it is easy to conflate these two issues because they superficially appear to be the same. There is a substantive difference between blaming an addict for taking drugs because he wants to, and blaming him for not ceasing to take drugs when he cannot do so. This should be apparent from the above discussion of the nature of addiction. The true significance of this difference will be shown in Section 2.5.

Before concluding this section I would like to point out another of the problems with FPR. I have already considered the reasons why an advocate of FPR can claim that an agent may be morally responsible for identifying with an irresistible desire. However, one of the issues that I have not yet sufficiently considered concerns the validity of this line of argument if it is also true that the agent is hard-determined such that he cannot do other than identify with certain desires – what if the agent's second-order desires are irresistible (in the sense of his being unable to form an alternative second-order desire with sufficient motivational efficacy for him to do otherwise)? If the agent's identification with particular desires is also hard-determined, then it may still be possible that PMR can be used to counter the line of argument pursued by the advocate of FPR. Following this line of argument, it may also be impossible for the agent to form different second-order desires to those second-order desires he has, as he is hard-determined to have them by factors that are beyond his control. If this is the case, we may have difficulty in blaming him for identifying with morally inferior desires. I will return to this issue in Section 2.5.

2.3.6: Conclusion to Section 2.3

We may be uneasy about using the examples of addicts, due to their pathology, as a justification for the application of FPR or PMR. With this in mind, I will now proceed to discuss what I call 'Jones-style examples'. These examples build upon the foundation that I have laid in considering the moral responsibility of Frankfurt's addicts. They will also afford a greater understanding of interpersonal coercion and external compulsion. This will be shown to be especially relevant to any consideration of the implications of God's existence for the possibility of morally responsible agency. Furthermore, they may patch some of the holes that I have suggested may exist in the account of moral responsibility adopted

---

70   I will return to this point in Section 2.5.

by the advocate of FPR.

Section 2.4: Jones-Style Examples

2.4.0: Introduction to Section 2.4

This section introduces and analyses a type of example initially developed by Harry Frankfurt in an attempt to undermine the idea that it is necessary to have multiple actualisable alternatives to be capable of morally responsible agency, and to justify the compatibilist conception of freedom and moral responsibility.

2.4.1: An Introduction to Jones-Style Examples

I will call the specific type of examples that are about to be considered 'Jones-style examples' after a hypothetical scenario that Frankfurt has presented to show that:

> A person may well be morally responsible for what he has done even though he could not have done otherwise.[71]

Frankfurt contends, implicitly, that Regulative Control is not essential to moral responsibility and that the truth of determinism (I would also assume that this can be taken to include hard-determinism due to the nature of the examples presented) has no bearing on moral responsibility. A proponent of this claim could argue that whether or not the agent acts on irresistible desires is irrelevant to moral responsibility as long as he is responsive to reason in an apposite way and is not compelled by external factors such that he cannot make his strongest second-order desire his will – that is, can exercise Guidance Control.

An agent named Jones intends to act in a certain way – I will call the action that he intends to do X. A second individual named Black wants Jones to act in exactly the way that Jones intends. However, Black is not willing to gamble on the possibility of being frustrated by Jones choosing to perform an alternative action. He therefore implants a device in Jones brain that will allow him to manipulate the action that Jones actually performs.[72] Jones is not aware that the device has been implanted.

---

71 Frankfurt (1969), p. 829-830.
72 Ibid, pp. 835-836.

Black is content to allow events to unfold without his influence, unless he becomes conscious that Jones is about to form what would be an effective intention to act other than in the way desired by Black. Black would be aware of this through some sign that he would be able to successfully interpret as Jones being about to form an intention that runs counter to his own desire.

Frankfurt's scenario is a situation where there are different possible efficient causes for a predetermined act. The efficient cause that obtains is a result of the intention that Jones is about to form immediately prior to acting. What I mean is that the sign that occurs immediately before the formation of what would be Jones effective intention to act (that is, if Black were not to intervene), should be understood as the critical moment at which the actual efficient cause of the action becomes manifest.

There are two possible causal sequences that are sufficient for Jones to do X.[73] It must be allowed, irrespective of which one obtains, that Jones cannot do other than X (because of Black's device). The first possible causal sequence is the one where Jones does not deviate from his original intention (that is to act in the way that Black wants him to act) and there is therefore no impetus for Black to intervene. This is because Jones's intention is in accordance with Black's desire and so there is no sign that shows he is about to do otherwise (which would instigate Black's intervention). The second is where Black operates his device. Its activation, and consequent role as ultimate actual efficient cause, depends on the occurrence of a sign which shows that Jones's final intention would not coincide with Black's desire (in other words, Jones changes his mind). Only then will the intervention of Black ensure that his own desire is fulfilled.

However, we do not know which causal sequence for the predetermined action will obtain until Jones shows, or fails to show, some sign as to whether or not he will form an intention that is complimentary to Black's desire. One possible causal sequence will remain unrealised while the other becomes actualised. But, there can only be one outcome as the result of either possible causal sequence - there can be only one action actually performed: X (the action desired by Black).

If Black does not intervene then the role that he plays (in relation to the actual act performed) amounts to nothing more than that of an observer – and one can contend that a concealed observer (exercising no coercive or compelling influence) cannot detract from the responsibility of an agent with regard to his own action.[74] This is because, in this scenario, the observer and his actions do not interfere with the formation of Jones's intention and eventual action.

The point of this example is that even though Jones never has it within his power to actualise an alternative action (he never has Regulative Control over

---

73 See Glannon (1995), p. 261.
74 Frankfurt (1969), p. 836.

his action) this does not mitigate the status of the responsibility that he has for it, as long as Black does not in fact intervene.[75]

2.4.2: Jones-Style Examples and Irresistible Threat Contexts

Frankfurt suggests that the scope of this argument can be extended to threat situations. Suppose that Jones had been threatened such that if he didn't choose to act in a particular way, say for the purpose of example stealing from his employer, there would be a consequence that could not fail to impress him (that is, he is assuming that in light of the threat Jones is compelled to act in accordance with it).[76] By adopting the above reasoning, it is still possible to assert that Jones is morally responsible for the theft if he had decided to rob his employer in advance of the threat being issued, and did not deviate from that intention. Thus, even though he now has no choice but to act in accordance with the threat, there was a time, when he was forming his original intention to act, that he was free from the irresistible coercive influence of the threat.[77] Therefore, if he acts in the way he would have acted anyway, irrespective of the threat, the threat itself in no way mitigates his responsibility for his action.[78]

This line of reasoning can be applied to all sorts of scenarios, and is compatible with FPR. This, once again leads to the conclusion entailed by FPR; Jones should be considered to lack moral responsibility for his action if, and only if, the only reason that he performed it was because of the irresistibility of the threat that was issued. It is accepted that the threat would have to be of sufficient force to negate the possibility of all alternative actions. Thus, under the compatibilist criteria established through Jones-style examples, being compelled by an irresistible threat does not automatically exclude moral responsibility.

---

75 Kane (1998), p. 41.
76 Frankfurt (1969), p. 832.
77 Frankfurt recognises that the certainty of harsh punishment that a threat entails does not necessarily mean that it exerts an irresistible influence. The knowledge that an action will have very undesirable consequences does not mean that this in itself excludes the possibility of defying the threat. The possibility of doing other than the individual issuing the threat desires is still very much open. In many (if not all – depending on one's acceptance of libertarianism or determinism and one's understanding of the limits of human freedom) cases the threatened party may choose to defy the person attempting to coerce him and face the consequences, this leads to the conclusion that there is still moral responsibility involved in performing the action (however the degree of moral responsibility may be mitigated to some extent). See Frankfurt (1969), p. 834.
78 Ibid, p. 833.

2.4.3: Conclusion to Section 2.4

One of the crucial factors for moral responsibility in Frankfurt's Jones-style examples lies in whether Jones acts as a result of his own desires, or whether the action performed is a direct result of Black's controlling influence. Thus, on this model, moral responsibility is not dependent on Regulative Control over a specific action. The agent's moral responsibility for an act is dependent on whether or not he identifies with the act that he does – whether or not he has a second-order desire for the act to occur. This is part of what it means to say that an agent's moral responsibility for an act relies on his power to identify with his desires in an apposite way, and to act in accordance with them (that is, to make a second-order desire his will and to act such that that desire is fulfilled).

The compatibilist contends that this identification is the central locus of responsibility, and in Jones-style examples where Black does intervene Jones is not only deprived of the ability to act in accordance with his desire, he is also deprived of the ability to form an intention that reflects his strongest second-order desire. This is true irrespective of whether we accept an incompatibilist or a compatibilist characterisation of moral responsibility.

What of the Control Condition? If Jones does not have Regulative Control over his actions, does he have any control over them? In this section it has been shown that it is possible to contend that he does. This is because it may be that all that is necessary to fulfil the Control Condition is 'Guidance Control'.[79]

It is possible for the advocate of FPR to claim that what he sees as the fundamental truth of Jones-style examples (that the agent does not need multiple actualisable alternatives or Regulative Control) can be extended to the context of every morally significant action. It may be that, even though the agent can never perform anything other than a single hard-determined action, he is still responsible for every action that he does. In other words, in any situation in which he acts, there may be some factors that would come into play to ensure that Jones does a particular action if he were to give a sign that he was about to form the intention to do other than what he previously intended. However, it can be argued that Jones never does in fact form the intention to do other than what is hard-determined and therefore these factors never become efficient causes that force him to act contrary to his strongest second-order desire. This means that Jones would never come into conflict with the determining factors. There is nothing self-evidently incoherent about this account.

Although this account appears plausible, we may still be uneasy about the fact that in doing something morally inferior the agent is also refraining from doing something morally superior, and that this fact should be in some way

---

79   See Fischer and Ravizza (1998), Chapters 1-2 for a discussion of Regulative and Guidance Control.

reflected in a principle that attempts to account for the sufficient conditions of moral responsibility – thereby helping to define the type of control that fulfils the Control Condition. What I mean is that it may not be valid to blame an agent for doing something if he could not in fact have done anything else (including refraining from acting) given the state of affairs that comprised the world at the time of acting. This may be the case even if the agent acted in accordance with his strongest second-order desire, and identified with an irresistible desire that motivated him to action.

In the next section I will ask whether it is valid to blame the agent for doing something when it was impossible for him to form the intention to do anything else.

2.5: The Principle of Possible Action

2.5.0: Introduction to Section 2.5

Section 2.5 is devoted to the idea of 'possible action' and its ramifications for moral responsibility.

2.5.1: An Introduction to the Principle of Possible Action

Peter van Inwagen has formulated a principle of moral responsibility that attempts to show the necessity of actualisable alternative possibilities (and by implication Regulative Control) for moral responsibility in specific contexts. He calls it the Principle of Possible Action (PPA):

> PPA: A person is morally responsible for failing to perform a given act only if he could have performed that act. [80]

He believes that this principle can successfully counter the most cogent objections raised by Jones-style counterexamples to the incompatibilist thesis.[81] How does this principle avoid these difficulties?

In *Responsibility and Inevitability* Fischer and Ravizza offer an example that

---

80   Van Inwagen (1983), p. 155.
81   Glannon (1995), p. 252.

helps to illustrate van Inwagen's contention.[82] Jones was walking along a beach when he saw a child that was drowning, yet he was not interested enough to do anything to help. What Jones did not know was that there was a patrol of sharks nearby in the water. Had he tried to rescue the child he would certainly have been prevented from doing so by the sharks. He cannot be held morally responsible for failing to save the child as the possibility of doing so was never in his power – the situation was determined such that this possibility was never actualisable.

It should be noted that the claim is that Jones is not responsible for not saving the child, and not that he is devoid of responsibility for not attempting to save the child. These are two separate (although arguably related) issues. We cannot blame Jones for not actually saving the child, but we may be able to justifiably blame him for not attempting to save the child, even if the same result would have ensued independently of how he actually acted (that is, the child would have drowned).

It can be argued that this example shows a flaw in FPR and suggests that PPA is a more plausible principle. The reason for this is that even if Jones was controlled by Black so that he did not attempt to save the child, the ability to save the child would still not have been within his power, irrespective of whether or not his desire coincided with that of Black. Thus, the responsibility for failing to save the child is nullified irrespective of whether Jones's actions were determined.

2.5.2: PPA, FPR and Moral Responsibility

Even if we accept that we are in some sense morally accountable under the criteria of FPR, PPA helps to show that we are still not morally responsible in significant ways.[83] This is better explained by way of example. Jones stole a car last Monday. He wanted to steal the car for the pleasure of the theft and the thrill of driving it. He believed this desire to be of greatest benefit. His evaluative and motivational systems coincided. He formed the intention to steal himself and there were no external factors that forced him to do so. It is not true that he stole only because he could not do otherwise.

Yet, if Jones could not exercise Regulative Control over his actions, it was never possible that he do other than steal the car on Monday. Assuming Jones is hard-determined he could not do other than what the hard-determining factors (F) at play in the world entailed he must do. According to Frankfurt, we can still hold Jones morally accountable for his action because he does the action

---

82   Fischer and Ravizza (1991).
83   I would note that I am developing PPA for my own purposes and am not necessarily suggesting that my development will always be in harmony with what was originally intended by van Inwagen, or would be endorsed by him.

that he identifies with his will, wants to do it and identifies with that desire in an apposite way, and is not subject to the intervention of a Black-type coercive force. Is this argument valid?

The following helps to illustrate the greatest defect of claiming that Guidance Control is sufficient for Moral Control in light of FPR. If Jones is hard-determined by F, such that he could not exercise Regulative Control over his actions, and if he freely identifies with his desire to steal, then it is impossible to discredit the fact that his desire and identification with it are also hard-determined by F.

If it is hard-determined that Jones will do X at t, and if forming the second-order desire to X is integral to the actual performance of X, then his identification with the second-order desire to X must also be hard-determined (for otherwise F would not be effective). The same is true of any other factors that are essential to Jones performance of X (for example, he must also be hard-determined to have a particular conception of benefit or to fail to abdicate his ability to evaluate his action – whatever essentially contributes to the actual performance of X). Thus we must also accept that Jones's second-order desire is hard-determined. If this is the case, then it was never possible that Jones not identify with his desire to steal in this instance (given the state of affairs that comprised the actual world prior to his choice). This poses serious questions for the validity of judging Guidance Control to be sufficient for Moral Control. I will now proceed to explain why.

While it is true that Jones conformed to Frankfurt's FPR, if he is incapable of exercising Regulative Control over his action, and if he is hard-determined, a good act was never an actualisable possibility (because of his hard-determined disposition). He therefore cannot be blamed for failing to be morally praiseworthy (that is by not stealing) under PPA (as he can only be held responsible for failing to perform a morally superior act if he actually could have performed that act). But what is the significance of this for morally responsible agency and does it successfully undermine the claim that Guidance Control is sufficient for Moral Control? We should bear in mind that one can ask what difference does the contention of PPA make. Frankfurt never argues that it is possible to blame Jones for not doing something morally praiseworthy, he is merely arguing that he can be blamed for doing something morally deficient even if it is true that he could not do otherwise.

2.5.3: Possible Action and Moral Maxims

When one includes the failure to comply with an 'ought' or 'ought not' maxim as a justification for moral judgement, one assumes that the agent being judged has the ability to do, and not to do, what the prescription demands. Also, when one appeals to a principle such as 'It is wrong to steal', the maxim 'you ought not to steal' is included by implication. For what is the point of appealing to a moral principle for the justification of the application of praise or blame, if it is impossible for the agent to conform to it? The maxim 'you ought not to steal' is seen to be lacking in substance if, as in the example of Jones's car theft, one was incapable of contrary action. What this amounts to is the claim that the agent must have actualisable alternative possibilities in relation to what he does if he is to be held morally responsible for his actions (in the sense of having the power to do something morally superior at t, and also having the power to do something morally inferior at t).

In the earlier example, while Jones could not be held morally responsible for actually failing to save the child (as this was never a possibility), he could still be held blameworthy for failing to conform to the imperative that he should have tried to save the child (for *should responsibility* requires *could ability*, and the type of control necessary for such a form of responsibility requires that one have the ability *to do*, or *not to* do, in morally significant choice contexts, and that both options be actualisable at the time of choosing). However, to justifiably blame him for not conforming to a moral maxim would require that he had the actual ability to act in accordance with it.

> Barring cogent reasons to believe otherwise, if we assume that "ought" implies "can", there is little reason not to assume, too, that "wrong" (and "right") imply "can". For the freedom - or control-relevant presuppositions of obligatoriness, it would seem, should also be the very ones of wrongness and rightness. If we grant that "wrong" implies "can", then we can show that obligation requires alternative possibilities.[84]

Consider the following:

If we accept that Jones cannot be held morally responsible for failing to save the child because he did not have the power to save him irrespective of his desires (as in Jones-style examples), then how can we justify holding someone morally responsible for failing to adhere to a moral maxim if he does not even have the power to form the desire to adhere to that maxim? If hard-determining factors entail the second-order desires that the agent identifies with, and thereby has sufficient power to ensure that it is impossible to act contrary to what is hard-determined, then *the agent has absolutely no power to alter what he desires* unless that alteration is in accordance with what is hard-determined. This is obviously an argument for incompatibilism.

If the agent has no power over his second-order desires (that is, cannot exercise Regulative Control over them), then how can we justify the assertion that: 'A person is not morally responsible for what he has done if he did it *only* because he could not have done otherwise'. There is a very real sense, if hard-determinism obtains, that the agent does everything he does in virtue of the fact that he cannot do otherwise. His reasons for acting, and all other necessary

---

84   Haji (2003), p. 290.

components of making a second-order desire his will, are predetermined by F in the hard sense. Thus, although he does not act '*only* because he could not have done otherwise', in the sense proposed by Frankfurt, he does act as he does because it is the *only* way that he can act – he cannot do anything else because of the irresistibility of his desire (due to the power of F).

There is something contradictory in blaming an agent for doing what he does, if he cannot be blamed for what he does not do – for surely they are two sides of the same coin? The same is true of praising him for doing something when he did not have the power to do anything morally deficient. Thomas Reid illustrates this point with reference to Cato:

> He was good because he could not have been otherwise… This saying, if understood literally and strictly, is not the praise of Cato, but of his constitution, which was no more the work of Cato than his existence.[85]

In the shark example above, we do not blame Jones for not saving the boy, although we do blame him for walking past the drowning boy and not *attempting* to save him. However, if the agent were hard-determined such that he had no power to even form the intention to save the boy then there is a significant sense in which we cannot blame him for his failure.

Let us momentarily return to Jones-style examples to help to illustrate this point. In this type of example, Jones must show a sign that he is about to form what would be an effective intention that would result in an action contrary to Black's desire. One of the reasons that we do blame Jones in instances in which Black does not intervene is because he does not give a sign that runs counter to what Black wants to occur. The reason that we do not blame Jones when Black intervenes is because he has given such a sign before Black manipulates the effective intention that he forms, and consequently controls the action that he performs. This means that Jones cannot identify with his second-order desire in an apposite way. However, by having the power to do something such that he shows a sign that he is about to form an intention that is contrary to Black's desire, and by also having the power to do something such that he fails to show a sign that he is about to form an intention that is contrary to Black's desire, he has Regulative Control over whether or not these signs occur. After all, if the sign results in the fact that a particular intention is formed and becomes effective then there is a sense in which Jones can do otherwise, if left to his own devices. However, if Jones were hard-determined such that he did not even have Regulative Power over what sign was given then there is no convincing sense in which he could be blamed for not doing otherwise.

It is difficult to imagine what could constitute the sign that Frankfurt assumes Black would be able to successfully interpret. One could argue that if the sign

---

85 Reid ([1785] 1941), Essay 4, ch. 4.

results in an effective intention to act that it is part of the effective intention. What is the substantive difference, as relates to this argument, as to whether Jones has Regulative Control over the sign that precedes the formation of what would be an effective intention (if not externally manipulated) and the formation of the intention itself? It is my claim that there is none. What difference would it make to this argument if Jones were to form the intention to act in a fashion before Black's intervention? It is my contention that it would make no substantive difference to what I have argued in relation to Jones's moral responsibility for his action.

One must ask what is involved in the idea that you can blame an agent for killing, but that you cannot blame him for failing not to kill (in the same instance)? If there is no possible world that can be actualised where he does not perform this morally deficient action, and this fact has been hard-determined before his birth, then in what way can he be blamed for performing the action in question? We must acknowledge that he could exercise no power over its occurrence. If this is the case, it is my contention that Guidance Control is not sufficient for moral responsibility and is therefore not an apt candidate for fulfilling the criterion of Moral Control.

My claim is that in order to be morally responsible the agent must be praiseworthy and blameworthy with respect to both what he does and what he fails to do in each morally significant choice context. Thereby, I am contending that the agent's actions, and failures to act, are integrally connected – for each act involves the fact that he has not acted in a contrary fashion. Thus to be morally responsible for a theft it must be possible to blame the agent for stealing, and also to blame him for failing not to steal. This language may sound convoluted but it does help to illustrate my point.

2.5.4: Conclusion to Section 2.5

I have just demonstrated that Jones-style examples do not undermine the insistence that Regulative Control is essential to morally responsible agency.

I will therefore formulate what I will call the 'Regulative Principle of Responsibility' as follows, and add it to the criteria of morally responsible agency:

> (xii) In order to have moral responsibility for a specific act the agent must have Regulative Control over the second-order desire that motivates it (this is presuming that all of the conditions for morally responsible agency that have already been delineated are satisfied), and have the power to act in accordance with that desire, irrespective of the state of affairs that constitutes the world at the time of acting.

This principle accounts for PPA and FPR, fulfils the Control Condition and can counter the possible objections stemming from Jones-style examples. Thus, it is more comprehensive than either principle individually. This is one of the defining principles for moral responsibility that I will continue to utilise in the following chapters.

2.6: Conclusion to Chapter 2

In Chapter 2 I have offered the final criterion of the abilities and capacities that the agent must possess if he is to be capable of morally responsible agency. I believe that in so doing I have established a firm foundation from which to progress to the question of the ramifications that divine foreknowledge would have for the agent's ability to be morally responsible. The truth of this claim will be tested in the following chapters.

In the preceding pages I have introduced what I consider to be the most convincing approaches to satisfactorily defining the type of control essential to Moral Control. However, it has ultimately been shown that the agent requires Regulative Control, at a particular level of the process involved in performing an action, if he is to have moral responsibility for it.

What is the significance of this for an investigation of the consequences that divine foreknowledge would have for morally responsible agency? The answer is that if God's foreknowledge determines the agent's actions it must do so in a way that allows the agent Regulative Control over the formation of his intentions, and allows him to act in accordance with the intention that he freely forms (in the forking-paths sense). If God's foreknowledge entails that the agent must perform a specific action and hard-determines the second-order desire and conception of benefit (and any other factors essential to the performance of the act) with which the agent will identify at a particular time of acting, then the agent cannot be morally responsible for what he does. In other words, if God's foreknowledge is sufficient to hard-determine everything that must occur in the future then it may be the case that it is God who determines whether or not the agent is exposed to the correct moral standard and whether or not he identifies with it and acts in accordance with it. The reasons for this have been discussed in the course of this chapter and will be further explained and tested in the following sections.

However, I have not yet given any conclusive reasons to show that divine foreknowledge necessarily excludes the possibility of morally responsible agency. In the next Chapter, I will examine God's powers and begin an investigation of this issue.

3

God's Essential Attributes and the Power to do Otherwise

3.1: An Introduction to Chapter 3

Many of us may be concerned about the status of our moral responsibility if God has infallible foreknowledge of all that will occur. For example, we might wonder: 'Was Adam truly responsible for eating the forbidden fruit, if God knew in advance that he would do so?'[86] This then may lead to the question: 'Was Adam really free with regard to this act of defiance (or lapse of judgement)?' Any Christian attempt to address this concern will have to accommodate two fundamental beliefs. The first is that God does not necessitate the agent's actions, and the second is that even if God foreknows what the agent will do he is still morally responsible for his particular actions. These two beliefs are part of the grounding of the Christian theory of moral responsibility and essential to any plausible Christian theodicy. Yet the belief in human libertarian freedom and divine foreknowledge may intuitively appear at variance. This is a point about which the Fathers of the Church were all too aware.

For example, Augustine succinctly sums up the problem as follows:

> Since he foreknew that man would sin, the sin was committed of necessity, because God foreknew that it would happen. How can there be free will when there is such inevitable necessity?[87]

Boethius frames the concern thus:

> It seems... too much of a paradox and a contradiction that God should know all things, and yet there should be free will. For if God foresees everything, and can in no wise be deceived, that which providence foresees to be about to happen must necessarily come to pass. Wherefore, if from eternity He foreknows not only what men will do, but also their designs and purposes, there can be no freedom of the will, seeing that nothing can be done, nor can any sort of purpose be entertained, save such as a Divine providence, incapable of being deceived,

---

86   I think that the scenario involving Adam serves aptly as a paradigmatic example of any particular agent succumbing to the lure of temptation and performing morally deficient actions.
87   Augustine ([387-395] 1964). Bk. III, ii, 15.

has perceived beforehand.[88]

These and similar concerns have given rise to an idea that has become known as theological fatalism. Fatalism is the thesis that no agent has the power to do anything about what will occur in the future.[89] Even the agent's behaviour cannot be thought to be within his power in any significant respect. The fatalist in many ways thinks of the future similarly to the way in which many of us think of the past. He believes that just as what happened last century, or aeons ago, are not up to him, so too is the future beyond the scope of his influence (including his own personal actions, thoughts, intentions, values, goals and so forth). The theological fatalist believes that God has already hard-determined what will happen, in the sense of fatalistically necessitating all future occurrences, before any particular individual arrives on the scene, and that there is nothing that anyone can do about it.[90]

What consequences would the truth of fatalism have for morally responsible agency? While it is true that theological fatalism does not necessarily conflict with my criteria (i) – (xi) of morally responsible agency, one would have to admit that it does result in several problems. It is a fact that in the real world the vast multitude of individuals do not always act in accordance with the correct moral standard and moral norms, and do not always form the second-order desire to act morally. This being the case, if their actions are fatalistically necessitated, such that they cannot do otherwise in any meaningful sense when they act immorally, then one would have to accept that they cannot be held morally responsible for what they have done (because at the time of acting they could not satisfy all the criteria of morally responsible agency).

In regard to instances of action that are not in conflict with either theological fatalism or my criteria (x) – (xi), the agent will always be doing something morally superior (otherwise he would be fatalistically constrained such that he does not have the power to form the second-order desire to do something morally superior and to act on that desire). Thus, we are left with the unsettling position that the agent is only morally responsible for morally superior acts, and cannot be held responsible for morally inferior acts. This is not something that I would intuitively believe is sufficient to constitute moral responsibility. However, be this as it may, it is my final criterion that cannot be satisfied if fatalism obtains.

Theological fatalism is obviously in conflict with criterion (xii). The reasons for this should be apparent from the discussions of the previous chapter. It is

---

88 Boethius ([c. 522] 1897), p. 234.
89 For accounts of fatalism see, for example, Taylor (1962) and (1963), Helm (1975) and Cargile (1996).
90 Taylor (1962), p. 56. For a discussion of theological fatalism see also, Helm (1974), McArthur (1977), Hasker (1988), Haack (1974 and 1975), Craig (1992), Talbot (1993), Gaskin (1994a), Hughes (1997) and Hunt (1998).

impossible for the individual to be hard-determined and still have Regulative Control over his second-order desires. If theological fatalism obtains, there is no significant sense in which the agent has the ability (power) to do otherwise. Due to the fact that criterion (xii) is fundamentally incompatible with theological fatalism it is this criterion that I will primarily focus on in the forthcoming discussion. The power to do otherwise, in the sense of having Regulative Control over one's second-order desires, is the only one of my criteria that is necessarily in opposition to theological fatalism and any form of determinism.

In this introduction I have outlined several of the sorts of concerns that have prompted me to begin this investigation. I hope, by the end of this work, to have provided answers to the questions that stem from them, or at least suggested strategies for finding those answers. It is my belief that there may be a way to reconcile divine knowledge of all occurrences that are future *from our perspective* with libertarian freedom and morally responsible agency – but that this can only be achieved by sacrificing the idea that God exists in a succession of moments and by accepting that God has unmediated knowledge of human actions.

However, before proceeding to this issue, I would first like to engage with the possibility that there is compatibility between the foreknowledge of a temporally located God and the agent's having Regulative Control over his actions. If the idea of such compatibility is shown to be coherent, then it will be possible to confirm that God's foreknowledge allows for morally responsible agency. Christianity affirms on Biblical and theological grounds that God has foreknowledge of everything that will occur in the future (relative to any particular moment in time). This is traditionally thought to be part of what constitutes his omniscience.

In the course of this and the following chapter I will be dealing exclusively with a conception of divine existence that postulates that God exists in a succession of moments – according to this characterisation God is sempiternal, which means that there is in a significant sense in which he is located 'in' time. Thus, when I make reference to divine 'foreknowledge' I will intend an understanding of God's knowledge where the position of the knower is temporally prior to the occurrence of what is known (I will continue to adopt this characterisation until Chapter 5, when I will consider the Molinist understanding of divine foreknowledge). It is assumed by those who adopt such a characterisation of foreknowledge that God is not bounded by all of the same epistemic constraints that limit the agent - God is not limited by his temporal location relative to the object of his knowledge. God knows propositions that express future occurrences *before* those states of affairs have obtained. This is what I take to be the substantive difference between 'foreknowledge' of a fact and 'timeless knowledge' of a fact (where it is taken that in the latter the knower in question does not have this type of temporal relation to the object of his knowledge. I will later consider whether it is possible to have knowledge of everything that will occur at all times without sempiternality – however, I will argue that if it is possible then we are no longer referring to what would be properly known as '*fore*knowledge').

There is difficulty in providing a sufficient explanation of the way in which God foreknows, because of the cognitive differences between the creature and the creator. Nevertheless, if the question of the compatibility of divine foreknowledge and morally responsible agency is to make any sense, one must attempt to provide an account that is sufficient for one to appreciate the ramifications that sempiternal foreknowledge would have on the agent's Regulative Control.

The purpose of this chapter is to briefly delineate the characteristics that I assume that God possesses which are relevant to my investigation. I also offer an argument that attempts to show the incompatibility between divine foreknowledge and the agent's power to do otherwise. The points raised and the reasoning used in this argument will prove especially relevant to my discussion of Ockhamism. Before progressing further, I would first like to stipulate that in the following discussion when I say 'act' I mean 'form the second order desire to act and act in accordance with that desire'. The reason for this qualification will become more apparent in my final discussion of morally responsible agency. I will now proceed to give an account of the attributes that I will assume God possesses. I believe that the following account will not prove controversial.

3.2: The Attributes of God

3.2.0: Introduction to Section 3.2

This section is devoted to exploring God's essence and powers (in a very limited way that serves to ground the arguments of this and the following chapters). In later sections I will spend more time considering the way in which he exercises those powers, and whether they allow for my criteria of morally responsible agency. For the purposes of this investigation, unless otherwise stated, it has been assumed that God exists. It is beyond the scope of this book to offer reasons for arguing the existence, or non-existence, of God. Others have spent time and effort arguing the truth and falsity of this matter, and, if this is a point of interest, I would direct you to their work.[91] However, irrespective of whether God actually

---

91 See, for example, the works of Anselm and Aquinas. See also, for example, Jack (1965), Kordig (1981), Mackie (1982), Braine (1988), and Gale (1991).

exists, the validity of my arguments should hold at any possible world in which he does exist, and at which he has the characteristics that I attribute to him.[92]

I will presently introduce the attributes that I claim God possesses. In doing so I am assuming a classical version of theism, which I do not believe to be controversial. I do not attempt to prove that God must have these attributes, as once again, providing such proofs is beyond the scope of this work. It is my belief that every attribute God has he has necessarily. However, as this claim is not commonly assented to by either the Ockhamist or the Molinist, I will instead make the following weaker assumption, which I do not think the majority of religious philosophers would object to. I will assume that any attribute God has, he has essentially. To say that God has an essential property is to say that he has that property at every possible world in which he exists.[93] In the course of my investigations I will consider relevant oppositions to this view, or qualifications of it.

What do I mean by a 'possible world'? Worlds are universes that are spatio-temporal manifolds in which states of affairs obtain.[94] A possible world is a world that could logically be the case. To state that there is a possible world $W1$ is to state that there is a logically consistent universe in which the state of affairs that comprises $W1$ could obtain. However, the logical consistency of a possible state of affairs is not sufficient to make that state of affairs actually occur. Therefore, it is necessary to draw a distinction between the existence of the possible world $W1$ as a conception or a logical possibility and an actual world that actually exists. Just because $W1$ is conceptually and logically coherent does not mean that, given the state of the actual world at any moment in time, it will ever actually exist, or has ever actually existed. It is my claim that there is only one actual world at any given time (this actual world is what I will call the 'real world'). The actual world is a discrete possible world. Thus, only one possible world is ever actual.

Plantinga defines a possible world thus:

> A possible world is any possible state of affairs that is complete. If [$W1$] is a possible world, then it says something about everything; every state of affairs S is either included or precluded by it.[95]

A possible world is a world that logically could be the case and is correctly conceived of as a logically coherent totality in itself.[96] Just as the actual world is

---

92   Possible worlds are introduced below.
93   See Pike (1977), p. 209.
94   See Nolt (1986), p. 432.
95   Plantinga (1974), p. 36.
96   For the purposes of the following discussion, I will temporarily adopt Plantinga's characterisation of a possible world. I will, however, proceed to offer a more detailed account of possible worlds as my argument progresses in this and the following chapter. I will make this clear when appropriate.

the totality of all states of affairs that actually obtain, so a possible world is the totality of all the states of affairs that would obtain in that world (that is given all of the factors and conditions that comprise it).[97] There are an indefinitely large or infinite number of worlds that are possible.[98]

3.2.1: God's Essential Attributes

It will be my working assumption that God is omnipotent, eternal, immutable, omniscient, infallible and provident. As already stated, I will also assume that he has all of these attributes essentially.

What do I mean when I say that God is omnipotent? My working definition of an omnipotent being is: 'An omnipotent being can do anything that it is logically possible for a perfect being to do.'[99] This obviously allows for the fact that there are certain limitations to his power.[100] Rather than attempt to offer a comprehensive account of what God can and cannot do at this point in the discussion, I will instead examine these issues as they become pertinent to my investigation.[101] I will particularly focus on the limitations of what can be known by a perfect omniscient being.[102]

One of the characteristics that is traditionally attributed to God is necessary existence.[103] This is an attribution that I will accept.[104] This is, once again, an

---

97 For a discussion of possible worlds see, for example, Prior (1962a), Chisholm (1967), Stalnaker (1976), Hoffman (1979), Stillwell (1985), and Nolt (1986).
98 See Rescher (1999), pp. 403-420.
99 Morris (2000), p. 404 (edited extract from *Our Idea of God*, Ch. 4, 1991). For further discussions of omnipotence see Cargile (1967), Plantinga (1974 a), Hoffman and Rosenkrantz (1980 and 1999), Flint and Freddoso (1983), Wierenga (1989), pp. 12-.35 and Morris (2000).
100 See Swinburne (1993), Ch. 9, for an explication of many of the difficulties in providing a coherent account of omnipotence.
101 Geach (1977), p. 4 has noted that there are inherent difficulties in attempting to offer any definitive account of what an omnipotent being can do. Some philosophers also believe that when attempting to delineate omnipotence we should not speak in terms of what God can 'do', and that instead we should focus on the powers that he possesses. See for example, Kenny (1979) esp. p. 96, Flint and Freddoso (1983) and Wierenga (1989) esp. pp. 12-35.
102 Thus, I do not wish to extensively deal with the concept of 'omnipotence' except as it specifically relates to the question of divine foreknowledge. Therefore, I will principally focus on what a maximally powerful being can and cannot foreknow, as opposed to what he can and cannot do or the totality of the powers that he can and cannot exercise.
103 See, for example, Rainer (1949), pp. 75-77, Plantinga (1974 a, 1974 b and 1980), Adams, R. M. (1983), Morris (1987 c), Morris and Menzel (1987), Wierenga (1989), MacDonald 1991 and Swinburne (1993), esp. Ch. 14.
104 One could use some form of the ontological argument to attempt to justify

assumption whose validity I will not argue. I am allowing that God must be necessary, because I am also assuming that without his sustaining power nothing created could endure.[105] I will therefore assume that God is metaphysically necessary.[106] What I mean is that God must exist if any possible world is to be actual. This is because the world that is actual is ontologically dependent on God (no world could in fact be actual without God's sustaining power).[107] I will, in essence, be proceeding on the assumption that God is the very grounding of the existence of the actual world and all that it contains. This puts the restriction on God that he cannot actualise a possible world at which he does not exist, for God is not the exemption of all metaphysical properties; he is rather their exemplification.[108]

It is also my claim that God is essentially eternal.[109] As I have defined metaphysical necessity, essential eternality follows from it. The life of God can be defined as 'illimitable' – it has neither a beginning nor an end. However, there is much debate over whether the eternal existence of God should be understood as sempiternality – the limitless duration through successive moments of time, or whether it should be understood as atemporality – eternal existence construed as being roughly analogous to an unchanging static state.[110] One can also question whether either of these conceptions do justice to the type of eternal existence that is essential to God. I will initially proceed on the assumption that God is sempiternal.[111] I will do so as my primary concern is with a God who has foreknowledge. If God is presumed to have temporally anterior knowledge of an occurrence in the historical world, then that knowledge bears a temporal relation to its object. It is my intention to argue that any attempt to reconcile sempiternal divine foreknowledge with libertarian freedom and morally responsible agency will ultimately prove untenable.

I further assume that God is immutable – in a particular qualified sense. The

---

this point of view, but I shall not do so as it is not my intention to engage in such a justification. For an exploration of this issue see Penelhum (1960).
105   See Adams (1988), p. 19.
106   For a related discussion see Hick (1960), esp. p. 726.
107   For example, Aquinas states: 'God cannot make a thing to be preserved in being without himself', *Summa Contra Gentiles*, 2.25.10. In Anderson (trans.) (1956).
108   Whitehead (1978), p. 363.
109   For an account of the eternal nature of God, and what it involves, see Swinburne (1993), esp. Ch. 12. For a discussion of divine eternity see Pike (1970), Stump and Kretzmann (1981), Helm (1988 and 2000), Yates (1990), Leftow (1991a and 1999), Padgett (1992) and Swinburne (1993), Craig (2000) and Stump and Kretzmann (2000).
110   See Stump and Kretzmannn (1981), esp. pp. 431-433.
111   As already stated, I am doing so because my thesis is primarily concerned with a God whose knowledge bears a temporal relation to its object – a God who has *fore*knowledge.

question of divine immutability is somewhat contentious.[112] Therefore, I will only contend that the content of God's knowledge does not change over time, as this is sufficient for my forthcoming discussion[113] Thus, nothing is ever added to, or subtracted from, the sum of God's knowledge.

I will also proceed on the assumption that God is essentially omniscient. What exactly does this mean? The following definitions of omniscience and God's essential omniscience are offered by Nelson Pike in 'A Latter Day Look at the Foreknowledge Problem':

> (I) If y is omniscient, then y believes all true propositions and believes no propositions that are false.[114]

> (II) God is essentially omniscient, i.e., the individual who is God possesses the attribute of omniscience in every possible world in which that individual exists.[115]

However, this definition can be criticised, as it does not explicitly account for, or explain, how God could know particular types of indexical propositions to be true (nor does it provide reasons why it should be assumed that indexical propositions can be reduced to non-indexical ones).[116] Providing an adequate account of omniscience has proven rather elusive.[117] Nevertheless, this is an issue with which I will not engage, as I will concern myself primarily with propositions of the form 'God knows at $t1$ that X will occur at $t2$'. Thus, the content of God's beliefs with which I am concerned (as they are the type of propositions relevant to my investigations concerning morally responsible agency) would be of the following form (or relevantly similar form): 'A (a particular agent) will X (perform a particular action) at t (a specific time)'. As a sempiternal God would have eternal knowledge of propositions of this form, it is true to say that for any particular moment in the entire history of time God foreknew (truly believed) these propositions (of course I am not suggesting that propositions of this type are the sole constituents of divine knowledge). Therefore, I will assume that an omniscient God knows all true propositions of this form (as part

---

112 See Creel (1999), esp. pp. 313-315.
113 For discussions of divine immutability see, for example, Morris (1984), Wienandy (1984), Creel (1986), Sarot (1992), Stump and Kretzmann (1992), Swinburne (1993), esp. pp. 219-223, and White (2000).
114 This is accepting that God's knowledge is propositional in nature.
115 Pike (1993), p. 130.
116 For a discussion of this issue see, for example, Wolterstorff (1982), Castaneda (1967) and Leftow (1991 a).
117 For discussions of omniscience see Prior (1962b), Kretzmannn (1966) and Swinburne (1993).

of the sum of his total knowledge) and believes no propositions that are false. I will further assume that an essentially omniscient God possesses the attribute of omniscience at every possible world in which he exists.

I will return in the next Chapter to the question of what is involved in the idea of divine providence.

3.3: The Question of the Compatibility of Divine Foreknowledge and the Power to do Otherwise

3.3.0: Introduction to Section 3.3

The publication in 1965 of Pike's paper 'Divine Omniscience and Voluntary Action' gave rise to a resurgence of interest in the question of the compatibility of divine foreknowledge and the ability to do otherwise, which is still much in evidence today. As this was such an influential paper, I believe that a discussion of it is warranted. This discussion will also help to establish many of the issues and problems that the Ockhamist account attempts to address and resolve.

3.3.1: Pike on Divine Foreknowledge and the Power to do Otherwise

Pike presents us with a paradigmatic scenario in which it is claimed that an agent is incapable of exercising Regulative Control over his actions, due to God's anterior knowledge of what he would do.

> Last Saturday afternoon, Jones mowed his lawn. Assuming that God exists and is (essentially) omniscient… it follows that (let us say) eighty years prior to last Saturday afternoon, God knew (and thus believed) that Jones would mow his lawn at that time. But from this it follows, I think, that at the time of action (last Saturday afternoon) Jones was not able—that is, it was not within Jones's power—to refrain from mowing his lawn.

In order to argue to his conclusion (i.e. that Jones is incapable of doing otherwise) Pike makes the following assumptions:

    a)   Being omniscient involves being infallible, and believing that p if and only if it is true that p.

    b)   God is essentially omniscient and infallible (this means that if a given entity is God he not only has never held a false belief, but cannot hold one. If a given entity does hold a false belief then that entity cannot be God).

c) God knows all future states of affairs.

d) God is sempiternal.

Pike believes that it follows from God's essential omniscience that the following proposition must be treated as an a priori truth.

> For any natural event (including human actions), if a given person is God, that person would always have known that that event was going to occur at the time it occurred.

He proceeds to offer the following argument as a justification for his incompatibilist position:

1. "God existed at $t1$" entails "If Jones did X at $t2$, God believed at $t1$ that Jones would do X at $t2$."

2. "God believes X" entails "X is true".

3. It is not within one's power at a given time to do something having a description that is logically contradictory.

4. It is not within one's power at a given time to do something that would bring it about that someone who held a certain belief at a time prior to the time in question did not hold that belief at the time prior to the time in question.

5. It is not within one's power at a given time to do something that would bring it about that a person who existed at an earlier time did not exist at that earlier time.

6. If God existed at $t1$ and if God believed at $t1$ that Jones would do X at $t2$, then if it was within Jones's power at $t2$ to refrain from doing X, then (1) it was within Jones's power at $t2$ to do something that would have brought it about that God held a false belief at $t1$, or (2) it was within Jones's power at $t2$ to do something which would have brought it about that God did not hold the belief He held at $t1$, or (3) it was within Jones's power at $t2$ to do something that would have brought it about that any person who believed at $t1$ that Jones would do X at $t2$ (one of whom was, by hypothesis, God) held a false belief and thus was not God - that is, that God (who by hypothesis existed at $t1$) did not exist at $t1$.

7. Alternative 1 in the consequent of item 6 is false (from 2 and 3).

8. Alternative 2 in the consequent of item 6 is false (from 4).

9. Alternative 3 in the consequent of item 6 is false (from 5).

10. Therefore, if God existed at $t1$ and if God believed at $t1$ that Jones would do X at $t2$, then it was not within Jones's power at $t2$ to refrain from doing X (from 6 through 9).

11. Therefore, if God existed at tl and if Jones did X at $t2$, it was not within

Jones's power at *t2* to refrain from doing *X* (from 1 and 10).[118]

Let us now take a closer look at 6, which is the step in this argument that is most frequently criticised. This states that in order to have the ability to do otherwise (and thereby show the falsity of theological fatalism/incompatibilism), given the existence of a God who has the characteristics that Pike has presumed, one of the following propositions must be true[119]:

(1) It is within Jones's power at *t2* to do something that would have brought it about that God held a false belief at *t1*

(2) It is within Jones's power at *t2* to do something which would have brought it about that God did not hold the belief He held at *t1*.

(3) It was within Jones's power at *t2* to do something that would have brought it about that any person who believed at *t1* that Jones would do *X* at *t2* (one of whom was, by hypothesis, God) held a false belief and thus was not God - that is, that God (who by hypothesis existed at *t1*) did not exist at *t1*.[120]

Is Pike's model valid – is he correct in his assertion that the agent must have the power involved in at least one of his three propositions, if he is to be capable of doing otherwise, given the existence of a God with sempiternal foreknowledge and essential omniscience and infallibility? I will answer this question by looking at each proposition individually. In doing so, I will consider arguments which propose that the fact that God has foreknowledge does not necessarily mean that theological fatalism is true, and that it is possible to show that Jones can have the power involved in one of these propositions.

3.3.2: 'It is within Jones's power at *t2* to do something that would have brought it about that God held a false belief at *t1*.' (Pike's Proposition 1)

It is an impossibility that this proposition is true, as it is beyond the power of Jones to bring about a state of affairs that involves a logical contradiction. It has been claimed that to be God is to be essentially omniscient and infallible. To be omniscient is to know all true propositions (at least of the form that I have specified) and to believe no propositions that are false. To be infallible is not just to believe no false propositions, but for it to be impossible to believe a

---

118   Pike (1965), pp. 33-34.
119   It should be noted that Pike explicitly states that he is not attempting to argue the truth or falsity of fatalism, but is rather attempting to construct an argument that is valid if particular assumptions about the existence and nature of God are made. His focus is essential omniscience and infallibility – he does not refer to the other divine attributes that I have assumed God possesses.
120   Pike (1965), pp. 31-33.

false proposition. It is incoherent to state that Jones could do something that would entail an essentially omniscient and essentially infallible being held a false belief.[121] It is logically impossible for Jones to have the requisite power to act at $t2$ such that God would have existed and held a false belief at $t1$.

I will now proceed to Proposition 3 before considering Proposition 2, as the latter is essential to much of the argument of the remainder of this and the following chapter. Examining the propositions in this order should help the argument to flow smoothly.

3.3.3: It was within Jones's power at $t2$ to do something that would have brought it about that any person who believed at $t1$ that Jones would do X at $t2$ (one of whom was, by hypothesis, God) held a false belief and thus was not God - that is, that God (who by hypothesis existed at $t1$) did not exist at $t1$. (Pike's Proposition 3)

Pike defends the idea that Jones cannot have the power suggested in this proposition as:

> No action performed at a given time can alter the fact that a certain person existed at a time prior to the time in question. This, too, seems to me to be an *a priori* truth.[122]

This assertion is reliant on the truth of what has become known as The Principle of the Fixity of the Past (PFP):

> All facts about the past are over done with in the sense that they cannot be subject to revision or alteration as a consequence of later events.

If we accept that the Principle of the Fixity of the Past applies to the fact that an individual entity existed at a particular time, then Pike's above assertion appears self-apparently valid. God's existence at $t1$ is taken to be a fixed fact relative to $t2$ (in the sense of not being subject to alteration due to anterior events). I too would accept that this is an *a priori* truth. However, even though I would accept that it is self-evident that no one has the ability to bring it about at some later time that God did not exist at $t1$ (given that he is metaphysically necessary and sempiternal), I will now examine a strategy that attempts to refute the idea that it would be necessary to have such a power, in the sense suggested by Proposition 3, in order for Jones to be able to act contrary to X (the act that God foreknew would occur at $t2$).

If we accept the assumption that 'God' is a *non-rigid designator*, it may be possible to argue that a particular entity that was 'God' at $t1$ ceased to be so due

---

121   Ibid, p. 32.
122   Ibid, p. 33.

to the actions performed by Jones at *t2*. This may sound unusual, but if we are working upon the assumption that 'God' is a non-rigid designator then we are committed to the view that 'God' refers to a role rather than a person.[123] One can then claim that the divine attributes are essential to the role of God, and not to the individual who happens to occupy that role. Thus, in order to fulfil the role of God, an entity must be omniscient, eternal, infallible and so forth.[124]

However, if we take it that 'God' is a non-rigid designator and that 'Yahweh' is the proper name of an individual entity that occupies the role of God, then 'Yahweh' is not the proper name of an entity who is necessarily God.[125] Thus, Yahweh does not necessarily personify the divine attributes – there is the logical possibility that some other entity who is not Yahweh could be God (however, some entity must be God, as he is metaphysically necessary in all possible worlds that could be actual).[126] Let us suppose that Yahweh occupies the role of God in a particular way at t1, and that it is Yahweh who believes that Jones will X at *t2*. Yahweh is God only in so far as he actually does exemplify the divine attributes – were he to cease to exemplify them then he would no longer be God.

Following this line of reasoning, Fischer points out that there are two ways in which to interpret the power involved in the claim that Jones could act contrary to X at *t2*: (i) Jones has the power to act such that God did not exist at t1 (ii) Jones has the power to act at *t2* such that Yahweh was not God at *t1*.[127] It is the former formulation that is essential to Pike's argument. If it is possible to successfully argue that the latter is a viable option, it may be possible to show that Jones can operate Regulative Control over his actions at *t2*, irrespective of the existence of God and his foreknowledge at *t1*. How would this differentiation help?

The claim is that in order to exercise Regulative Control it is not necessary that Jones be capable of causing God to cease to exist at *t1*. It may be the case that all that is needed is the weaker power to act at *t2* such that Yahweh would not have been an appropriate candidate for the role of God at *t1*. If Jones acted contrary to the beliefs of Yahweh this would not require that the person Yahweh cease to exist – it would rather mean that the person Yahweh would no longer personify the divine attributes and would thereby no longer fulfil the role of God. Yahweh would not have had infallible foreknowledge at *t1*, as one of his beliefs would fail to obtain at *t2*, and therefore some other entity would have been God. Some other entity would still actually fill the role of God, as this is a metaphysical

---

123   See Pike (1969), pp. 208-209.
124   See Fischer (1983), p. 69. He does not refer to each of the different divine attributes that I am discussing, but if his argument is valid it should hold even taking these into account. He primarily focuses on omniscience.
125   For an account of using 'God' as a proper name see Swinburne (1993), pp. 234-238.
126   This strategy is employed by Martin (1964), in Chapter 4.
127   Fischer (1983), p. 78.

necessity. It is only the entity that is capable of successfully foreknowing what Jones will in fact do at *t2* that can be God.

In his reply to Fischer, Pike attempts to illustrate the possibilities allowed by such a differentiation through his discussion of what he calls a 'Jones-Predictor'.[128] Smith is a Jones-Predictor at t1 and believes that Jones will do *X* at *t2*. To be a Jones-Predictor is to hold no false beliefs about what Jones will do. Can Smith do something other than *X* at *t2*, given the fact that Smith is a Jones-Predictor at *t1*? The answer is that there is no incoherency in affirming that he can. Smith is a Jones-Predictor at *t1* only because he has formed a belief at this time about what Jones will do at *t2* that is proven true by Jones's later action. Jones does proceed to *X* at *t2* and this affirms Smith's status at *t1*.

However, there is nothing that prevents Jones from acting contrary to *X* at *t2* - there is nothing about Smith's status as a Jones-Predictor that logically entails that Jones must *X* at *t2*, or causes him to do so. It is rather that Jones has the power to do something other than *X* at *t2* if he so chooses, but this is a power that he does not actually exercise. It is in virtue of Jones not exercising the power to act contrary to *X* that Smith retains his role as Jones-Predictor – if Jones were to have done otherwise, Smith would no longer have satisfied the criterion of being a Jones-Predictor, although some other entity possibly could.

Fischer's argument is based on similar reasoning. He merely substitutes 'Yahweh' for 'Smith' and 'God' for 'Jones-Predictor'. According to this model, it is not necessary for Jones to make Yahweh cease to exist for him to be able to do other than *X* at *t2*. If he does some action other than *X* then Yahweh will still exist – it is just that, in lieu of Jones's action, he will no longer satisfy the criterion of being God, as he would have held a false belief at *t1*. Therefore, we could contend that if Yahweh does occupy the role of God at *t1* that Jones still has the capacity to perform some action other than *X* at *t2*, but that this is a capacity that he does not exercise.

The conclusion that we reach, as a result of Fischer's argument, is that an entity who has historically displayed the attributes of omniscience, and eternality is not sufficient to prevent the agent from exercising Regulative Control over his actions at any time. This appears to pose a difficulty for the denial of Proposition (3) as advocated by Pike. However, I will now show that, if we accept the characteristics that I have attributed to God, but can reach a different and coherent understanding of what it is to be God than that proposed by Fischer, it is possible to illuminate a fundamental flaw in his thesis.

On closer analysis there appears to be a discrepancy in the application of the terms used in the two accounts. The term 'essential omniscience' is understood in

---

128   Pike, (1984) pp. 602-604. The remainder of the paragraph is a synopsis of his point.

different ways by both parties. Pike understands the term to be integrally linked to the individual Yahweh, while Fischer understands it to be tied only to the role that Yahweh is presumed to occupy.[129] Pike does not need to make the assumption that Yahweh occupies the role of God, because in his understanding this fact is already packed into the very concept of the individual named 'Yahweh'. Pike understands 'Yahweh is essentially omniscient' *de re* and asserts that 'if Yahweh is essentially omniscient *de re* then his existence *includes* his omniscience'.[130] Fischer has a weaker *de dicto* analysis of 'essential omniscience' where 'God' in 'God is omniscient' is a non-rigid designator and the proposition 'God is omniscient' is a necessary truth.

Given that in Pike's model Yahweh's essence includes his omniscience and infallibility, Jones cannot act such that Yahweh was not God at *t1* by doing some action other than *X* at *t2*. Yahweh is not akin to a Jones-Predictor, as a Jones predictor can be mistaken in his belief and can thereby cease to be a Jones-Predictor at any time as a consequence of the actions that Jones chooses to perform. However, Yahweh, as understood by Pike, cannot cease to be omniscient. Not only does he hold no false beliefs at *t1*, he cannot hold any at any time, due to his essential infallibility.[131] It is not just that he has been inerrant up until *t1*, it is rather that he can never err – and that this fact is included in his essence. If this is the case, then Pike is correct in his argument that Jones cannot act contrary to *X* at *t2* due to God's sempiternal foreknowledge.

It is my belief that Pike's understanding of God is more in accord with our general understanding than that of Fischer. Therefore, on this understanding, we must conclude that Proposition (3) does not allow for Jones-Predictor type qualifications and cannot be sidestepped by adopting Fischer's understanding of essential omniscience as being only tied to a role and not a particular individual.

In light of the preceding discussion of Proposition (1) and Proposition (3), if one is to argue that Jones has Regulative Control over his effective second-order desire at *t2* (and thus has the possibility of being morally responsible for his actions) irrespective of God's foreknowledge, one will have to consider the possibility of marrying this claim with Proposition (2).

3.3.4: 'It is within Jones's power at *t2* to do something which would have brought it about that God did not hold the belief He held at *t1*.' (Pike's Proposition 2)

If Jones were to have the power to act such that God would have held a different

---

129   See Pike (1965) Section 1 and (1970) Ch. 4.
130   Pike (1984), p. 610.
131   Ibid, p. 611.

belief to the actual belief that he held (for example that Jones would form the intention to not mow his lawn at $t2$ and would proceed to act on that intention), then Pike maintains that he would have to have the power to alter the past. This is precisely because he contends that the fact that God believed at $t1$ that Jones would mow his lawn at $t2$ is a 'fixed' fact about the past. What is meant by 'fixed' in this context is that it is a fact that cannot be subject to alteration, qualification, or revision by any later occurrence.

> No action performed at a given time can alter the fact that a given person held a certain belief at a time prior to the time in question. This last seems to be an *a priori* truth.[132]

This is a restatement of the cogent aspects of the Principle of the Fixity of the Past as it relates to an agent's past beliefs. It can be argued to be an *a priori* truth, as it is taken as an unalterable fact that God's mind was in state m at $t1$, and m included the belief that 'Jones will mow his lawn at $t2$' (this is a claim whose validity I will consider in much greater detail in the next chapter). Therefore, in order to have the power to refrain from doing so Jones would have to be able to do something such that God's mind would have been in some other state $m+$ at $t1$.

The state of God's mind would have to have been different because God is omniscient, it is assumed that future-oriented propositions have truth operators, and God cannot believe any false propositions. Pike's claim implicitly takes it for granted that the state of God's mind at $t1$ is over and done with relative to $t2$ - that is, cannot be subject to any subsequent alteration or qualification (I will later show that there are moves that can be made to argue that this is not the case).

Pike argues that it is impossible to alter the past and that therefore Jones does not have the power suggested in Proposition (2) (as the belief that God had at $t1$ is a fixed fact about the past relative to $t2$). The validity of his argument relies on the truth of the following: (i) it is impossible for Jones to act at $t2$ such that God's belief would have been different at $t1$ (ii) the fact that God foreknows that Jones will X at $t2$ entails that it is logically impossible that Jones could proceed to do something contrary to X.[133] This consequently implies that Jones never had the actual power to do something other than X (which is what is claimed by the theological fatalist).

3.4: Conclusion to Chapter 3

Pike's rebuttal of the possibility that Jones has the power involved in Proposition

---

132 Pike (1965), p. 33.
133 I will return to the question of the validity of this assumption.

(2) is considered to be the weakest link in his argument by those who do not agree with his incompatibilist suppositions, and it is the one that is most frequently attacked. I will therefore deal extensively with this proposition in the following Chapter, as its validity is contentious.

If none of the above three propositions, or some variant of them, are true then it appears as though the outcome of any morally significant choice has in fact been hard-determined (necessitated) by God's foreknowledge. This would exclude the possibility of Regulative Control and would destroy genuine moral responsibility.

I began my discussion by providing an account of the traditional divine attributes that I have taken as a basic assumption in my critical explorations. These assumptions are common to the majority of Christian theological thought. I earlier stated that it was my personal belief that any attribute that God has he has necessarily. However, because of the controversial nature of such a position I made the weaker, and more acceptable claim, that any attribute God has he has *essentially* – I defined this as God having each of the attributes in question at every possible world in which he exists. I then provided an account of what I meant by a possible world. My account of possible worlds and their relationship to the actual world will be further developed in the following chapter.

I next introduced Pike's incompatibilist argument. In the introduction to this chapter I had already explained what is involved in the idea of fatalism and the related concept of theological fatalism. In his argument, Pike had insisted that the agent would require the ability to exercise one of three powers, if he were to be capable of voluntary action (which involves the ability to do otherwise) given the existence of an omniscient God with perfect foreknowledge of all future states of affairs. I extracted three propositions from his argument which expressed the powers in question. I then subjected them to critical evaluation. I found that it could be successfully shown that the agent could not have the power at $t2$ to do something that would have brought it about that God held a false belief at $t1$ – as this would involve a logical impossibility. I also found that it was not within the agent's power at $t2$ to do something that would have brought it about the person who was God at $t1$ held a false belief and thus was not God – that is the agent could not act such that God did not exist at $t1$.

I considered Fischer's objection to the way in which Pike had presented his argument to this effect. However, I found Fischer's alternative account unsatisfactory as it involved a way of understanding God that does not sit with our common and intuitive understanding of God. However, it was the final power that caused most difficulty – the claim that it is within the agent's power at $t2$ to do something which would have brought it about that God did not hold the belief that he held at $t1$.

If Pike's argument is correct one is led to the conclusion that divine foreknowledge is incompatible with free will (in the sense that involves Regulative Control). This is theological fatalism resting on the foundation that the unchanging knowledge of God necessarily cannot ever have comprised of even one false belief. As God's foreknowledge necessarily includes all true propositions, including all future-oriented propositions, and because he is essentially infallible, the agent can never form the intention to act other than in the way that has been fatalistically necessitated by that knowledge. This would obviously negate the possibility of morally responsible agency. However, the Ockhamist argues that there is a viable alternative to theological fatalism, or any form of incompatibilism. I will therefore proceed to examine the Ockhamist's strategy in the next chapter.

4

Ockhamism

4.1: Introduction to Chapter 4

I have already claimed that Ockhamism offers one of the most convincing accounts of the compatibility between divine foreknowledge and the agent having the power to do otherwise. If the Ockhamist account is successful in its argument to this effect then it may be possible to show that divine foreknowledge does in fact allow the possibility of morally responsible agency. After all, if the agent has the power to otherwise with regard to the formation of his effective second-order desires in morally significant contexts, even if a sempiternal God with infallible foreknowledge exists, then that agent will be capable of fulfilling all of my criteria of morally responsible agency. In this Chapter I will attempt to offer a comprehensive account of the modern Ockhamist position and then proceed to critically evaluate it. The Ockhamist must be capable of offering a convincing alternative to incompatibilist arguments, such as those of Pike, if his thesis is to prove tenable. By the end of this chapter I hope to have established whether or not the ideas essential to Ockhamism are in fact plausible.

4.2: The Ockhamist

Pike's argument relies heavily on the validity of his understanding of the Principle of the Fixity of the Past. The Ockhamist attempts to undermine incompatibilism by appealing to the idea that there are facts that constitute the 'past' that have different levels of fixity. By introducing this qualification, he believes that it is possible to show the compatibility of the idea that the agent can exercise the power to do otherwise with the fact that God has infallible foreknowledge of all future states of affairs. In investigating this claim, I will test whether the ideas embodied in the Ockhamist position will allow for morally responsible agency, given sempiternal divine foreknowledge.

What is an Ockhamist? 'Ockhamism', as I will understand it, is a direct or indirect development of the thought of William of Ockham. He introduced the idea that it is possible to differentiate between propositions about the past that are necessary and propositions about the past that are not so.[134] He proceeded to argue that there are certain propositions involving God's beliefs that are not necessary. The idea is that all propositions about the past whose truth also involves the occurrence of future contingents are not necessary until those contingents have come to pass. Such propositions refer to what modern Ockhamists have called 'soft' facts about the past. These facts may be subject to later qualification in a particular way (this will be explained below) by the actions of the agent. Making use of this idea, recent Ockhamists have introduced the hard/soft fact distinction and used it as a tool to undermine arguments such as the incompatibilist thesis of Pike.

It should be noted that in the following investigation I am attempting to characterise a broad Ockhamist position. I will therefore make use of the thought of many philosophers who have contributed to the discussion of hard and soft facts. I attribute many of these ideas to 'the Ockhamist'. I occasionally do this in cases where the author does not consider himself/herself, strictly speaking, an Ockhamist. My purpose in doing so is to construct a comprehensive base from which to proceed. Under my characterisation, I will include under the title of 'Ockhamist' those philosophers who believe that there is a way to use the distinction between hard and soft facts, and the idea of accidental necessity (term is explained in the next section), to allow the reconciliation of divine foreknowledge with the agent's ability to do otherwise (in the sense of the forking-paths model).

4.3: Necessity

4.3.0: Introduction to Section 4.3

In this Section I consider how the idea of necessity should be understood in relation to God's foreknowledge. I delineate several ways in which it can be understood and critically expound them. I consider how the idea of necessity is used by Pike. Finally, I introduce and discuss the idea of 'accidental necessity'.

4.3.1: Pike's Use of the Idea of Necessity

Pike's argument assumes that God's omniscience and infallibility hard-determines

---

134   See Ockham ([1321-1324] 1969).

the agent due to the necessary consequences of these essential attributes. Thus, the argument is structured such that it assumes that if God believed eighty years prior to Jones's action that he would mow his lawn at a specific time, then it was not within Jones's power to do other than mow his lawn at the time in question – Jones necessarily must mow his lawn.

However, there are several ways in which to understand necessity in relation to God's sempiternal foreknowledge. Consider the following:

i. Necessarily, if God foreknows X, then X will occur.

ii. God foreknows X.

iii. Therefore, X will necessarily occur.

However, Aquinas has made us aware that there is a scope fallacy here.[135] The fallacy stems from transferring the scope of the necessity from the consequence to the consequent.

Consider the following:

iv. Necessarily, all bachelors are unmarried.

v. Fred is a bachelor.

vi. Therefore, Fred is necessarily unmarried.

It is apparent that Fred is not necessarily unmarried. The fact that he is unmarried is a contingent state of affairs that he is free to change. He is not constrained by necessity such that he must be unmarried.

Having noted the scope fallacy we can now validly restructure i – iii as follows:

vii. Necessarily, if God foreknows X, then X will occur.

viii. God foreknows X.

ix. Therefore, X will occur.

This reformulation accounts for the fact that X is not necessitated. On this model it is possible that X not happen.

Consider the following:

x. Necessarily, if X will (contingently) occur, God foreknows X.

xi. X will (contingently) occur.

xii. Therefore, God foreknows X.

The idea here is that there is a necessary correspondence between what

---

135 Aquinas, *Summa Theologica*, I, q. 14, a. 13.

actually occurs and what God foreknows. In the case of Jones's mowing or not mowing his lawn, whatever contingent action occurs is the product of his free exercise of his Regulative Control. It follows from x-xii that Jones's power to do otherwise is not inevitably compromised by the fact that God's foreknowledge necessarily corresponds with what Jones does. If this is correct, then it is possible that such a relation of correspondence holds between all of the agent's free actions and God's foreknowledge of them. This is an account that will need much greater depth of analysis and clarification. I will therefore attempt to offer this throughout the course of this chapter.

In Pike's argument the idea of necessity is related to the involuntariness of Jones's action – due to God's temporally anterior knowledge it is not within Jones's power to refrain from mowing his lawn (it could be argued that this follows from i-iii). It is from this conception of necessity that we are left with the three propositions outlined above. However, Pike does not give an exact formulation of the necessity that he assumes in his account. He clearly states that it is not causal necessity.[136] The closest that we come to such a definition is his insistence that in God's foreknowledge truth is analytically connected with divine belief such that it constrains Jones's ability to act voluntarily. However, the inability to hold a false belief does not necessarily mean that the object of the belief is necessitated (as can be extrapolated from x – xii).

4.3.2: Accidental Necessity

In Pike's account Proposition 2 is rejected on the assumption that God's belief is a fixed aspect of the past. I would therefore like to briefly extrapolate what is involved in the idea that particular propositions that express facts about the past are fixed - in the sense of being necessarily true at all subsequent times.

Let us presume that it is a fact that Jones bought a mobile phone at $t1$, some particular moment in the past. Thus, the corresponding proposition 'Jones buys a mobile phone at $t1$' is now necessary, as it is impossible after $t1$ to act such that Jones did not buy his phone at the specified time (and thereby act such that the proposition in question is false). But what kind of necessity is it that is involved in this claim? It is not metaphysically, physically or logically necessary that he have bought his phone at the time in question.

The type of necessity in question is what has become known as 'accidental'. A certain class of propositions that express contingent states of affairs which are now in the past are what the Ockhamist (amongst others) calls 'accidentally necessary'. It should be noted that an adequate definition of this concept has been rather

---

[136] Pike (1965), p. 35

elusive and attempting to offer one has frequently led to intractable problems.[137] I will therefore only attempt to offer the most salient features of the concept of accidental necessity, and will attempt to be as uncontroversial in this endeavour as possible.

When I speak of a proposition being accidentally necessary I mean that the state of affairs that it expresses is completely fixed. Accidental necessity is indexed to the specific time of the occurrence of a contingent – a proposition is only accidentally necessary once the state of affairs that it relates is fully accomplished. Accidentally necessary propositions are to be further understood as expressing those contingent facts that have obtained at any possible world that has an identical history with the actual world up to the present moment. Thus, the proposition 'Jones buys his first mobile phone at $t1$' was not accidentally necessary prior to $t1$, but the fact that he did do so at $t1$ makes it accidentally necessary immediately after this time and at all subsequent times $t2+$, and at all possible worlds that share an identical history to the actual world. Furthermore, once a proposition is accidentally necessary, there is nothing that anyone can do to alter the truth-value of that proposition.

Consider the following three propositions:

a) Jones bought his mobile phone at $t1$ (a particular time last week).

b) Jones bought his mobile phone at $t1$ and used if for the first time yesterday ($t2$).

c) Jones bought his mobile phone at $t1$ and will not use it for the first time until $t3$ (5pm next Tuesday).

We can state that proposition (a) is accidentally necessary as it expresses a state of affairs that has fully obtained (it is 'over and done with' – a permanently fixed aspect of the past). Proposition (b), although it makes reference to two different moments in time, is now also accidentally necessary, as the two instants that it involves are now an enduring feature of the past. However, proposition (c) is not accidentally necessary, as it expresses a state of affairs that has not fully obtained. It is possible that this proposition may prove false in virtue of Jones's free use of his Regulative Control when deciding when he will use his mobile phone for the first time. There is nothing that prevents him from making his first call at any time prior to 5pm next Tuesday.

From the above discussion we can state the following about accidental necessity:

i. Accidental necessity only applies to propositions that correspond to logically contingent states of affairs.

---

137 For accounts of accidental necessity see, for example, Plantinga (1974a, 1974b and 1987), Freddoso (1983), and Robinson (2004).

ii. Accidentally necessary propositions become necessary immediately after he states of affairs to which they correspond have occurred.

iii. Once a particular state of affairs has occurred there is nothing that anyone, including God, can do to change the truth value of the corresponding proposition (this obviously involves the denial of the possibility of retro-causing an accidentally necessary proposition to be false).[138]

Plantinga offers the following characterisation of the claim essential to (3):

> ... p [a particular proposition that expresses a contingents state of affairs] is accidentally necessary at t if and only if p is true at t and it is not possible both that p is true at t and there exists an agent S and an action A such that (1) A is basic for S [S has the power at t or later to perform A], and (2) if S were to perform A at t or later, then p would have been false (3) necessarily if S were to perform A at t or later, then p would have been false.[139]

Thus, Plantinga defines the accidentally necessary in terms of lack of counterfactual power.[140] p is accidentally necessary if and only if it is impossible for anyone to exercise a power by performing an action A, in virtue of which p would prove false and thereby the past would be counterfactually affected. I will return to the question of counterfactual powers in much greater detail. However, in order not to stray too far from the current line of investigation, I will now return to the question of Pike's Proposition 2.

Pike implicitly takes it for granted in Proposition 2 that propositions expressing the fact that God had particular beliefs are accidentally necessary once the moment in which those beliefs are fully established has occurred. As God has eternal immutable foreknowledge, Pike assumes that it is true at any (and every) moment in the past that God believed that Jones would mow his lawn at the specified time. He therefore takes it that this belief is a fully fixed aspect of the past.

How would this result in the impossibility of the agent exercising Regulative Control over his actions?

Suppose that $t3$ is some time in the future and that Jones's mowing his lawn at $t3$ is a paradigmatic example of a future contingent that involves the agent's power to do otherwise. Let us also suppose that:

1. God believed 100 years ago ($t1$) that the proposition 'Jones will mow his lawn at $t3$' (p) is true.

2. Thus (the incompatibilist could insist) the proposition 'God believed

---

138 See Song (2002), esp. p. 43.
139 Plantinga (1987), p. 198. This principle can also be reformulated to accommodate cooperative venture freely undertaken. See p. 199.
140 Ibid. Plantinga provides an extensive account of accidental necessity in this paper.

that Jones will mow his lawn at $t3$' ($p2$) was accidentally necessary at $t1$ (the idea being that the state of affairs that is God having a particular belief has completely obtained at $t1$, and that therefore the proposition that expresses it is accidentally necessary at all subsequent times).

3. $p2$ entails the proposition 'If $t3$ is the present moment, then Jones is mowing his lawn' ($p3$).
4. But if $p2$ was accidentally necessary 100 years ago then no one will ever have the power to cause $p3$ to be false (or act such that $p3$ is false) at $t3$, and thus Jones is not free to refrain from mowing his lawn at $t3$.

If the above line of argument is valid then it follows that divine foreknowledge and free will are fundamentally at variance.

However, by exploiting the idea that accidental necessity does not apply to propositions that express God's beliefs about future contingents, the Ockhamist believes he can evade arguments of the form that I have just presented. He claims that the propositions that express the beliefs that comprise divine foreknowledge relate to states of affairs that are future, relative to the time at which the beliefs are held – and therefore are not accidentally necessary. I will further expand upon this idea in the section devoted to hard and soft facts. But suffice it to say for now that this may allow for a coherent compatibility theory.

Section 4.3.3: An Ockhamist Response to Pike's Proposition 2

Plantinga believes that Pike's formulation of step 6 in his argument is fundamentally flawed. He is convinced that the claim that in order for Jones to have the power to refrain from mowing his lawn at $t2$ it would have to be 'within [his] power at $t2$ to do something which would have brought it about that God did not hold the belief He held at $t1$' is unwarranted. He argues that there is an alternative to this claim that Pike has not considered in his account. This is the possibility that Jones might have the ability to exercise a power in virtue of which the past would be counterfactually affected.

In his argument Plantinga presents the following as obviously false:

> It was within Jones's power at $t2$ to do something such that if he had done it, then God would not have held a belief that he in fact held.[141]

It is self-evidently true that no one has the power to act such that a contradictory state of affairs obtains. This appears to be the only prospect that Pike entertains and so he feels he has offered a complete account when he dismisses it as an impossibility. However, Plantinga offers us the following alternative:

---

141   Plantinga (1974a), p. 71.

It was within Jones's power at *t2* to do something such that if he had done it, then God would not have held a belief that he did in fact hold.[142]

The idea here is that in order to exercise such a power Jones would not have to change the actual past. There is nothing that can be done such that a completely fixed aspect of the past can be altered (see iii in Section 4.3.2: Accidental Necessity). One cannot change the past such that an event that actually occurred did not occur - one cannot act such that an accidentally necessary proposition is false. However, this is not what Plantinga is suggesting. He is rather claiming that it is possible to act such that the past would have been different than it in fact was. What I mean is that the actual past would have been different in the sense that some particular aspect of it would never have occurred (i.e. a counterfactual state of affairs would have comprised the world at the time in question).

There is no need to claim that Jones must have the capacity to exercise a retro-causal power (as the idea of retro-causation is fraught with difficulties). Instead, Saunders asserts that we should understand that:

> Jones's power so to act at *t2* is simply his power to perform an act such that if that act were performed, then certain earlier situations would be different from what in fact they were.[143]

If we allow that Jones has the capacity to freely perform an act in virtue of which a counterfactual state of affairs would have comprised the past then this bypasses Pike's concerns.[144] There is no challenge to God's foreknowledge, essential omniscience or infallibility. The reason for this is that essential omniscience and infallibility make it impossible for Jones to act in a particular way and for God to have believed that he would do something else.[145] God cannot hold a false belief. Thus we can return to one of our earlier models of the necessity involved in divine foreknowledge (vii – ix with some additional qualifications).

 i. Necessarily, if Jones (freely) does X (a contingent action that is under his Regulative Control) at *t2*, then God foreknows at *t1* that he will do X at *t2*.

 ii. Jones (freely) does X at *t2*.

 iii. Therefore, God foreknows at *t1* that Jones (freely and contingently) will do X at *t2*.

The particular action X occurs as a consequence of Jones's exercise of his

---

142 Ibid, p. 71.
143 Saunders (1966), p. 220.
144 We will see that Plantinga's assertion is dependent on the assumption that God's past belief is not accidentally necessary. An account of hard and soft facts is given below. For a refutation of Plantinga see Alston (1985).
145 See Saunders (1966). Pike (1966) also appreciates the strength of this position, see pp. 369-370.

Regulative Control. There is no question of the free exercise of his power to do otherwise being in conflict with the divine attributes. The attribute of essential omniscience ensures that if Jones performs a particular contingent action then God would have foreknown that he would do so. It appears that those who wish to offer a comprehensive refutation of Plantinga's Ockhamist conception will have a significant amount of work to do.

However, one may object, if the proposition 'God knows at *t1* (a specified time in the past) that Jones will mow his lawn at *t2* (a specified time in the future)' is accidentally necessary immediately after *t1*, then it is impossible, because of the constraints of accidental necessity, for anyone to change the truth-value of this proposition (making it impossible to do something that would have a counterfactual affect on the past). In order to consider whether the Ockhamist can offer a convincing response to this objection I will now introduce the ideas of 'hard facts' and 'soft facts'.

4.4: Hard and Soft Facts

4.4.0: Introduction to Section 4.4

In order to refute the above incompatibilist objection, the Ockhamist introduces a distinction between different types of facts that are in distinctive ways 'situated' in the past. The Ockhamist does not want to deny that a certain class of propositions that express facts about the past are accidentally necessary. Rather he claims that a specific class of God's past beliefs are not 'genuine' facts about the past and, as such, the propositions expressing them are not accidentally necessary. In order to argue this, he divides facts about the past into two distinct classes – 'hard' and 'soft'. The substantive difference between these categories is that propositions that express hard facts about the past are completely fixed and that propositions that express soft facts about the past are not so.

Pike, in his reply to Saunders, was perhaps the first to attempt to adequately articulate the distinction between different types of past facts. Saunders had asserted the following:

> Although it is true that if I had refrained from writing this paper in 1965, Caesar's assassination would have been other than it is in that it would not have preceded by 2009 years my writing of this paper, it would be absurd to argue that I therefore did not have it in my power to refrain from writing his

paper in 1965.[146]

While critical of Saunders' overall account, Pike takes advantage of the fundamental insight that it offers. He proceeds to offer us the following observation:

> Caesar was assassinated 2009 years before Saunders wrote his paper. Yet it was within Saunders' power at the time of writing his paper to refrain from so doing. Thus, at the time of writing his paper, it was within Saunders' power so to act that Caesar would not have died 2009 years before he wrote his paper. Saunders thus had the power (at one time) so to act that the past (relative to that time) would not have been as it was.
>
> Contrast Saunders' case with another. Caesar died on the steps of the Senate. It was never within Saunders' power so to act that the past would have been other than it was as regards this item.[147]

Proceeding from the above insight he offers us the following classification: 'hard facts' are facts about the past (for example, facts about Caesar's death) which were 'fully accomplished,' 'over-and-done-with, and so forth' at a specific time in the past (for example in 44 BC). These are contrasted with facts that were not 'over and done with' at the time in the past to which they in part relate. Thus, it was not 'fully accomplished' in 44 BC that Saunders would write his paper 2009 years later. Pike takes it for granted that God's past beliefs are hard facts about the past. Unfortunately, he does not offer us sufficient reasons to assume that this is the case. At this juncture we are still lacking a sufficient criterion by which to differentiate hard and soft facts.

I will begin to address this situation by offering the account of hard and soft facts offered by Marilyn McCord Adams. However, I will proceed to show that this analysis is flawed. Therefore, I will conclude by introducing Hoffman and Rosenkrantz's alternative and more comprehensive distinction.

4.4.1: Adams's Hard and Soft Fact Distinction

It was Marilyn McCord Adams who in 1967, in her influential (and controversial) paper 'Is the Existence of God a 'Hard Fact'?', attempted to remedy the fact that no comprehensive analysis of the distinction between hard and soft facts had yet been offered. I will call her analysis the Hard and Soft Fact Distinction (HSFD):

1. A fact F is about a time $t1$ if, and only if, F's obtaining entails that something occur at $t1$.

2. A fact F about $t1$ is a soft fact about $t1$ if, and only if, F's obtaining

---

146 Saunders (1966), p. 224.
147 Pike (1966), p. 369.

entails that something (contingent) occur at some later time $t2$.

3. A fact F about $t1$ is a hard fact about $t1$ if, and only if, it is not a soft fact about $t1$.

1. This is a characterisation of a fact's relation to a specific time. A fact can only be credited with being about a specific time if it entails that a particular state of affairs occur at the time in question.

2. A fact about $t1$ is a soft fact relative to $t1$ if it entails that some contingent fact occur at some later time.

3. A hard fact is a fact about $t1$ if and only if it is not a soft fact about $t1$. By implication, a hard fact is a fact about a time $t1$, if, and only if, at the time of its occurrence, it is in some meaningful sense 'over and done with' (by this I mean completed in the sense that the proposition that expresses it has a truth value that has been fully and unalterably established. Thus, a proposition that expresses a hard fact is accidentally necessary immediately after the time that the hard fact obtains). Any fact that is not over and done with at $t1$ is a soft fact relative to $t1$.

Proceeding from this classification, hard facts can be described as 'non-relational' facts that are permanently fixed and immune to subsequent alteration or qualification. I will speak of these facts as being 'completely fixed'. Propositions that express soft facts are not accidentally necessary until all of the times to which they refer have obtained. Any proposition that expresses a hard fact I will call a 'h-type proposition' and any proposition that expresses what may prove to be a soft fact I will call an 's-type proposition' (whether or not an s-type proposition proves to express a fact is dependent on the occurrence of a future contingent that has not yet obtained, and possibly may not obtain). An s-type proposition does not have a fully established truth-value until all of the times that it relates have elapsed – therefore we cannot definitively state whether or not the possible state of affairs expressed in this type of proposition is actually a fact until the latest time to which it is indexed has transpired.

Let us now consider the following example. Jones decided to buy a mobile phone and proceeded to purchase it at a particular time $t1$. The fact that Jones bought a mobile phone at $t1$ (a time that has already elapsed) is a hard fact (I will call this fact h-F) – there is nothing that can now be done by any agent such that this was not the case. The fact has obtained and is impervious to alteration or qualification by subsequent events – it is unalterably true at every moment following $t1$ that Jones bought his phone at this time. Thus the truth-value of the proposition which expresses this fact is immutably fixed – the proposition 'Jones buys a mobile phone at $t1$' is accidentally necessary immediately after $t1$ and at every succeeding moment.

However, the fact that Jones bought the phone a week before making his first call is a soft fact about $t1$. At $t1$, and at each successive moment up to $t3$ (the time when he actually makes the call), it is possible that the s-type proposition which expresses this soft fact could have proven true, or could have proven false, in virtue of Jones's free action. This is because the factual status of the state of affairs in question was not fully established until $t3$, and accordingly the truth value of the proposition that expresses it was dependent on a future contingent occurrence until $t3$ obtained. This is what I mean when I say that a soft-fact has 'future relationality'. To falsify the corresponding s-type proposition at $t2$ would not require changing a fact about the past – as it was not an immutable aspect of the past that Jones would make his first call at $t3$ until immediately after $t3$.

To this extent, soft-facts are not 'over and done with' until all the times to which they are indexed have passed – only once they have fully obtained do they alter their status by becoming hard. In other words, once Jones actually makes the call, it is then a fixed fact about the past that he made it one week after he purchased his phone. It is only after the actualisation of the future contingent that completes the soft-fact that its status changes. If a proposition expressing a state of affairs that may have proven to be a soft fact is falsified by subsequent contingent events (such that it cannot be true at all of the times to which it relates) then it is thereafter completely fixed (it is accidentally necessary) that the proposition is false (and is therefore not reflective of an actual fact). For example, if Jones had decided to make a call after only two days and proceeded to do so, then it is a completely fixed fact that it was not a week before he made his first call and the proposition 'It was not a week before Jones made his first call' would be accidentally necessary.

It is argued by the Ockhamist that the truth of the proposition that involves the claim that it is a fact that he will make his first call a week after his purchase can either be verified or falsified right up until $t3$. Thus the verification at $t3$ of a proposition pr that expresses a soft fact s-F (which is also related to $t1$), does not mean that it was not possible at $t2$ that this proposition would prove false. This is because the agent could have acted before $t3$ in such a fashion that the state of affairs expressed in pr would not have been a fact (the factual status of s-F was dependent on how the agent would choose to act at $t3$). The Ockhamist argues that the only reason that it is true at $t1$ that Jones will make his first call a week after purchasing his mobile phone is because, through exercising his Regulative Control, he does in fact proceed to make his first call after one week has elapsed. However, if Jones had chosen (in the sense that involves free will) not to make his first call a week after making his purchase, then it would have been true at $t1$ that Jones would not make his first call a week after purchasing his new phone. Thus, there is a sense in which a future contingent occurrence has a factual consequent on the truth of a proposition that expresses what may prove to be a fact and that is, in the particular sense I have been discussing, situated in the past (relative to that contingent).

4.4.2: A Flaw in Adams's Hard and Soft Fact Distinction

It appears that Adams's HSFD has gone a long way towards giving a sufficient justification of the difference between hard and soft facts. One of the problems that still remain though is explaining the coherency of asserting that a hard fact is 'over and done with' once it has occurred. According to HSFD, hard facts are all of those facts that do not fit the criterion of soft facts. We have seen that soft facts are those facts about the past that involve the occurrence of a future contingent. However, one may now ask if there are any facts that do not involve the occurrence of a future contingent. Do not all propositions that express a past fact entail the truth of another proposition (or other propositions) that corresponds with a subsequent contingent state of affairs? Fischer states the problem thus:

> The problem with [HSFD] is that is appears as though [it] must classify all facts as soft. Consider the fact, "Jack is sitting at $t1$". Intuitively, this should be classified as a hard fact about $t1$. But notice that "Jack is sitting at $t1$" entails that it is not the case that Jack sits for the first time at $t2$. Thus, in virtue of [HSFD's] embodying the Entailment Criterion of Soft Facthood, it must classify "Jack is sitting at $t1$" as a soft fact about $t1$. Because this sort of result is clearly generalizable, it appears as if [HSFD] will classify all facts as soft, and it is therefore evidently unacceptable.[148]

Hoffman and Rosentkrantz make a similar point when they state the following:

> If there are necessary "actualities," that is, existents which must exist at every time, then their existence at any time t is a necessary condition of the truth of any statement whatsoever. This implies that for any statement p, and any time t, p is at least in part about t. Then ... p does not express a hard fact about t; that is, no statement is a hard fact about any time t. But this makes the hard fact/soft fact distinction an empty one. But are there any such necessary actualities?... The existence of even one such necessary actuality is enough to refute Adams's analysis [HSFD].[149]

Consider the following propositions:

  (1) Jones buys a mobile phone at $t1$.

  (2) Jones does not buy his first mobile phone at $t2$.

Even though it is intuitive to assert that (1) is a hard fact about $t1$, under HSFD it turns out to be a soft fact. This is because, under Adams's criterion, (1) entails (2) and (2) is indexed to $t2$, a future time relative to $t1$. There are an indefinitely large number of propositions of the form of (1) that would entail propositions

---

148   Fischer (1991), p. 358.
149   Hoffman and Rosenkrantz (1984). It should be noted that they are only pointing this out as a problem, and they do not suggest that it is actually the case.

of the form of (2). Thus, what initially appeared to be a promising account will need further modification in order to be coherent, for it appears that under HSFD anything that we would intuitively understand as a hard fact turns out to be soft.

4.4.3: Hoffman and Rosenkrantz's Solution to the Flaw in Adams's HSFD

Hoffman and Rosenkrantz attempt to address this situation by offering yet another way of distinguishing hard and soft facts.

They begin by distinguishing 'eternal states of affairs' such as:

(3) Socrates is walking at t.

(4) $2 + 2 = 4$.

(5) It never rains on the plains of Spain.[150]

from what they call 'Unrestrictedly Repeatable Present' (URP) states of affairs, such as:

(6) Mt. St. Helens comes into existence.

(7) Socrates is walking.

(8) Mt. St. Helens is erupting.[151]

An eternal state of affairs must either always obtain or always fail to obtain. However, a URP state of affairs may obtain, then fail to obtain, then obtain again, indefinitely many times throughout all of time.[152] Using the idea of URP states of affairs they offer us the following means of deciding whether a particular fact is a hard fact about the past.

A state of affairs r is hard fact about time $t = df$.

a) r is the state of affairs, s at (in) t;

b) s is a *URP* state of affairs;

c) s obtains throughout (throughout some part of) t;

d)   either s is a simple state of affairs, or if it is complex, then all of its parts are *URP*;

e)   neither r nor s nor any of s's parts entails that either a simple URP state of affairs are indexed to a time which does not overlap with t, or a

---

150   Ibid, p. 423.
151   Ibid, p. 424.
152   Ibid, p. 423.

complex URP state of affairs of whose parts are RP and which is indexed to a time which does not overlap with *t*;

and

f)   *t* is a past time.

Armed with this new criterion for distinguishing hard facts let us return to (1).

In order to facilitate ease of understanding it will first be prudent to introduce the idea of 'kernel' states of affairs. If *r* is the state of affairs, *s* at (in) *t*, then *r* consists of a kernel state of affairs, *s*, and a temporal suffix or prefix, at *t* (in *t*), which indexes *s*.[153] Thus, for example, if the state of affairs, expressed in the proposition 'Jones buys a mobile phone' is indexed to *t1*, this yields the state of affairs 'Jones buys a mobile phone at (in) *t1*', whose kernel is the state of affairs expressed as follows:

(1*)   Jones buys a mobile phone.

Let us also introduce a proposition that expresses the kernel state of affairs for 2:

(2*)   ¬(Jones buys a mobile phone for the first time).

Now let us consider whether, under Hoffman and Rosenkrantz's criterion, (1) qualifies as a hard fact.

a)   (1) is the state of affairs, (1*) at *t1*;

b)   (1*) is a URP state of affairs;

c)   (1*) obtains throughout *t1*;

d)   (1*) is a simple state of affairs;

e)   (1) does not entail a simple URP state of affairs indexed to a time that does not overlap with *t1*; and

f)   *t1* is a past time.

(2*) is not URP as it may obtain at one moment because Jones has never bought a mobile phone, then fail to obtain at another moment because he is buying a mobile phone for the first time, and then obtain again at a subsequent moment when he is no longer buying his phone. However, immediately after this moment it will obtain at all following times. Thus, even though under HSFD (1) entails (2), under this analysis it remains a hard fact, as (1) can sufficiently satisfy (e).

---

153   Ibid, p. 426.

4.5: Are God's Beliefs About the Future Hard or a Soft Facts? The First Attempt to Find an Answer

Now I will consider the most significant application of Hoffman and Rosenkrantz's model for this investigation. I will apply their analysis to a proposition that expresses God's past belief about a future contingent.

We have seen that because s-type propositions are dependent on the occurrence of a future contingent for their truth-value they may prove false, in virtue of the way in which the agent exercises his Regulative Control. The Ockhamist is committed to the claim that God's beliefs are soft facts about the past and as such are not immutably fixed, as they are not accidentally necessary (until the occurrence of the future time to which they relate). Thus, any proposition of the form 'God believes at $t1$ that an agent will X at $t2$' is not accidentally necessary (until immediately after $t2$).

Let us take the following proposition as a paradigmatic example:

(9) God believes at $t1$ that Jones mows his lawn at $t2$.

This would include the kernel state of affairs expressed in the following proposition:

(9*) God believes that Jones mows his lawn at $t2$.

(9) satisfies (a), (c), (d) and (f). However, because God is metaphysically necessary and essentially omniscient, (9*) does not turn out to be URP. This is because it relates to an eternal state of affairs: the state of affairs that it expresses always obtains (throughout the whole of time there is no moment at which it does not obtain). Hence (9*) fails to satisfy condition (b), and is a soft fact about $t1$. Also, (9*) entails that Jones exists at $t2$, that Jones mows his lawn at $t2$, and so forth, which are indexed to a time later than $t1$ (i.e. $t2$).[154] Consequently, (9*) fails to satisfy (e). Therefore, this further justifies the assertion that (9*) is not a hard fact about $t1$.

This account has many advantages over HSFD. However, it is my claim that it does not entirely reflect the complexity of the state of affairs that is God having a fore-belief about what will occur at a future moment in time. It is my contention that God's foreknowledge does necessitate the actions of the agent. We saw that there was a scope fallacy in the following account of the necessity involved in

---

154   It may be argued that these states of affairs are not strictly speaking simple. However, this is of little consequence as (19) fails to be a hard fact because of all of the other reasons provided. Hoffman and Rosenkrantz do provide an argument to justify their assertion that these are simple states of affairs. See (1984), footnote 12, pp. 427-429.

divine foreknowledge:

   i. Necessarily, if God foreknows X, then X will occur.

   ii. God foreknows X.

   iii. Therefore, X will necessarily occur.

I think that this is self-apparently valid. However, with a slight modification we can remove this scope fallacy and strengthen the incompatibilist argument. Consider the following:

   xiii. Necessarily, if God foreknows X, then X will occur (follows from essential omniscience).

   xiv. The proposition 'God believes Jones will mow his lawn at $t2$' is accidentally necessary at $t1$.

   xv. Therefore, X (the future state of affairs expressed in p) will necessarily occur at $t2$.

This is a more formidable argument than i – iii. If God has foreknown from eternity what an agent will do at a particular moment in time, then for every moment in the past it was true that God foreknew what the agent would do. If propositions expressing God's beliefs can be shown to be accidentally necessary prior to the future occurrence to which they in part relate, then for any particular action that the agent performs at any specific moment in time, it is true that that action must necessarily occur. However, in order to justify my thesis it will be necessary to show that there is something about the propositions that express God's sempiternal foreknowledge that allows us to assert that they are 'genuine' facts about the past (that accidental necessity attaches itself to them in some way[155]). If it is true that God's knowledge is soft, according to the characterisation offered above, then the Ockhamist can simply argue that the agent has the power to act such that the past would be counterfactually affected – and thereby insist that my conception of necessity is unwarrantedly strong. In order to counter the Ockhamist, I will initially attempt to engage with him on his own terms, and to show that his position is unconvincing.

4.6: Hard and Soft Facts and Intuitive Plausibility

I believe that Hoffman and Rosenkrantz's attempt to characterise the differences

---

155   It should be noted that even though propositions that express hard facts are accidentally necessary, it may be true that certain propositions that express facts that qualify as soft under Hoffman and Rozenkrantz's criterion are also accidentally necessary. I will return to this point as part of my justification for my incompatibilist thesis.

between hard and soft facts shows great ingenuity. Unfortunately, I think that they begin with the premise that sempiternal divine foreknowledge is compatible with libertarian free will and then attempt to construct a model according to which God's prior beliefs about future contingents are shown to be soft facts – irrespective of whether that model is reflective of our intuitive understandings. However, as Zagzebski notes:

> Given some set of clear examples of hard facts and clear examples of soft facts, it is surely possible with enough ingenuity to devise a definition of hard facts that is consistent with the set and that has as a consequence that God's past beliefs are soft facts.[156]

I am in agreement with her when she proceeds to state:

> To present a definition is not to show that it bears any connection to a distinction in the nature of things.[157]

I believe that it is not sufficiently convincing to provide a model according to which a theory is coherent, unless the model is also in accordance with our intuitions.[158] One can accuse that those, like Hoffman and Rosenkrantz, merely offer a way in which divine foreknowledge and freedom may be shown to be compatible, without giving any sufficiently convincing reasons for accepting that God's beliefs should be understood according to their characterisation – a characterisation that has been expressly constructed to accord with their motivating thesis. It is obvious that propositions that express God's beliefs about future states of affairs that involve an agent's actions are a special class of propositions. However, I do not believe that they can be accounted for by, and incorporated into, the Ockhamist's account as easily as many Ockhamists would have one believe. Hoffman and Rosenkrantz merely provide a negative solution without actually giving sufficient positive reasons as to why one should subscribe to it.

Zagzebski is convinced that the incompatibilist's thesis has strength in that its suppositions are reflective of our intuitive understanding:

> Incompatibilists about divine foreknowledge hold that the claim that God's past beliefs are either not really past or are such that our power is unaffected by them violates necessary truths about the structure of time. I have not defended the intuitions the incompatibilist relies on, but I argued… they are common enough and strong enough to be considered common sense. I think,

---

156   Zagzebski (1991), pp. 70-74.
157   Ibid, p. 74.
158   Zagzebski alludes to a number of articles in this paper, not all of which support compatibilism, including Adams, M. (1967), Fischer (1983) and (1989), Zemach and Widerker (1987), Freddoso (1983), and Kvanvig (1986), Ch 3. She does not explicitly make reference to Hoffman and Rosenkrantz, but I believe that her points apply equally to their writings.

then, that even a negative solution to the foreknowledge dilemma of the type we are considering must attack these intuitions directly. The supporters of this approach, unfortunately, do not do this. Until they do, we have no reason to think their distinctions are more than purely nominal.[159]

Thus, I think that it would be prudent to consider whether the Ockhamist account does in fact have intuitive plausibility, or whether it is merely an attempt to construct an internally coherent theory. In order to address this question, I will consider whether it is intuitive to believe that the propositions that express God's past beliefs are not accidentally necessary. If the position advocated by the Ockhamist is intuitively plausible, then his position will be fortified. However, if we come to the conclusion that it is more intuitively plausible to understand these beliefs as accidentally necessary, then I believe that the onus will be on the Ockhamist to give reasons why we should accept that they are not fixed, other than the fact that a counterintuitive Ockhamist model can be constructed according to which they prove to be so.

I have presented these challenges as in the forthcoming discussion I will speak of certain proposals or ideas as being intuitively implausible. I believe the above account should help to add significance to such assertions.

4.7: Fischer on God's Beliefs

4.7.0: Introduction to Section 4.7

Although, on Hoffman and Rosenkrantz's distinction between hard and soft facts, God's beliefs about future contingents are soft, Fischer believes that they are part of a class of soft facts that are fixed.[160] Thus, Fischer is not attempting to undermine the idea that there are hard and soft facts. He is rather committed to showing that any Ockhamist account (such as that of Hoffman and Rosenkrantz) that does not discuss the possibility that there are hard elements (this is explained in the following two subsections) in particular types of soft facts is insufficient. In this section I introduce and criticise his argument to this effect.

4.7.1: Fischer's Incompatibilist Constraint

Fischer asserts that a soft fact is a fact *in virtue* of events that occur in the future.

---

159   Zagzebski (1991), p. 76.
160   Fischer (1986), p. 592.

He calls this a soft fact's 'future dependence'.[161] Now, let us suppose that Smith knows at $t1$ that Jones will mow his lawn at $t2$. Fischer argues that this is a soft fact about $t1$, because one and the same state of Jones's mind at $t1$ would count as knowledge if Jones does X at $t2$, and would not count as knowledge if Jones does not do X at $t2$ (see my previous discussion of Jones-predictors). Thus, human foreknowledge of a future contingent is not a hard fact about the past (assuming that human foreknowledge is possible – a possibility about which I am personally dubious[162]). It is the future dependence of the fact in question that lets us classify it as soft. Following from this observation, Fischer introduces an 'incompatibilist constraint' on any account of the hard and soft fact distinction:

> The only way in which God's belief at $t1$ about Jones at $t2$ could be a soft fact about the past relative to $t2$ would be if one and the same state of the mind of the person who was God at $t1$ would count as one belief if Jones did X at $t2$, but a different belief (or not a belief at all) if Jones did not do X at $t2$. But it is implausible to suppose that one and the same state of the mind of the person who was God at $t1$ would count as different beliefs given different behaviour by Jones at $t2$.[163]

There is, on Fischer's account, an asymmetry between soft facts such as Caesar dying 2009 years prior to Saunders writing his paper and Smiths knowledge that Jones will X at $t2$ on the one hand, and God's belief that Jones will X at $t2$, on the other. But it was the assimilation of these sorts of facts that was the initial ground for the claim that God's belief at $t1$ is a soft fact about $t1$.[164] On Fischer's analysis we can say that there is at least a hard component to God's beliefs – which is constituted by the state of his mind at the time when he holds any particular belief.

Fischer believes that:

> God's omniscience would be seriously attenuated if the same state of God's mind at $t1$ would constitute different beliefs about Jones, depending on Jones's behaviour at $t2$.

Let us suppose that Jones did X at $t2$. Y (God) believed at $t1$ that Jones would do X at $t2$. Let us call the state of Y's mind at this time $m1$, and allow that $m1$ was (in part) constituted by the belief that Jones would X at $t2$. However, it appears

---

161   Fischer (1983), p. 76.
162   I am personally not convinced that a human agent can have *knowledge* of future contingents. I believe that he can have a well-founded belief that may prove to be true in virtue of future occurrences. However, I think that knowledge involves certainty – and a human agent cannot be certain about what contingents will come about due to epistemic and cognitive constraints. I mention this only in passing, and do not attempt to offer sufficient justification of this theory, as it is not a point that is vital to the forthcoming discussion.
163   Fischer (1983), pp. 76-77.
164   Ibid, p. 78.

that if Y's mind was in *m1* at *t1* and Jones did not do X at *t2*, that Y's mind being in *m1* at *t1* would still be (in part) constituted by the belief that Jones will X at *t2*. Hence, it can be argued that Y's mind being in *m1* at *t1* would *not* count as one belief if Jones did X at *t2*, and another belief (or not a belief at all) if Jones did not do X at *t2*.[165]

Is there any way for the Ockhamist to counter Fischer's incompatibilist constraint? I think that we can construct a response by returning to the idea that there is an analytical connection between God's anterior belief and the truth of the future contingent to which it relates. I will call the following line of reasoning 'Ockhamist Strategy 1' (OS1). I have already introduced the idea that due to essential omniscience and infallibility it is not only the case that God holds no false beliefs, but it is also the case that he cannot hold any. From this it follows that if it is true that Jones will mow his lawn at *t2* then God would have truly believed at *t1* that he would do so, and that if Jones refrained from mowing his lawn at *t2* then God would have truly believed at *t1* that he would refrain from doing so. We can then proceed to the point that if God truly believes (knows) that Jones will do X at *t2*, then Jones will in fact proceed to do X at *t2*. However, in order to avoid fatalistic conclusions, the Ockhamist argues that God knows with certainty what Jones will do *in virtue* of the fact that Jones will choose to do it. Thus, it is not that one and the same state of God's mind would count as one belief *if* Jones does X at *t2*, and another belief if Jones does *not-X* at *t2*. God is certain that Jones will X at *t2* in virtue of the fact that Jones will in fact X at *t2*, and what Jones does at *t2* is the only thing that God has ever believed he will do. God's prior beliefs and the future states of affairs to which they relate are co-dependent. God's belief does not determine the object of the belief, and the state of affairs that constitutes the object of belief does not determine God's prior belief – the relationship is one of correspondence. This, it can be argued, is one of the fundamental epistemic differences between divine belief and human belief – human belief about what will occur at a specific future time will not of necessity correspond with what will actually occur at that time. However, God's belief about what state of affairs will constitute the world at a particular time will necessarily correspond with the state of affairs that occurs at the time in question (as God's beliefs are analytically connected to the truth. I will call this idea 'belief as correspondence').

In summary, the compatibilist can insist that the state of God's mind would have been counterfactually affected, if Jones had proceeded to perform some other action not-X. Thus, it could be argued that God's mind would have been in some other state *m2* at *t1*, which would have corresponded with the truth of the fact that Jones did not-X at *t2*. Putnam points out that meanings 'ain't in the head'.[166] According to him, my belief that water is wet (and the state of my mind

---

165   Ibid, p. 77.
166   Putnam (1975), esp. pp. 223-227.

which is in part constituted by this belief) would have been a different belief – the belief that *XYZ* is wet – if lakes and oceans on earth had been filled with *XYZ* rather than water. Thus, by analogy, it can be argued that the state of God's mind at *t1*, which is (partly) constituted by his belief that Jones will do *X* at *t2*, is in that state (partly) in virtue of the fact that Jones does in fact proceed to do *X* at *t2*.

4.7.2: Fischer's Hard-Core Soft Facts

I would now like to introduce the possibility that there are two categories of soft fact. The first covers those soft facts of which it is true that there was nothing within the agent's power to do such that they would not have been facts at all. The second covers soft facts that would have proven not to be facts at all, if the agent had done otherwise with respect to the exercise of his Regulative Control. Thus, Fischer can assert in his paper, 'Hard-Type Soft Facts', that even though under Hoffman and Rosenkrantz's analysis God's beliefs turn out to be soft facts, that they are soft facts which are nevertheless fixed. He defines the fixity in question as follows:

> A fact *F* is 'fixed' at a time *t* (relative to an agent) just in case there is no action such that the agent can at *t* perform the action and if he were to do so, *F* would obtain.[167]

I will call a fact that is fixed according to the above characterisation 'counterfactually fixed'. This is an innovative approach on Fischer's behalf, as he is no longer committed to refuting the claim that God's fore-beliefs are soft. Fischer believes that God's fore-beliefs fall under the first category of soft facts. As such he believes that they are also what he calls 'hard-core soft facts' and 'hard-type soft facts' (see below).

Let us consider the following propositions:

(11)   God believes at *t1* that Jones will mow his lawn at *t2*.

(12)   Yesterday Jones woke up a day prior to the sun's rising in the east today.

(13)   At eight Jones wakes up four hours prior to eating lunch.

(12) is a soft fact about the past that is counterfactually fixed. What is it that fixes this fact? Fischer states:

> …the fixity of the fact about yesterday does not arise from the fixity of genuine

---

[167] Note the similarity between this description of fixity and Plantinga's formulation of accidental necessity. He is essentially claiming that in relation to fixed soft facts there is no action that the agent has the power to perform in virtue of which the past would be counterfactually affected. Fischer (1986), p. 591.

features of the *past*; rather, it comes from my inability to affect the sun's rising in the east (which is a necessary condition of affecting the fact about yesterday). If falsifying fact *F1* would require falsifying fact *F2*, and one cannot falsify *F2*, then one cannot falsify *F1*.[168]

Thus, even though proposition (12) expresses a soft fact, it was never within Jones's power to perform an action in virtue of which the proposition expressing it would have been falsified (that is, he could not do something in virtue of which the state of affairs expressed in (12) would not have been a fact). This is because falsifying (12) would require the power to perform an act in virtue of which the proposition 'the sun rises in the east today' would be falsified (and correspondingly in virtue of which the state of affairs that it expresses would never have been a fact). Given that it is beyond Jones's power (at any time) to falsify this last proposition, it is also beyond his power to falsify (12). Therefore, we can conclude that (12) is counterfactually fixed. A soft fact that is counterfactually fixed is what Fischer calls a 'hard-core soft fact'.

The existence of God is a hard-core soft fact. The proposition 'God exists' expresses an eternal state of affairs. It is a proposition that can be stated at any time and will still be true at the time at which it is stated – it always obtains. Because it expresses a metaphysically necessary state of affairs there is nothing that the agent can do such that the status of its truth would be affected. God's existence can be argued to be a soft fact because the fact of his metaphysically necessary eternal existence always entails that there will be a future time at which he will exist (this assumption is obviously reliant on the claim that God is essentially located in time). However, the existence of God is a hard-core soft fact because it is counterfactually fixed (no agent can act such that it would have been the case that there was no God at any earlier time – follows from metaphysical necessity).

However, I think I would have to agree with the Ockhamist that it can be argued that propositions such as (11) are not self-evidently hard-core soft facts. This is because, if we accept that God's belief as correspondence, we can argue that the agent can act such that God would have held a different belief about what he would do at a particular time (as delineated above). Thus, we have been given no convincing reason to suppose that God's belief is counterfactually fixed.

OS1 is a powerful argument and not easily countered. Nevertheless, I believe that it is not entirely convincing. In order to show that this is the case it will be necessary to provide reasons why we should consider God's belief a hard-core soft fact, irrespective of the appeal of OS1, and provide reasons why the agent does not have the power to act such that God's past beliefs would be

---

168 Fischer (1986), p. 595. It should be noted that it is common in the literature to speak of falsifying a fact. However, facts cannot be falsified – it is rather the propositions that express them that can be falsified.

counterfactually affected. However, Fischer has not yet given up. He believes that he can provide just such a reason. In order to argue his incompatibilist position he next introduces the idea of hard-type soft facts.

4.7.3: Fischer's Hard-Type Soft Facts

In order to explain the idea of hard-type soft facts Fischer differentiates two distinct ways in which soft facts can be broken up into 'parts'.[169] He maintains that in each soft fact there are at least the two components of 'object' and 'property'. Within the subclass of property there are also what he calls 'hard-properties' and 'soft-properties'. A hard-property is non-relational or temporally genuine (does not relate to a future state of affairs – it is future indifferent), for example, 'waking up at eight o'clock'. When one combines a hard-property with an ordinary object one gets a hard fact. For example, 'In 44 BC Caesar dies on the steps of the Senate'. A soft-property is relational or temporally non-genuine. Therefore, a property P is a soft property relative to t just in case if anything were to have P at t, then it would follow that some immediate fact obtains after t (an immediate fact is to be understood as a state of affairs that will completely obtain at a particular time).

However, Fischer maintains that if you combine a hard-property with a special kind of object you get a soft fact. He believes that to have a belief is to be in a temporally genuine state. In so far as God's beliefs are similar to human beliefs, God's having a belief at a particular time means that he is in a particular dispositional state at the time in question. Fischer believes that a dispositional state's counting as a belief does not depend on the truth of the object of the belief. He claims that it follows from this that, 'believing that Jones will mow his lawn at $t2$' ($prop1$) is a hard-property relative to $t1$.[170] A human agent's having this belief does not entail that anything immediate occurs after $t1$. However, in relation to God his belief does entail that something immediate occurs after $t1$, but this does not mean that in virtue of this fact his belief is not a hard property. Fischer asserts that God can have a hard property at a time, although his having it is a soft fact about the time in question.

Fischer then introduces what is perhaps the definitive part of his argument:

(i) It is logically possible for some individual to be in the same kind of dispositional state at $t1$ and for Jones not to mow his lawn at $t2$.

(ii) Being in that state would count as believing that Jones will mow his lawn at $t2$, even if Jones *doesn't* mow his lawn at $t2$.[171]

---

169 The remainder of this paragraph is a synopsis of the argument presented by Fischer (1986), p. 597.
170 Ibid, p. 597.
171 Ibid, p. 598.

Fischer acknowledges that (11) expresses a soft fact about $t1$. However, he believes that the softness in question does not stem from the softness of the constituent property (*prop1*), but from what he calls the 'interaction' between a hard property and the special bearer of the property – God. Therefore, God's belief is a hard-type soft fact – in that it is a soft fact that has a hard-property (as it involves an essentially eternal entity being in a temporally genuine state).

Fischer then proceeds to argue that in order for Jones to perform an act at $t2$ in virtue of which (11) would have proven false; he must have the power to perform an act in virtue of which God would not have possessed *prop1* at $t1$. However, under Fischer's analysis this is a hard property relative to $t1$ and is therefore fixed. He believes that it follows from this that no agent has the power to act such that God would have had a different belief at a particular time. He then attempts to drive his argument home by stating:

> ...it seems to me plausible to suppose that no human can at $t2$ so act that some bearer of a hard property relative to $t1$ wouldn't have possessed that property at $t1$.[172]

However, one can easily envisage an objection to Fischer's account. It can also be argued that *prop1* is a soft property when combined with the object that is God. *Prop1* is not a universally hard property because whether or not it is future indifferent depends on the bearer of the property. Thus, if Smith believes that Jones will X at $t2$ this fact is future indifferent, as Smith's belief does not entail that anything immediate occur at any future time. But God's believing that Jones will mow his lawn at $t2$ does entail the occurrence of an immediate fact in the future (due to essential divine omniscience). Fischer argues that certain features of God's belief and man's belief are analogous. They are analogous in the sense that, in both cases, having a particular belief involves being in a particular dispositional state, and that a dispositional state's counting as a belief is not dependent on the truth of the object of belief (whereas a states counting as knowledge does so depend).[173] Fischer argues that when God believes at $t1$ that Jones will mow his lawn at $t2$ he is in a particular dispositional state, and that it is logically impossible for God to be in the same dispositional state and for Jones not to mow his lawn. It is God's dispositional state that is a hard property, and this is true irrespective of the fact that God's belief is itself a soft fact.

However, if we accept Fischer's claim that God's belief is analogous in the suggested ways to human belief, we are left in the predicament of not having adequately accounted for an obvious epistemic difference. The claim that 'a dispositional state's counting as a belief is not dependent on the truth of the object of belief' seems true when applied to human belief but inappropriate when applied to God's belief. Due to essential omniscience God's beliefs are analytically

---

172 Ibid, p. 598.
173 Ibid, p. 598.

connected to the truth – God's beliefs do in fact constitute knowledge, as if it is true that X, God necessarily believes that X and cannot be mistaken in this belief (infallibility). Therefore, we can state that God knows that his beliefs are true (hence 'foreknowledge' and not just 'fore-belief'). This seriously undermines Fischer's account, as if God's knows his beliefs to be true, there is no way that he could be in a dispositional state that involves having a belief which does not correspond with the future state expressed in that belief. However, instead of insisting, as Fischer does, that this leads to theological fatalism we can instead introduce an argument similar to OS1. One option appears to be to deny that God's beliefs about future contingents are soft facts. This, however, calls into question the whole point of introducing the idea of hard-properties in the first place.

I am convinced that God's beliefs do involve a hard property. However, I do not think that Fischer's account is sufficiently convincing to sway those who are unsure about the status of divine belief. I will therefore attempt to supply additional reasons as to why God's beliefs are a genuine aspect of the past. It is worth emphasising that it is very difficult for an incompatibilist to enter into a refutation of Ockhamism when the terms and definitions that are used are subject to constant revision. However, I believe that our intuitive understanding of the world, the nature of belief, and God will allow us to assess the plausibility of the Ockhamist thesis as a whole. However, to be fair, the incompatibilist position that I have been outlining is not yet entirely convincing either.

Section 4.8: Hasker on God's Beliefs

4.8.0: An Introduction to Section 4.8

The incompatibilist is left with a lacuna that needs to be filled. At this point Hasker steps in. He believes that there is a fundamental problem with Hoffman and Rosenkrantz's criterion of hard facts. If he is correct this means that arguments grounded on their account will need revision or will be proven unsatisfactory. In this Section I delineate his reasons for this belief and his attempt to offer a solution to the problem.

4.8.1: Hasker on Future Indifference

In order to show the flaw that Hasker finds in Hoffman and Rosenkrantz's analysis, it would be first prudent to introduce some of the terminology that he utilises. 'Future indifferent' propositions are propositions that are:

> ...wholly about the past and the present, and that are such that their truth or falsity cannot be affected by anything that happens in the future.[174]

He defines future indifference as follows:

> [A proposition] is future-indifferent iff it is consistent with there being no time after the present, and also with their being times after the present.

Thus, future indifferent (FI) propositions are counterfactually fixed and are accidentally necessary (these are my observations and this terminology is not used by Hasker). What does he mean by 'consistent with there being no time after the present'? He means that an FI proposition would be true even if 'the entire universe should disappear there be nothing at all after the present moment'.[175] Any proposition that is consistent with there being no times after the present would also have to be consistent with there being times after the present (if the truth of a proposition is fixed at one particular moment, then it will also be true at all subsequent moments).

He describes the category of hard facts as:

> ...facts, or true propositions, such that, with respect to a given time, it is impossible that anyone at or after that time should have the power to render them false.[176]

So, it can be claimed that hard facts, like FI propositions, are counterfactually fixed and accidentally necessary.

It follows from the account offered by Hasker that Hoffman and Rosenkrantz's criterion of hard facts allows that many propositions that intuitively express hard facts (and which I think that they too would want to classify as hard) turn out to be expressions of soft facts, if it is taken that God exists. Before progressing to this issue however, let me first give an illustration of the difference between FI propositions and non-FI propositions.

Consider the following:

(14) Jones finished mowing his lawn at one pm yesterday (*t*).

This proposition satisfies the criterion of future-indifference, as it would be true even if time were to cease immediately after one pm. Furthermore, there is nothing that can be done at any subsequent time such that Jones did not finish mowing his lawn at the specified time.

(15) Today, Jones said truly that he will mow his lawn tomorrow.

---

174 Hasker (1989), p. 83.
175 Ibid, p. 84.
176 Ibid, p. 83.

This is obviously not an FI proposition, as it is not consistent with there being no time after the present – the actual temporal world must continue until at least tomorrow if this proposition is to prove true.

Now let us reconsider (14) – taking it for granted that a sempiternal God exists. It can be argued that (14) gives rise to the following propositions:

(16) God exists after Jones mowed his lawn.

(17) God created Jones.

(18) God remembers the fact that Jones mowed his lawn at t.

(19) God will pass judgement on Jones's soul *after* his death.[177]

If it is correct that (14) gives rise to (16), (17), (18) and (19) then it turns out that what would have proved to be a hard fact under Hoffman and Rosenkrantz's criterion is actually a soft fact – as it implies a URP state of affairs that is indexed to a time that does not overlap with one pm yesterday – for example, 'God remembers that Jones mowed his lawn at $t1$ (some specified moment after t)' or 'God judges Jones's soul after his death (which is obviously a URP state of affairs that occurs after t)'.[178] Why does (14) entail (16), (17), (18) and (19)? If God exists, then Jones has particular essential properties that metaphysically entail the existence of future moments in time. The problem that we now encounter is that every proposition about present or past facts appears to metaphysically entail that God exists. Hasker relates this idea as follows:

> If God is a metaphysically necessary being (i.e., exists in all possible worlds) and is also essentially everlasting (as compatibilists suppose), then we immediately get the result that no proposition whatever is future-indifferent for any proposition metaphysically entails "God exists," which in turn entails the existence of times after the present. If, on the other hand, God's existence is not thought to be logically necessary, it is still reasonable to suppose that in a theistic universe every contingent being has essentially the property, "being created by God." And so, given God's everlastingness, we get the result that any proposition entailing the existence of contingent beings likewise metaphysically entails the existence of God and hence of future time. Furthermore, any proposition describing an event of the past, present, or future entails that God will remember that event for all time to come - so, no proposition can be future-indifferent. Finally, I propose as a plausible opinion the view that, once God has undertaken to create a world of contingent beings and, in particular, a world containing rational spirits capable of communion with himself, it would be inconsistent with his nature for him to annihilate his creation and

---

177 Proposition (19) is of my own invention and should not be ascribed to Hasker.
178 This is different from the proposition that expresses the eternal state of affairs 'God exists' – as it is not eternally true that God remembers anything – as remembrance places the person remembering in a temporal location that occurs only after the event being remembered has occurred. Similarly it is not eternally true that God created Jones – 'God creates Jones at $t1$' is a URP state of affairs

allow it to fall into nothingness. If this is so, then any proposition entailing the existence of contingent beings (or at least, of created rational spirits) will be non-future-indifferent.[179]

Can we not simply side-step this line of argument by insisting that it is possible that God can exist even if time were to cease? Thus, even though (14) implies (16) and (17) that does not mean that time cannot cease immediately after t. It can then be argued that (18) would not be implied by (14) as if time were to cease God would have timeless knowledge of the truth of (14) – and would not 'remember' it. This conception would also address the issue of whether there was a moment before creation (as God can exist outside of time). However, I believe that this conception would lead to unnecessary complication. If we take it for granted that God does not have to exist in the temporal continuum then it would be far more appropriate to think of him solely in terms of atemporality (rather than atemporal then sempiternal and then atemporal again). I believe that by thinking of God solely in an atemporal fashion we can avoid many of the difficulties that arise due to the idea of *fore*knowledge. I also believe that if we allow that God is, or can be, sempiternal then arguments for theological fatalism can be countered more successfully by using a Molinist approach. I will fully expand and justify this claim in the next chapter. Furthermore, I believe that if we are discussing a God who is, at any stage, sempiternal that (19) is most intuitively understood in terms of a temporal continuum. It is also my opinion that most people envisage the life of the soul after death in temporal terms – at least in so far as there is a temporal interlude before the soul is judged.

4.8.2: Hasker on Conceptual Consistency

Hasker argues that the 'consistency' involved in FI should not be understood in terms of metaphysical consistency because 'if this notion is explicated using the notion of metaphysical necessity, the distinction [between future-indifferent and non-future-indifferent propositions] collapses as all, or virtually all, propositions become non-future-indifferent'.[180] In what terms then should this consistency be understood? Hasker believes that the idea of 'conceptual consistency' is most appropriate.

What is 'conceptual consistency'? Hasker offers us a distinction between two of the ways in which logical necessity can be understood:

> In one sense, a proposition may be said to be logically necessary if it is conceptually necessary, or true in virtue of the terms in which it is expressed. In another sense, a proposition is logically necessary if it is metaphysically

---

179   Hasker (1989), pp. 86-87.
180   Ibid, p. 85.

necessary, or true in all possible worlds.[181]

Thus, Hasker can offer his final and most comprehensive definition of FI.

> (CFI) An elementary proposition is future-indifferent iff it is conceptually consistent with there being no times after the present.[182]

How can Hasker argue to the conclusion that propositions expressing God's beliefs about future occurrences are future indifferent in a way that accords with CFI? Is a proposition such as the following future-indifferent according to Hasker's final characterisation?

> (20): God has always believed that Jones will mow his lawn at $t2$ (where $t2$ is a future moment).

Hasker asserts that 'the word 'God' expresses those properties that are definitionally included in our conception of God'.[183] Let us assume that God has always believed that Jones will mow his lawn tomorrow. It is necessarily true that if God believed that something will occur, then that state of affairs will occur. However, this leads us to the conclusion that if God believed that something will occur, it is metaphysically and conceptually necessary that that thing will in fact occur at the specified time. It is metaphysically necessary because, under Hasker's own understanding, omniscience and infallibility are definitionally included in the concept of God. It is conceptually necessary because if we assume that God is infallible then this conceptually entails that what is believed to be true is true. Thus, if an infallible entity believes the proposition 'Jones will mow his lawn at $t2$' to be true, it is necessarily true that Jones will mow his lawn at $t2$. However, this has the effect of making proposition such as (20) non-future-indifferent under Hasker's own characterisation.

Hasker does not surrender his position at this point though. He believes that by substituting the name 'Yahweh' for 'God' in 'God has always believed p' he can evade the problems that were presented above.[184] He adopts the theory of non-connotative proper names.

> (21) If Yahweh exists, Yahweh is God.[185]

He offers the following justification for doing so:

> Consider the name 'Yahweh', which was used by the ancient Hebrews to refer to their God. They used this name (as a reading of Genesis will confirm) with no thought or connotation of such metaphysical attributes as essential omniscience, essential everlastingness, and the like... We will use the name, as

---

181   Ibid.
182   Ibid.
183   Ibid, p. 91.
184   For a discussion of this issue see, Craig (1992).
185   Hasker (1989), p. 91.

the ancient Hebrews did, simply as a non-connotative proper name referring to that individual who in fact was, and is, the God of Abraham, Isaac, and Jacob.[186]

Thus, the contention is that under the non-connotative theory of proper names the name 'Yahweh' has none of the connotations with the essential divine attributes that the word 'God' does. Thus, if we modify proposition (20) to read:

(22) Yahweh has always believed that Jones will mow his lawn at $t2$

We can then argue that this latter proposition refers to a hard fact, as it is future-indifferent according to CFI. However, this is not as clear-cut as Hasker makes it appear. We can dismiss the scholarly debate about the way in which the ancient Hebrews used the word 'Yahweh' as irrelevant to our immediate concerns, as it is possible to simply substitute a newly invented proper name for God and argue that this will suffice for the argument at hand (all that matters is that there is some proper name which can be non-connotatively understood to represent the proper name of God). The more serious objection is that Hasker has not even considered the possibility that there may be more compelling alternatives for the way in which the name Yahweh should be understood, such as those based on the Fregean understanding[187] (according to this theory, it is possible that it is due to conceptual limitation that one does not appreciate that the proposition 'Yahweh has always believed that Jones will mow his lawn at $t2$' actually expresses the proposition 'God has always believed that Jones will mow his lawn at $t2$').

Although one may be dubious about applying the theory of non-connotative proper names to God, I will temporarily allow that Hasker is correct in order to reach what I consider to be a more important conclusion. Even if we accept that (22) is future indifferent under CFI, Hasker still has to face the following objection:

> Whatever is or is not expressed by the name "Yahweh", you are forced to admit that infallibility is an essential property of Yahweh himself. As you yourself admit, there is no possible world in which Yahweh holds a false belief, no possible world in which he believes [Jones will mow his lawn at $t2$ but the lawn is not mowed at this time]. So [22] does entail a fact about a future time, and it cannot be a hard fact. It does no good at all first to pretend to forget this, as you do in order to classify [22] as hard, and then suddenly to remember it in order to derive [20] from [22].[188]

Hasker believes that this difficulty can be resolved by using the 'ordinary methods' of logical inference, without recourse to *de re* modalities.[189] He believes

---

186   Ibid, p. 87.
187   See, for example, Plantinga (1978).
188   Hasker (1988), p. 433. I have modified the contents of the quotation in order to fit with the examples and numbering that I have been using.
189   Hasker (1985). p. 133.

that '*de re* modalities' are roughly akin to metaphysical necessity.[190] However, it can be argued that Hasker is not playing by his own rules, as it appears as though he has already allowed the use of a *de re* modality in his assertion that 'Yahweh is God' as he takes it as given that Yahweh is essentially God – there exists no world at which Yahweh is not God. This has already been asserted by him in the proposition that I have numbered (21).

In response to this issue Reichenbach makes the following observation:

> Granted that a universal admission of *de re* considerations effectively destroys the usefulness of making a distinction between hard and soft facts, in that few hard facts would remain, still does it follow that they are always irrelevant? It would seem that they are relevant in those cases where *de re* considerations are directly germane to the determination of the hardness or softness of a fact ... The compatibilist then can argue that *de re* considerations are relevant to and cannot be excluded from considerations regarding Yahweh's beliefs about the future.[191]

Thus, Reichenbach suggests that the Ockhamist can legitimately allow a limited use of *de re* considerations. Hasker, however, is not at all impressed. He is quite forceful in his response, but seems assuredly oblivious to his own limited use of *de re* considerations:

> As Reichenbach recognizes, my criteria for the hard-soft fact distinction require that *de re* necessary truths not be considered in identifying future-indifferent propositions. The reason for this, as I clearly indicate, is that considering de re necessary truths in determining this would eliminate virtually all candidates for the status of future-indifferent propositions, thus making the hard-soft fact distinction pointless. Reichenbach seems to see this, at least in part; he admits that "a universal admission of *de re* considerations effectively destroys the usefulness of making a distinction between hard and soft facts" (H O, p. 88), so he wants to consider only some of the *de re* necessary truths as relevant. But so far as I can see, he gives us no clue as to how we should determine these, and distinguish them from the others which must be excluded in order to preserve the hard-soft fact distinction.[192]

The effect of allowing these limited *de re* considerations is that (22) turns out to be a non-future-indifferent proposition under CFI. This is because, if we understand 'Yahweh is God' to express an essential attribute of God, it is true that Yahweh's having a belief metaphysically and conceptually entails a future time (as in the case of God's having a belief – see above). It appears that if Hasker accepts (21) he must also accept the Direct Reference Theory, under which (20) and (22) substantially express the same proposition. This is because they have the same referent (Yahweh is essentially God) and the name that is substituted for the referent does not change the substance of the proposition. Therefore, given that 'Yahweh' and 'God' are different names (signs) for the same referent,

---

190   See Hasker (1989), p. 85, footnote 9.
191   Reichenbach (1987), p. 88.
192   Ibid, pp. 337-338.

irrespective of which sign is used the meaning is identical.

However, I think that his brings us to a much more important point. I do not believe that it is possible for the Ockhamist to consistently account for the difference between hard and soft facts without adding arbitrary qualifications. I think that it is very difficult for us to be convinced by the Ockhamist account when Ockhamists cannot even offer comprehensive definitions of their terms which are not specially and arbitrarily modified to suit their purposes. How can it be convincingly argued that the agent has the power to do otherwise with respect to his particular actions, because God's prior beliefs about what he will do are soft facts relative to the times at which they are held, when the Ockhamist cannot even tell us exactly how to characterise hard and soft facts? This brings me back to the comments of Zagzebski that I previously introduced. If it is true, as I maintain, that the incompatibilist's position is more reflective of our intuitions than the Ockhamist's, then the Ockhamist will at least have to provide a better account of the terminologies and distinctions that he uses. However, I will offer further reasons why the Ockhamist position is unconvincing through the following analysis of counterfactual power, before introducing my final reasons for rejecting Ockhamism.

4.9: More Problems, Zagzebski and Counterfactual Power

4.9.0: An Introduction to Section 4.9

I begin this Section by attempting to show the intuitive implausibility of the Ockhamist account by way of example. I then proceed to introduce Lewis's ideas on the truth-conditions of back-tracking counterfactuals. I finally consider Zagzebski's argument that the agent cannot exercise a power in virtue of which God's beliefs would have been counterfactually affected. This Section serves to ground many of the claims that I make in the Conclusion to this chapter.

4.9.1: Counterfactual Power and Plausibility

I have already considered the possibility that the agent may be able to exercise a power in virtue of which a counterfactual state of affairs would have comprised the world at a particular time. Thus, if Jones had actually exercised the power to refrain from mowing his lawn at $t2$, the truth of the following proposition would never have obtained:

(23) God believed at *t1* that Jones would mow his lawn at *t2*.

Instead the counterfactual state of affairs expressed in the following proposition would have obtained in its place:

(24) God believed at *t1* that Jones would refrain from mowing his lawn at *t2*

I have already considered how the Ockhamist can argue that the exercise of such a power would not involve an objectionable power to affect the past.

However, I would now like to consider a possibility that may detract from the plausibility of the Ockhamist defences that I have just sketched. In the following I am taking it for granted that Jesus is God. I am also going to rely on our intuitive understanding of the past and its limitations. In Matthew 26:34 – it is reported that Jesus said to Peter:

(25) Verily I say unto thee, that this night, before the cock crows, thou shalt deny me thrice.

I am going to take this quotation as a paradigmatic example of any situation in which God reveals the future to man – in the sense that he predicts how a particular individual will proceed to act (of which many can be found in the Bible).

In this passage Christ is making a certain revelation to Peter about the future. I will call the time that the cock makes his third crow *t3*. I will call the time when Jesus makes this revelation *t1* and I will call the interim time *t2*. Now consider the following proposition:

(26) At *t1* God affirms, by stating (25), that Peter will deny him three times before *t3*.

The question that I would like to ask is whether or not (26) should be considered an accidentally necessary aspect of the past which is counterfactually fixed? It is my contention that it is implausible to simply classify it as a soft fact and assert that this is explanatorily sufficient, as it is intuitive to think that (26) is accidentally necessary immediately after *t1*. Let us consider (26) in light of Hoffman and Rosenkrantz's criterion.

Let us introduce the kernel state of affairs:

(26*) God affirms, by stating (25), that Peter denies him three times before *t3*.

(26**) ¬(God affirms, for the first time by stating (25), that Peter denies him three times before *t3*).

(26*) satisfies Hoffman and Rosenkrantz's (a) – (d). (26**) is not URP as it may obtain at one time because God has never stated (25), then fail to obtain at another moment because he is stating (25), and then obtain again at a subsequent time because he is no longer stating (25). However, immediately after this moment it will obtain at all future times. It can be argued that 26* does entail a future URP state of affairs, because of the fact that if God asserts a true belief it entails that time must continue until the time when the URP state of affairs that is Peter denying Christ three times obtains.

When a human agent asserts that he believes that something is going to happen at a future time it is not necessarily the case that anything will occur after the time in question. The fact that one had a belief at $t1$ is 'future indifferent' (it does not entail that anything will happen at a future time). The fact that Black believes at $t1$ that Jones will X at $t2$ is a hard fact about the past. The question of whether the content of the belief is true is future relational (in order for it to be true some future contingent must occur that is in accordance with the belief), but the fact that Black had a belief at a particular time in the past is future indifferent. I have already shown why things are not identical in the case of God. When God believes that X will occur at $t2$ it is necessarily the case that time continue until at least $t2$, in virtue of the entailments of God's omniscience and infallibility. Therefore, God's belief at $t1$ about an occurrence at $t2$ entails a URP state of affairs indexed to a time which does not overlap with $t1$. Hence, (26) cannot satisfy (e). However, I think that this shows the above model to be significantly counter-intuitive, as according to it one can maintain that an agent can now perform an act in virtue of which something that has been asserted would not have been asserted.

In order to illustrate my contention let us suppose that I am currently temporally located at $t2$ and I am certain that it is a fact that God did assert (25) at $t1$. However, if the fact that God asserted (25) is soft (and that the proposition that expresses it is not accidentally necessary) then it can be claimed that at $t3$ Peter can do something in virtue of which it would not have been the case that God asserted (25) at $t1$. However, this would have the effect of making it untrue at $t2$ that I was certain that God asserted (25) at $t1$. I think that this runs contrary to our intuitive understanding of time and its limitations and what it means to be certain about something at a particular time. There is also another associated problem. It is argued that God's certainty with regard to the object of his beliefs is analytically connected to the truth of the future occurrence of those states of affairs (i.e. it must correspond with those states of affairs). However, could it not also be argued that my certainty at $t2$ that God stated (25) at $t1$ is also connected to the truth of the fact that God did assert (25) (qua certainty and not incompletely justified belief)? To be certain that (25) was stated, it must be the case that (25) actually was stated.

The Ockhamist could argue that if Peter proceeds to not deny Christ three times then God would never have stated (25) and I would therefore have never been certain that God had stated (25). However, given that I am certain at $t2$ about something that was stated at an earlier time, and given that $t2$ has obtained before Peter makes his choice, it seems highly implausible that Peter could act at *t3* such that both God's statement, and my certainty concerning that statement, never occurred.

However, I believe that any such insistence to this effect would merely serve to highlight the intuitive implausibility of the Ockhamist position. I think that Ockhamist claims look far more plausible when considered in a sterile abstract fashion. Now I will try to make things a little more personal and therefore clear. Let us suppose that you are in fact Peter. You were just speaking to Jesus, and he said that you will betray him three times before the cock crows for the third time. The cock has now crowed twice and you have betrayed him twice. You decide however that you will not betray him a third time. Do you think that in virtue of your not doing so the past would be counterfactually affected such that he never made the statement in question? I think you would have to admit that it is not at all plausible that you can do so. Why? Because it is in accordance with our intuitive understanding to believe that once a statement of this type is made there is nothing that can be done such that it was not made. I think that one of the most curious things about the whole Ockhamist and incompatibilist debate is that the issue of accidental necessity is often unclear – with the entire focus being placed on the question of hard and soft facts – as though hard facts are the only accidentally necessary facts (some exceptions to this have been outlined above). It is my belief that the proposition that expresses the fact that Jesus told Peter that he would betray him before a specified time is accidentally necessary immediately after Jesus has spoken – and that this is intuitively obvious.

The fundamental issue is not whether the proposition in question is hard or soft, or has hard or soft components (or any other similarly convoluted way of classifying facts); it is rather to do with accidental necessity. If the proposition is accidentally necessary then we can construct and fit it into whatever category we like, but it will nevertheless be true that there is no power that any agent can exercise in virtue of which the proposition was not true at the time in question. Thus, if the proposition 'Jesus says (25) to Peter at *t1*' is accidentally necessary, then it is necessarily true at all subsequent times. If (26) is accidentally necessary, then it is necessary that Peter will betray Christ three times before the indicated time, as following from essential omniscience, infallibility and the impossibility that God would lie (do something morally deficient) it follows that the truth that is expressed in (25) is a necessary truth. If it is necessarily true that Peter will deny Christ three times before *t3* then we cannot credit him with Regulative Control over his actions, although we can credit him with Guidance Control (in the sense that he still does what he most desires to do). However, we would have to come to the conclusion that, under my criteria of morally responsible agency, he is not responsible for the action that he performs at *t3*. I will further justify these claims below. First, however, I would like to consider another issue that is not dealt with in the literature.

Consider the fact that Jesus said (25) to Peter at *t1*. Now what if at *t2* Peter were to say:

> (27) Jesus just said that I will betray him three times before the cock crows for the third time.

to one of the other apostles. Now, it appears that this statement is accidentally necessary immediately after $t2$, as Peter's uttering of this proposition does not entail that anything occur at any future time, and there is nothing that can be done after $t2$ such that he did not say it. But this statement is based upon a revelation made by Christ which the Ockhamist may want to insist is subject to counterfactual qualification. Thus, we would need to now claim that any statement that is accidentally necessary, but which arises as the result of a statement which can be counterfactually affected can also be counterfactually affected by Peter's action at $t3$. This, however, makes the whole scenario even more implausible.

Now let us consider the possibility that an agent asks God at $t1$ what it is that he believes an agent A will do at $t2$? Are we to assume that a sempiternal God does not have the ability to answer such a question? Surely not, for if we made such an assertion this would surely call into question divine omnipotence. So, let us assume that God can answer such a question – does it appear plausible that if God replies that A will X at $t2$, that the agent has the power to do other than X at $t2$? One can make the standard Ockhamist reply that the agent has such a power, and by exercising such a power God would have stated at $t1$ that A would do some other action *not-X* at $t2$. However, let us now suppose that you are the agent in question. You pray to God for a revelation of the future and God decides to tell you that you will X at $t2$, does it now seem plausible that you can proceed to *not-X* at $t2$? I think that it does not seem so, and the reason for this is that you implicitly intuitively understand accidental necessity to have attached to the proposition expressing the revelation in question. Suppose further that you have told all of your friends, who have in turn told all of their friends, what it is that God revealed will happen at $t2$. Let us further suppose that $t2$ is in 50 years time and you found a church based upon the revelation. Do you suppose that by refraining from doing what God has revealed will occur 50 years in the future you can counterfactually affect this entire past? After all, if you proceed to refrain from doing X at $t2$ this would, under the Ockhamist thesis, counterfactually affect the past such that God would have made a different revelation. Of course, one could insist that you would only have imagined that God made such a revelation or some such, however, this once again stretches plausibility.

The most important point that I think emerges from this discussion is that God has the power to state at any particular moment in time what it is that he believes will occur at any specific future time. I also think that this is because God has occurrent foreknowledge of what will occur at any future time – and what is occurrently known can also be stated - as there is a significant sense in which the object of knowledge is consciously affirmed by the knower to be true. However, can one who disagrees with my claim merely insist that God's beliefs about future contingents are dispositional? I will now attempt to address this contention. I will begin by outlining the substantive difference between occurrent and dispositional knowledge. Occurrent knowledge involves knowledge of propositions that are consciously affirmed at a given time t to be true. Dispositional knowledge involves knowledge of propositions that would be consciously affirmed to be true at t (thereby becoming occurrent) if there were sufficient conditions for them to be considered.

God's knowledge could potentially be occurrent or dispositional depending on the way in which his mind operates. Thus, his mental state m could theoretically be comprised of occurrent or dispositional knowledge, or a combination of both. If God is such that he is capable of having dispositional knowledge, then it may be that his knowledge regarding the future actions of the agent remains dispositional until those actions actually occur, and thereby provide sufficient conditions to make them occurrent. According to this model, God is essentially dispositionally omniscient. Therefore, it may be claimed that God's mental state at any moment does not include occurrent knowledge of future contingent states of affairs that have been consciously affirmed to be true.

How does this counter the incompatibilist arguments I have just proposed? It is a subtle move but potentially allows for the possibility of Regulative Control. At any given time $t1$ God's knowledge will not consist of the certainty that Jones will mow his lawn at $t2$, because the sufficient conditions for God making his dispositional belief occurrent will not in fact be present until $t2$. Only at $t2$ will God actually occurrently know that Jones mows his lawn, for at any time prior to this all that God possessed was a true disposition to know such. It is argued that because God is not occurrently aware of the content of his mental state with regard to the agent's future actions, this foreknowledge does not fatalistically entail what the agent must do (there is a sense in which God has not revealed to himself what will in fact happen – he has in a certain sense not 'stated' to himself, or anyone else, what the future holds).

But is this not a mere semantic equivocation? In order to answer this I will take a look once more at the relationship between dispositional and occurrent knowledge of the same action X. On the proposed model it appears as though we can define dispositional knowledge as a precursor to occurrent knowledge, in the sense of being potential occurrent knowledge. The disposition is nothing more than the ability to form correct occurrent knowledge, but the occurrent knowledge does not yet exist and as such the status of the dispositional knowledge can be thought of nothing more than an ability. An ability, however, is not something that actually manifests itself until it is exercised. So to say that God had the ability to form the correct occurrent knowledge is not at all the same thing as to say that God had actually formed and consciously affirmed a particular proposition to be true at $t1$. It can be argued that only if a temporally situated

God had occurrently known that Jones would mow his lawn at $t1$, would it have been fixed knowledge relative to $t2$.[193] It can then be argued that this is not the case with dispositional knowledge, as it relies on a future occurrence for its transformation to occurrent knowledge.

One might insist that this is a good model of knowledge, as it accounts for the way in which things are still known even when one is not consciously focusing on what it is that one knows. The problem with this account becomes more obvious however when one revisits what exactly it is that constitutes dispositional knowledge. I will now argue that what initially looked promising can be shown to be lacking. I am in agreement with Goldman when he observes that to say that a dispositional belief is nothing more than a power or ability is to miss a vital aspect of the way in which it is a constituent of knowledge.[194]

> To say that a person believes proposition p at t is to say that p is somehow lodged in the mind at t - in memory if not in consciousness.[195]

In other words, for God to have dispositional knowledge would require that in some sense there is an internal mental state that satisfies the criteria of knowledge. Thus, knowledge would have to have some sort of content. An unexercised power is in a significant way 'empty'.

Any particular agent (including God) may have the ability to form a correct occurrent belief about a particular fact because of knowledge that he already possesses, but until he forms the occurrent belief we should not think of him as having knowledge of the fact in question. For us to say that the agent has a dispositional belief about a fact or proposition which is not now, or ever was, present to consciousness, is not the same as to say that he has knowledge of the particular fact or proposition in question. For it to be knowledge requires that it have been occurrent in the past and stored as memory (or be currently occurrent). For instance, to say that I know a mathematical theorem because I have the ability to understand all of the components of the argument, and were I to find occasion to consider them all in a specific relational context, would reason to the theorem, is not the same as my actually knowing the theorem. For it is very possible that I might go through life without ever having had such an occasion, and as such I can hardly say that I knew the theorem in question. A capacity to know is not the same thing as knowing, just as an unexercised power

---

193 That is, accidental necessity cannot attach to dispositional foreknowledge as in such knowledge nothing has been affirmed to be true. However, it does attach to propositions expressing God's occurrent knowledge. As God only has occurrent knowledge of the agent's actions immediately after the time that he acts, it can then be claimed that God's foreknowledge does not result in theological fatalism.
194 Goldman (1986) speaks of 'dispositional beliefs' rather than 'dispositional knowledge' but his point will still hold for my argument.
195 Ibid, p. 526.

to form correct beliefs is not the same thing as knowledge. I believe that given divine omnipotence there is no reason to assume that all of God's knowledge is not occurrent at all times (I also think that this is more plausible, given the idea of divine immutability, than the idea that God's knowledge moves from dispositional to occurrent states).

I believe that propositions expressing God's occurrent foreknowledge of future contingents is intuitively understood to be an accidentally necessary aspect of the past. Therefore, I think that the above argument has lent intuitive credence to Fischer's assertion that God's beliefs have a counterfactually fixed hard component. I believe that the argument involved in OS1 is intuitively implausible when considered in this light.

4.9.2: Zagzebski, Lewis and Counterfactual Fixity

I would now like to consider what Zagzebski has to say about the power to counterfactually affect the past, and thereby further re-enforce my contention that a sempiternal God's prior beliefs are counterfactually fixed.

In order to claim that the agent has libertarian freedom the following two propositions must be true:

(28) It is within Jones's power to mow his lawn at $t2$, and if he exercises this power, then God would have had the belief at $t1$ that he would mow his lawn at $t2$.

(29) It is within Jones's power to refrain from mowing his lawn at $t2$, and if he exercises this power, then God would have had the belief at $t1$ that he would refrain from mowing his lawn at $t2$.

I am introducing the past-tense 'had the belief' in relation to God's beliefs into these propositions intentionally, as I think it will help to further illustrate the implausibility of the Ockhamist thesis. The Ockhamist generally prefers to form the propositions that he discusses such that they use the present-tense 'believes' in relation to God's beliefs – for example:

(30) If Jones mows his lawn at $t2$, then God believes at $t1$ that he will do so.

However, I think that the Ockhamist would have to accept that God actually had some belief at $t1$. And, as I have attempted to illustrate above, it would have been possible for him to state exactly what belief he had at this time – irrespective of whether or not the statement of such a belief would entail that a future state of affairs would occur. However, it is very difficult to justify the truth of (28) and (29). As Lewis notes:

Seldom, if ever, can we find a clearly true counterfactual about how the past would be different if the present were somehow different. Such a counterfactual, unless clearly false, normally is not clear one way or the other.[196]

Lewis helps to illustrate his argument with the use of an example that he borrows from Downing:[197]

> Jim and Jack quarrelled yesterday, and Jack is still hopping mad. We conclude that if Jim asked Jack for help today, Jack would not help him. But wait: Jim is a prideful fellow. He never would ask for help after such a quarrel; if Jim were to ask Jack for help today, there would have been no quarrel yesterday. In that case Jack would be his usual generous self. So if Jim asked Jack for help today, Jack would help him after all.[198]

One may be tempted to assume that this back-tracking argument is true. However, this would be too quick an assumption. According to our usual method of counterfactual reasoning, we would state that it would be useless for Jim to ask Jack to help him, since Jack would not do so. It is claimed that Jim would never ask for help after a quarrel. However, it can be further claimed that if Jim did ask Jack for his help today the only way that this could occur, given the actual past, would be if he overcame his pride. This would not, however, mean that the quarrel would not have taken place. Thus, it can be claimed that Jim does not have the power to act today such that yesterday's past would be counterfactually affected.

Lewis makes the following claims:

L1: Counterfactuals are infected with vagueness.[199]

In order to illustrate this point, he calls our attention to the following scenario. Suppose that Caesar had been in command in Korea. Now consider the following propositions:

(a) If Caesar had been in command in Korea, he would have used the atom bomb.

(b) If Caesar had been in command in Korea, he would have used catapults.

Which of these two counterfactual statements is true? There is obviously an inherent vagueness in any attempt to resolve this issue. If we allow for the resolution of this vagueness in terms of Caesar's willingness to use the best weapons at his disposal, and his taking the time to become fully informed by his (modern) advisors, then we could assert that (a) is true. However, if we were to attempt to resolve this vagueness in terms of his knowledge of weaponry, taking it for granted that he only had knowledge of the weapons of the Roman era, then

---

196 Lewis (1979), p. 455.
197 Ibid, p. 456 from Downing (1959).
198 Lewis (1979), p. 456.
199 Ibid. L1 to L4 are quoted from p. 457.

we could assert that (b) is true. However, given that both counterfactuals depend on a particular and controversial resolution of their vagueness it is not possible to assign a definite truth-value to either of them.

> (L2) We ordinarily resolve the vagueness of counterfactuals in such a way that counterfactual dependence is asymmetric. Under this standard resolution, back-tracking arguments are mistaken: if the present were different the past would be the same, but some past causes would fail somehow to cause the same present effects.

As in the above example, if Jim asked Jack for help today, this would mean that somehow Jim would have overcome his pride and asked for help despite yesterday's quarrel.

> (L3) Some special contexts favour a different resolution of vagueness, one under which the past depends counterfactually on the present and some back-tracking arguments are correct. If someone propounds a back-tracking argument, for instance, his cooperative partners in conversation will switch to a resolution that gives him a chance to be right. But when the need for a special resolution of vagueness comes to an end, the standard resolution returns.

> (L4) A counterfactual saying that the past would be different if the present were somehow different may come out true under the special resolution of its vagueness, but false under the standard resolution. If so, call it a back-tracking counterfactual. Taken out of context, it will not be clearly true or false. Although we tend to favour the standard resolution, we also charitably tend to favour a resolution which gives the sentence under consideration a chance of truth.

Lewis attempts to provide a non-vague account of counterfactuals as follows:

> Analysis 2: A counterfactual "If it were that A, then it would be that C" is (non-vacuously) true if and only if some (accessible) world where both A and C are true is more similar to our actual world where A is true but C is false.[200]

This is a fully general analysis. But Lewis believes that this has strength in that counterfactuals are both vague and various. He believes that different resolutions of the vagueness of overall similarity are appropriate in different contexts.[201]

Zagzebski helps to clarify Lewis's position as follows:

> The inherent vagueness of counterfactuals consists in the vagueness in specifying which worlds count as the closest A-worlds. In some contexts it may be natural to say that the closest A-worlds are worlds in which the past is different from the actual world in various ways. This is because the assumption that the world is now different in some way is to assume that past causally relevant conditions did not lead to actual present events. A world that preserves sensible causal connections between the present and the past but that has a different past may be more like the actual world for the purposes of a certain discussion than one

---

200   Ibid, p. 465.
201   Ibid, p. 465.

that has the same past but an unexpectedly different present. So we may say that to imagine a world just like this one except that *A* is true is to also imagine a causal history for *A* that is different from the actual past.[202]

The question that I believe is now most important is whether the following proposition should, or should not, be allowed a special resolution of vagueness (see L3 and L4 above).

> (31) If Jones had refrained from mowing his lawn at $t2$, then God would have had the belief at $t1$ that Jones would refrain from doing so at $t2$.

Zagzebski believes that there should be no special resolution allowed, as the standard resolution is more reflective of our intuitive understanding of the asymmetry between past and future. However, the Ockhamist can insist that his understanding also does not violate this asymmetric understanding – as he argues that no aspect of the past is changed from what it actually was in virtue of Jones's action – rather, the actual past would have been different. I have already attempted to give reasons why such an idea is in itself intuitively implausible. Nevertheless, let us briefly entertain this idea in order to meet another objection. The Ockhamist can claim that, given his theory of divine belief as correspondence, there is no sensible alternative to his account. Consider the following:

> (32) Even if Jones had refrained from mowing his lawn at $t2$, at $t1$ God would have believed that Jones would mow his lawn, and this belief would have been false in virtue of Jones's subsequent actions.

The Ockhamist can legitimately demand to know what becomes of essential divine omniscience and infallibility if (32) is true – a consequence that could stem from adopting the standard resolution – and which does appear to stem from many of the incompatibilist accounts that have already been introduced. However, let us now consider the alternative possibility that is proposed by the fatalist. If God believes at $t1$ that Jones will X at $t2$, this belief will of necessity be reflective of the truth of the state of affairs to which it relates. If one subscribes to fatalism, omniscience and infallibility can be preserved - but at the cost of libertarian free will. According to the theological fatalist, there is never the question that God's prior belief would have proven false in virtue of Jones's subsequent action – rather, Jones would never have had the ability to do other than what is foreknown by God. I am not suggesting that theological fatalism should be openly embraced. I am rather suggesting that it is more plausible than Ockhamism, given the existence of a sempiternal God.

The Ockhamist, however, may simply respond that he does not accept Lewis's account of backtracking counterfactuals and attempt to provide another account that is at least as equally convincing. However, I believe that Lewis's account

---

202   Zagzebski (1991), p. 101.

is sufficiently reflective of our intuitive understandings for us to embrace it. Alternatively, they can exploit the point made by Lewis in L4 – that we should charitably allow a special resolution of vagueness in order that the proposition in question has a chance of truth.

Let us temporarily suppose that it is legitimate to allow a special resolution of counterfactuals that have the form of (31). Zagzebski claims that even if we were to allow such a resolution the powers expressed in propositions (28) and (29) are not sufficiently strong to allow the counterfactual power over the past that is essential to the Ockhamist account. Zagzebski introduces the following example to show the strength of her argument:

> (33) If I ran instead of skipped at $t2$, my decision at $t1$ would have been different.
>
> Saunders claims that since it is plainly true that I have the power to run even if I am skipping, and since (33) is true, I have the power to do something that is such that were I to do it, the past would have been different. So this case is apparently supposed to be a true instance of (31).[203]

However, we may now ask, how can we convincingly allow a special resolution such that not only is (33) true, but I also have the power at $t1$ to do other than skip. I do not see a problem in allowing that *if I had the power* to run at $t2$ then my decision at $t1$ would have been different. I do however see a problem in insisting that *I actually have the power* at $t2$ to act such that my decision at $t1$ would have been different – when I actually made a decision at $t1$. The temptation is to conflate these two issues because of superficial similarity. Zagzebski sums this point up as follows:

> But I think that our discussion of Lewis shows that the context in which (33) is true is quite different from the context in which the issue is my power to do something (i.e. run), which is such that if I did it the past would have been different.[204]

I think that it is intuitive to understand that at $t1$ I have actually made a decision and that the proposition that expresses this decision is accidentally necessary immediately after $t1$. The Ockhamist might object that Zagzebski has been selective in her interpretation of what it means to allow for a special resolution of vagueness. However, I would respond that insisting that at $t2$ I have the power to act such that my earlier decision was not a fixed feature of the past is to enter the realm of the highly implausible (I would also suggest the realm of the impossible). Zagzebski is convinced that what is true of (33) is also true of (31). Thus, it can be insisted that propositions of the form of (31) do not allow for a special resolution of vagueness that is sufficiently strong for the power claim that they implicitly involve. However, if we do not allow for such a special

---

203   Ibid, p. 103. This proposition is taken from Saunders (1966). I have changed the numbering in this quotation in order to accommodate my own argument.
204   Ibid, p. 103.

resolution then we are once again left with fatalism – as it is necessarily the case that God cannot hold a false belief.

Let us now try a different Ockhamist objection – it is not legitimate to claim that (33) is sufficiently similar to (31) for us to reach the conclusion suggested by Zagzebski. Why can the Ockhamist not simply claim that by comparing the following proposition to (31) it becomes apparent why the counterfactual power that Zagzebski denies is a possibility?

> (34) It was true at t that Caesar was assassinated 2009 years before Saunders wrote his paper.

There is no question that Saunders could have exercised a power in virtue of which this proposition would not have been true. Why not attempt to liken this to (31)? The reason that I believe any such strategy will fail is because the Ockhamist must allow that God believed something at $t1$. If he did not then the question of foreknowledge becomes redundant. This is different to examples such as (34), as (34) was never true in virtue of what a person believed or knew or decided at an earlier time. I have already argued that it is intuitively plausible to claim that God had a particular belief that he was capable of stating (or which he occurrently knew – affirmed to be true) at a particular past moment about what an agent will do at a future moment. I think that attempting to force (31) into the mould of (34) is just unconvincing. I therefore think that we must assent to the idea that there are intractable problems that arise as a consequence of claiming that God exists sempiternally and has foreknowledge of all that will occur.

4.10: Conclusion to Chapter 4

Once again, I would like to stress the fact that this chapter has been solely devoted to an investigation of the compatibility of the ability to do otherwise with a sempiternal, omniscient and infallible God. Following from the investigations of this chapter, it is my conclusion that the Ockhamist account fails in terms of intuitive plausibility.

In order to argue to this conclusion I considered the various ways in which necessity can be understood in relation to the content of God's foreknowledge. It appears that in Pike's argument truth is analytically connected with divine belief in such a way that it constrains the agent's ability to do otherwise (or, in Pike's terminology, to act voluntarily). However, I showed that the inability to hold a false belief does not necessarily mean that the object of the belief is necessitated.

I next introduced the idea of 'accidental necessity' and delineated what it involves. I also explained how it 'attaches' to certain types of propositions. The question of accidental necessity, and whether or not it should be thought to attach to particular types of propositions about the past, is a question that is integral to the issue of compatibilism as understood by the Ockhamist. I briefly showed how an incompatibilist could argue that, on the basis of the accidental necessity of propositions expressing God's beliefs about the occurrence of future states of affairs, the agent does not have the capacity to do otherwise. However, this argument was shown to be susceptible to criticism by the Ockhamist.

I proceeded to offer an Ockhamist criticism of Pike's incompatibilist argument. This criticism involved the idea of 'hard' and 'soft' facts. The issue of how to classify hard and soft facts has been one of the most difficult to resolve for the Ockhamist. I am highly critical of Ockhamism in virtue of this fact. I will further explained why, after briefly recounting the difficulties that various Ockhamists have encountered when trying to provide an adequate analysis of the distinction between hard and soft facts. Adams was one of the first to attempt to provide an account of the way in which facts about the past can be classified. However, after outlining her distinction, I showed why every fact about the past would have to be classified as soft, if we were to use her criterion of differentiation.

I then considered Hoffman and Rosenkrantz's alternative formulation. This model was more comprehensive and appeared to offer a more compelling account of the distinction. Unfortunately for the incompatibilist, it also classified God's beliefs about the agent's future actions as soft. Thus, the Ockhamist could exploit this analysis to argue the compatibility of divine foreknowledge and the power to do otherwise. The ball was now in the incompatibilist's court – he had to show why the analysis provided by Hoffman and Rosenkrantz was flawed or incomplete.

Fischer was the first to attempt to do so. He argued that it is impossible for the state of God's mind at $t1$ to count as one belief if Jones did X at $t2$, and another belief (or not a belief at all), if Jones did not-X at $t2$. I am convinced that he is correct in his insistence. However, there is an Ockhamist response which serves to undermine Fischer's argument – and I recounted this. Fischer attempted to counter this objection by introducing the ideas of 'hard-core soft facts' and 'hard-type soft facts'. However, if one accepts the Ockhamist account of God's foreknowledge as 'belief as correspondence', then Fischer's arguments may not prove sufficiently persuasive. I believe however that through the use of illustrative examples Fischer's position can be shown to be intuitively correct. I attempted to provide such examples in a later section.

I proceeded to consider Hasker's attempt to undermine Ockhamism. He insisted that if one allowed *de re* considerations in one's account of the hard and soft distinction that every fact involving the agent would turn out soft, if it were taken that God exists. I examined this contention and the objections to it. However, the objections in question suggested that certain *de re* considerations should be arbitrarily permitted. This is what I consider to be perhaps the greatest flaw in Ockhamism – it has not proven possible for the Ockhamist to provide an adequate account of the difference between hard and soft facts without making arbitrary allowances that are introduced for no good reason, other than to make his compatibilist thesis non-contradictory. One might respond that the incompatibilist cannot give an account of why God's beliefs should be considered hard facts about the past in a fashion that is not subject to criticism using the Ockhamist thesis. This is where my most important claims become relevant. The reason that the incompatibilist thesis has greater credence than the Ockhamist one is because it is reflective of our intuitive understandings of concepts such as time, belief, knowledge and the ability to counterfactually affect the past.

In order to show that it is most plausible to assume that accidental necessity attaches to the propositions that express God's beliefs about the future I offered an extensive example involving revelation and occurrent knowledge. It is my fundamental argument that if at any moment a sempiternal God was asked what he believes a particular agent will do, he could state exactly what he believes that agent will do at the time in question (as he has already occurrently aware of this information). I provided examples to show why this fact should lead us to the conviction that such beliefs do necessitate the action of the agent and do not allow for the power to do otherwise in any particular instance. I also attempted to show why insisting that God is dispositionally omniscient is incoherent – or at the least unconvincing.

Thus, I am in basic agreement with both Fischer and Hasker. However, I think that their accounts are subject to Ockhamist criticism because they attempt to qualify and re-qualify the hard and soft fact distinction. However, I believe that it may be impossible to offer a sufficiently comprehensive account of the distinction between hard and soft facts (and their sub-categories) if the existence of a sempiternal God is taken as a given – at least without adding arbitrary allowances and qualifications. When one enters into dialogue with the Ockhamist there is an extent to which one must assume his terminology and system of classification. However, once again, it is my belief that the various formulations of this system of classification is in many way unreflective of our intuitions, and has no merit other than being a counterintuitive negative solution to the problem of sempiternal divine foreknowledge and libertarian free will.

However, if this is not deemed a sufficient reason to be highly sceptical of the Ockhamist project, I conclude by offering another reason why the agent does not have the counterfactual power to affect the past in the way that the Ockhamist assumes. Given that God can state what he believes at any moment in time (because his knowledge is occurrent), it must be true that he had a belief at each and every moment in time. By introducing Lewis's account of the resolution of vagueness of overall similarity between possible worlds, I argued that the agent could not have the power to act such that God's prior beliefs would be counterfactually affected in virtue of his action. This is of course, once again, reliant on the argument that God's belief is a fixed fact about the past. However, as already suggested, if God is asked at *t1* what he believes an agent *A* will do at *t2* it is plausible to suppose that he can answer. Given that *t1* is prior to *t2*, I believe that what occurs at *t1* intuitively has explanatory priority over what occurs at *t2*. Thus, I believe that in this case what occurs at *t1* cannot be counterfactually affected by what occurs at *t2* – and that Lewis's standard resolution of vagueness is appropriate.

One might very well argue that if we do not allow a special resolution of vagueness God could be wrong in his belief about what will occur at *t2*. This, however, is not the case. Given that God necessarily cannot be mistaken about what will occur at *t2*, what he believes will occur at *t2* must occur. However, if we deny that the agent has counterfactual power over God's past beliefs, then we must accept that what occurs at *t2* is not contingent, but is rather entailed by God's foreknowledge (which I believe has not only temporal but also explanatory priority). Thus, divine omniscience and infallibility are retained at the cost of free will.

It is one of my ultimate conclusions that our intuitions should not be compromised by any compatibilist account – unless that account can show sufficiently persuasive reasons as to why those intuitions are wrong. The Ockhamist does not do so, and even the negative solution that he provides is fraught with inadequacies. For this reason, I believe that the idea that infallible sempiternal foreknowledge would fatalistically necessitate future action is more plausible than the Ockhamist's compatibilist thesis.

It is therefore my final claim that the foreknowledge of a sempiternal, omniscient and infallible God would not plausibly allow for morally responsible agency as intuitively it would negate the possibility of the agent having Regulative Control in an apposite way. It is only my final criterion of morally responsible agency that is fundamentally at variance with theological fatalism, but this is sufficient to ensure that no agent can be morally responsible for his actions, if God's foreknowledge prevents him from having and exercising the power to do otherwise (with respect to the formation of his second-order desires).

5

Molinism

5.1: Introduction to Chapter 5

I believe that Molinism offers a superior (if flawed) account of divine knowledge of the agent's actions to that of Ockhamism. In the course of this chapter I will attempt to show why this is the case. The Molinist contends that God has eternal knowledge of all that will be, and that part of this knowledge is (in a particular sense, which will be explained below) logically prior to the creation of the actual world. What he means by 'eternal knowledge' is knowledge that does not unfold in time – has no temporal phases; is an unchanging state of knowing.[205] The Molinist also believes God to be perfectly providential.[206] I will understand the traditional Christian conception of providence to consist in the idea that God knowingly and benevolently directs each and every event, involving each and every creature, towards specific ends that he has ordained for them.[207] Thus, nothing ever occurs in the actual world that is not under God's control (what this control involves is explained below). Molinists are dedicated to defending the idea that there is compatibility between the traditional Christian conception of providence and the libertarian picture of free will (from here onwards when using the term 'free' I will mean free in the libertarian sense, unless otherwise stipulated).[208] Therefore, the Molinist insists that the agent can exercise the power to do otherwise, even if God knows all that will occur in the actual world and exercises control over all the occurrences therein.

The Molinist primarily deals with the question of the 'creature's' free will. However, I will refer primarily to the agent's free will, as the morally responsible agent is my principal concern. This should not cause any controversy though, as the agent is obviously the creature about which the Molinist is most concerned.

The traditional Christian picture that the Molinist wants to defend also includes the idea that God has infallible foreknowledge of all that will occur. It should be noted that when the Molinist refers to God's 'foreknowledge' he

---

205 See introduction of Freddoso (1988).
206 Freddoso (1998), p. 463.
207 Ibid, p. 2.
208 Ibid, p. 1.

is referring to knowledge of all that is future *from our perspective* and is not necessarily making the claim that God is sempiternal. The majority of Molinists believe that God is atemporal. I will discuss what it means for God to have foreknowledge according to this model below.

It will be my contention that understanding foreknowledge in a non-temporal fashion will solve many of the difficulties that were encountered when considering the foreknowledge of a sempiternal God. I believe that the problems that generally arise in relation to the idea of divine foreknowledge stem from that fact that the true beliefs that comprise God's knowledge are conceived of as temporally situated (for example, it was true at *t1* that God truly believed that Jones would *X* at *t2*).

Molinism attempts to provide a foundation from which God's omniscience, infallibility and omnipotence can be married with free will and morally responsible agency – but it does so at the expense of the idea of God as a sempiternal entity (which is not necessarily of itself problematic). I will further explain this assertion in due course. I believe that Molinism is not without its difficulties and I will highlight and discuss these where appropriate. It will also be my intention to attempt to offer a solution to some of the problems that are often associated with Molinism.

5.2: The Four Moments of God's Knowledge

5.2.0: Introduction to Section 5.2

As with the Ockhamist, the principal challenge that the Molinist must overcome is providing an account of divine foreknowledge that would still allow the agent to exercise the ability to do otherwise (libertarian free will). I have already pointed out that the Molinist is also concerned with the question of divine providence. However, I will discuss this latter issue only as it relates to divine knowledge of the agent's actions. It may initially appear implausible to insist that the agent has freedom if God immutably knows what he will do and exercises control over what he does. One might assert that if Jones can exercise Regulative Control over whether he will do *X* in *S* (a specific state of affairs) at *t* (a particular moment in time), or whether he will refrain from doing *X* in *S* at *t*, then God can hardly also foreknow and control what he will proceed to do. Surely, one can ask, if God allows the agent Regulative Control, does he not thereby surrender much of the control that he exercises over the agent? Does God's knowledge of the agent's actions not ultimately lead to the various problems that I discussed when considering Ockhamism, and which I attempted to show that the Ockhamist account is incapable of adequately addressing? The Molinist insists that this is not the case. He attempts to justify his claim through his account of the way in which God knows what the agent will freely choose to do and the way in which he actualises a possible world in which the agent's actions are free. I will attempt to critically evaluate the success of the Molinist strategy in the course of this chapter.

According to Molina, there are four 'Moments' essential to God's knowledge of the events that will occur in the world that he creates (actualises). These Moments, or stages, are not to be thought of as temporally phased, but rather are ordered according to logical primacy.[209] The Molinist believes that for each of these Moments God has a particular type of knowledge, or exercises his will. The Molinist also believes that God's knowledge 'moves' from prevolitional to postvolitional phases. His account of the contents of God's prevolitional knowledge is fundamental to his strategy for arguing that infallible divine knowledge of the agent's actions is compatible with the agent having the capacity to do otherwise. In order to allow a comprehensive appreciation of the Molinist thesis I will begin by describing the four phases of perfect divine knowledge.

5.2.1: The First Moment: Natural Knowledge

In the First Moment, God knows all metaphysically necessary truths.[210] This knowledge is what the Molinist calls 'Natural Knowledge'. It is not restricted to logic, mathematics and natural laws, but also applies to the total set of all possible contingent states of affairs. This latter is included in Natural Knowledge as it is necessarily true that a contingent state of affairs is possible. This type of knowledge is independent of God's will, as he does not determine metaphysically necessary truths (the Molinist believes that these truths are not a consequence of God's activity).

Through Natural Knowledge God knows all the possible actions that *could* be performed by a free agent in any possible circumstance. According to the Molinist, there will not, however, be a sufficient set of causal or necessary conditions for any particular possible world to become actualised until God directs his will.[211]

Through Natural Knowledge God only knows that if an agent with Regulative Control were instantiated in a situation S, he *could* freely X and he *could* freely *not-X* (he knows that there are possible worlds at which the agent does X in S

---

209   Freddoso calls them 'nontemporal stages'. See introduction of Freddoso (1988).
210   See Gaskin (1993), pp. 412-413, and (1994b) p. 551. See also Pike (1993), p. 150, and Flint (1998), p. 38.
211   See Perszyk (2000) pp. 13-14.

and possible worlds at which he does *not-X* in *S*). However, what the agent would actually *freely* proceed to do, if instantiated in *S*, is reliant on the way in which he would choose to exercise his free will (Regulative Control).

We have seen that for the agent to have the capacity involved in Criterion (xii) of morally responsible agency certain conditions must be satisfied.

These were stated as follows:

> In order to have moral responsibility for a specific act the agent must have Regulative Control over the second-order desire that motivates it and have the power to act in accordance with that desire, irrespective of the state of affairs that constitutes the world at the time of acting.

Therefore, the agent must have the power to form the effective (second-order) desire to X and the power to refrain from forming the effective desire to X if instantiated in S, irrespective of the conditions that would constitute the world prior to S. Thus, for example, in the case of Eve, it must be true that:

S: the complete state of affairs that is constituted (in part) by the devil tempting her to eat the forbidden fruit, in the guise of a snake, when she is alone in the Garden of Eden. Q: eat the forbidden fruit.

(a) If Eve is tempted in S she has the power to form the second-order desire to Q and to act in accordance with that desire (X).

(b) If Eve is tempted in S she has the power to refrain from forming the second-order desire to Q and to thereby refrain from acting on a desire to X.

These are the conditions that must be fulfilled if Eve is to be capable of freedom and morally responsible agency (if we are to credit her with Regulative Control over her actions in an apposite way – as expressed in Criterion (xii)).[212]

When God understands through his Natural Knowledge what contingent possibilities exist, he knows that a free Eve could exercise the power stated in (a), and that she could exercise the power stated in (b). If Eve is to have the capacity involved in Criterion (xii), the fact that she is tempted cannot necessitate her fall, irrespective of her desires and intentions, although it can provide a contribution to the sufficient set of conditions that result in her fall.

This, however, is not very providentially useful, as God would not know what she *would freely* do if in the actual world she were instantiated in S (we will see, when considering Middle Knowledge, that the Molinist believes that this capacity is essential to the compatibility of free will, God's knowledge and providence). In order to exercise perfect providential control it would be insufficient for God to

---

212 This is a point made by Gaskin (1998), p. 420, although he arrives at it via a different route of reasoning.

know that, if he were to actually instantiate Eve in S, she would have the power to X and the power to *not-X*. If God only knew what powers Eve *could* exercise, he would, in a sense, have to wait and see what Eve actually *would* proceed to do in any concrete state of affairs – he would not know in advance (either temporally or in terms of logical primacy) what she would in fact freely do if instantiated in the state of affairs in question.[213]

Consider the following: God knows that if he were to instantiate a free Eve she would have the power referred to in (a) - let us call this power *p1* - and he knows that she would also have the power referred to in (b) – let us call this power *p2*. Through Natural knowledge God knows that Eve could freely exercise *p1* and that she could freely exercise *p2*. He also knows that if she exercises *p1* a world of type *W1* will result (a world that is part of the set of all possible worlds at which Eve freely chooses to eat the forbidden fruit in S) and if she exercises *p2* a world of type *W2* will result (a world that is part of the set of all possible worlds at which Eve freely chooses to refrain from eating the forbidden fruit in S). Now let us suppose that God actually instantiates Eve in S. It is true that in the actual world Eve could freely exercise *p1* and that in virtue of this a possible world of type *W1* would prove to be the actual world, and it is true that she could freely exercise *p2* and that in virtue of this a possible world of type *W2* would prove to be the actual world. Neither of these eventualities are in conflict with God's Natural Knowledge – as he knows from eternity that both are possibilities – it is metaphysically necessary that both possibilities exist.

However, what Eve actually *would* do if instantiated in S is not metaphysically necessary – it is contingent, as Eve has Regulative control over her effective desires. Therefore, through Natural Knowledge God does not know what Eve *would* freely proceed to do if instantiated in S.

Natural Knowledge is part of God's 'prevolitional knowledge'. It is prevolitional in so far as God does not intentionally determine the content of this knowledge through the direction and exercise of his will. It is assumed that possible states of affairs exist independent of whether or not God intends them.

5.2.2: The Second Moment: Middle Knowledge

The second Moment of God's knowledge is 'Middle Knowledge'. Through Middle Knowledge God does not merely know what the agent *could* freely do in any specific state of affairs, but knows, among other things (as explained below), what the agent *would freely* do if instantiated in any particular possible state of

---

213   From here onwards, when I use the term 'instantiated' – I mean 'if instantiated in the actual world'.

affairs.[214] Through Middle Knowledge God knows that if instantiated in S Jones (for example) *would freely* X (he would also know the set of possible worlds at which this is true). However, Middle Knowledge is not identical to knowledge of the occurrences that will constitute the actual world, as it logically precedes the intentional act of will that is essential to the actualisation of any specific possible world. The contents of Middle Knowledge are expressed in subjunctive conditional propositions, which express what would happen under particular specified conditions.[215]

Let us now suppose that God knows (through his Middle Knowledge) that if Jones were instantiated in S he would *freely* do X. Given that God has eternal knowledge of this counterfactual; he would also know that some *W1-type* world would result.[216] It is argued that God's knowledge does not hard-determine the action that Jones would freely do if instantiated in S. The Molinist is committed to the claim that Jones's action would be contingent and under his Regulative Control. Correspondingly, if it were true that Jones would choose to exercise his Regulative Control in S such that he would Y, God would know this from eternity and would also know that a *W2-type* world would result. This type of knowledge allows God to know what any possible agent would freely do in any possible state of affairs, and to thereby know what world-type would result (in my example this would be a world of type *W1* or a world of type *W2*).

What has become known as a counterfactual of creaturely freedom (CCF) states conditionally what a creature would freely do if placed in particular circumstances. Any such counterfactual will have a complete antecedent which 'specifies the complete set of non-determining circumstances in which the creature is placed'.[217] As we have seen, Middle Knowledge is, in part, knowledge of CCFs. CCFs must be contingent for, if they were necessary, then the circumstances stated in the antecedent would necessitate the consequent and this would make libertarian freedom impossible.[218]

Middle Knowledge is the Moment that the Molinist alleges preserves the

---

214 See Adams (1977) p. 109 and Reichenbach (1988) p. 276.
215 Adams, R. M. (1991), p. 344.
216 There is some debate as to whether this should be called a 'counterfactual'. Kvanvig notes that 'if there are such truths and God considers them in determining what world to create, some of them will not be counter to fact – God will act so that the antecedent of the conditional is true' (1986), p. 124. In cases where they do not prove to be counter to fact I will occasionally call them 'subjunctives of freedom' (SFs). However, for the most part, and in keeping with the Molinist tradition, when speaking of God's Middle Knowledge, I will generally use the term Counterfactual of Creaturely Freedom and allow that this includes SFs.
217 Flint (1998), p. 40.
218 See Adams, R. M. (1991), p. 344.

agent's freedom (in the sense that I have argued is essential to morally responsible agency). It is claimed that Middle Knowledge is of contingent facts and is independent of God's will. Its purpose is to allow God knowledge of what 'would be the case if' so that he can decide what world to create in order to realise his desires. If God knows what any particular possible agent would freely do if instantiated in any particular possible state of affairs, he can use this knowledge to decide whether or not he actually wants to instantiate specific possible agents in specific states of affairs. Once again, Middle Knowledge constitutes part of God's prevolitional knowledge. This is, as with Natural Knowledge, because the content of this knowledge does not involve the direction of the divine will (it logically precedes it). Thus, the truth-values of CCFs are to be thought of as 'insulated' from God's volitional activity. Thus, the Molinist can claim that for any proposition that expresses a CCF (p), there is no choice or action that God has the power to exercise such that, were he to exercise it, p would be false.[219] This position, however, is not uncontroversial and I will proceed to discuss it further in Section 5.3.

It should be noted that Middle Knowledge does not just include CCFs. Flint offers us the following example. Let us suppose that God knows, through Middle Knowledge, that if he were to instantiate Adam in circumstances C, which includes God's promise that if he eats the fruit of a particular forbidden tree he will be expelled from the Garden of Eden. Let D stand for a proposition describing Adam's free act of disobedience. Middle Knowledge would tell God that ($C \to D$). Given that God does not make promises in vain, he would also know that expulsion would have to follow if Adam were to disobey in C – that is, he would know that [(C & D) => E], where E describes God's act of expelling Adam. But from ($C \to D$) and [(C & D) => E], it follows that ($C \to E$); so God would also know this truth. The Molinist argues that although God would know the truth of a proposition of the form 'If I were to instantiate Adam in circumstance C, I would expel him from the Garden', this does not mean that Adam's action would not be contingent. He believes that because the fact that Adam would disobey if placed in C can be expressed in a CCF, his choice to do so is not a necessary consequence of God's activity (the CCF is reflective of how Adam would freely choose to exercise his Regulative Control if instantiated in C). Thus, although ($C \to E$) is part of God's Middle Knowledge, it is not a CCF: it states what God, and not some undetermined creature, would do in a particular situation.[220]

When we think of CCFs we should not think that they necessarily relate to creatures that ever have actually existed, or will actually exist. CCFs do not involve assumptions about the actual existence of the creatures or states of affairs to which they relate. This is because in the total set of CCFs known by God through his Middle Knowledge he also knows counterfactuals about what

---

219 See Flint (1998), p. 175.
220 Ibid, pp. 42-43.

non-actual but possible creatures would freely do if placed in particular possible states of affairs.[221]

However, as Flint notes, it is 'notoriously difficult' to speak about beings that do not exist. He therefore suggests, in keeping with the tradition of Molinism, that when speaking about CCFs, we should think of them as not directly referring to particular creatures, but rather to the individual essences of such creatures. Keeping this in mind, he suggests that we should think of counterfactuals of freedom as having the following form:

> If creaturely essence P were instantiated in nondetermining [either logically or causally] complete circumstances C at time t, the instantiation of P would (freely) do A.[222]

Saurez believed that the fact that an agent with a particular essence would do X if in S is a primitive fact - a *habitude*.[223] This *habitude* is irreducible and cannot be explained in terms of intentions or dispositions, or more fundamental facts about the agent. An essence, so understood, is eternal. The fact that a creature with essence P would X, if instantiated in S, is a metaphysical property of P. It is my contention that the modern Molinist is committed to a very similar claim - the fact that the agent would *freely* X if instantiated in S is a primitive fact about the creaturely essence of the agent (I will return to the question of what constitutes a creaturely essence and how they should be understood in due course). One could argue that the truth of this claim would result in the agent's action being determined by his creaturely essence (or the creaturely essence to which he corresponds, depending on the way in which creaturely essences are understood). However, I shall not address this issue in full until the current investigation has proceeded further.

5.2.3: The Third Moment: The Creative Act of Will (The Divine Actualisation of a Particular Possible World)

In this Moment God decides what possible beings he will actualise and what particular possible states of affairs he will actually place them in. The divine will is directed in unison with this decision. The possible world that God actualises is the world that he most desires (given that he wants to actualise a world where his creatures are free - the question of what worlds God is free to create is addressed in Subsection 5.3.1). It is traditionally popular to speak of0 God as *creating* the

---

221   Ibid, p. 46.
222   Ibid, p. 47. However, for ease of understanding and fluidity of argument I will often refer to counterfactuals of creaturely freedom as referring to 'creatures' or 'agents' rather than individual essences of possible nondetermined beings.
223   Saurez (1620), Prol. 2.7.21.

world. However, if one is employing possible world semantics (as the modern Molinist does), this term is inappropriate – one should rather say that God actualises a particular possible world. This may seem like an equivocation, but it is important. Possible worlds are timeless – in the sense that as a possibility they do not have a beginning – they are possible from eternity (as already noted above, it is metaphysically necessary that they are possible). The language of creation implies that the actual world has a beginning, and it is true that it does have a 'beginning' in the sense that it has a temporal history that begins at one particular point. However, the world that is actual is part of the total set of possible worlds and did not have a beginning as a possibility - in the sense that it was a possible world from eternity. The importance of this distinction will become more apparent in the course of these investigations. Occasionally, in this chapter, I will still speak of God creating the actual world; however, this should be taken to mean that God actualises a particular possible world, unless otherwise stipulated.

At this stage of the enquiry it would be prudent to delineate the difference between *strong actualisation* and *weak actualisation*.[224] Strong actualisation is when a being acts such that it causally determines the occurrence of a particular event. Weak actualisation involves a being contributing to the occurrence of a particular event by situating a free creature in a state of affairs in which the creature in question will freely cause the event. The idea of weak actualisation has proven an important explanatory tool in the Molinist's compatibilist account. Due to the Molinist's insistence on the truth of CCFs, there will be limitations on exactly what states of affairs God can weakly actualise. I will return to this subject below.

The Third Moment gives rise to the fourth and final Moment which completes God's knowledge.

5.2.4: The Fourth Moment: Free Knowledge

The Fourth Moment is God's 'Free Knowledge'. Free Knowledge is God's knowledge of what contingent states of affairs will constitute the actual world; including the way in which he will intervene in history (such interventions are to be understood as part of his providential activity).[225]

In his prevolitional knowledge God knows the many states of affairs that constitute the various possible worlds that he could actualise, irrespective of the particular creatures and circumstances that he will in fact proceed to instantiate. God then decides what creatures and circumstances he will in fact instantiate

---

224 Plantinga (1974b), pp. 172-173.
225 See Gaskin (1993) pp. 412-413.

and directs his will in a creative act that actualises a particular possible world (in which CCFs and SFs are true and in which he instantiates a particular set of possible agents in particular states of affairs).

The final phase, or Moment, of God's knowledge is post-volitional, as the content of Free Knowledge involves knowledge of the direction of the divine will and everything that proceeds from it, or is in accordance with it. What God Freely knows will constitute the actual world at all future times will come to pass, because nothing can occur in the actual world that is in conflict with the divine will – as all the contingent states of affairs that comprise the actual world are, in a particular sense (explained below), under God's control. If God did not will, or allow, the actual world to be composed of particular states of affairs at any moment in time, then those states of affairs would never obtain.

In the Fourth Moment God's knowledge is no longer concerned with what *could* be the case in possible worlds, or what creatures *would* freely do *if* instantiated in particular circumstances – he now knows exactly what *will* be the case in the world that he has elected to actualise – and what his creatures actually will (freely) do. God's Free Knowledge is also known as his 'knowledge of vision' (in other words, 'his all seeing knowledge').[226]

Once God has exercised his will, and actualised the possible world that he desires to obtain, his knowledge of future occurrences is post-volitional. The Molinist believes that God's knowledge is eternal and not subject to change due to contingent occurrences. Thus, after God has decided what world he wants to actualise he will not change the direction of the divine will. God does not change his mind.

As Free Knowledge involves God's free action, it is contingent.[227] This is the only Moment of God's knowledge that is dependent on the direction of the divine will.[228] Flint notes that it follows from God's free exercise of his will that he knows what counterfactuals of divine freedom are true: 'he also freely decides what creative act of will would have been performed given any world-type which could have been true. His single act of will, then, makes infinitely many counterfactuals of divine freedom true.'[229] In other words, God knows what he would have done if other world-types (sets of worlds at which the set of true CCFs would have been different) had been true.

When we think of divine foreknowledge, it is usually something akin to Free Knowledge that we have in mind. Thus, Free Knowledge and the 'common' notion of foreknowledge can be thought of as roughly analogous. However, it

---

226 Freddoso (1998), p. 463.
227 I am taking it for granted that God does not create out of necessity.
228 Pohle (1911), p. 440.
229 Flint (1998), p. 57.

should be noted that there is a substantive difference in that Free Knowledge is not located in time – God's knowledge does not bear a temporal relation to its object, as God is thought of as atemporal and therefore not part of the temporal continuum. I realise that this may cause confusion and therefore this is a point that I will return to in much greater detail.

By the stage that God's knowledge has proceeded to Free Knowledge he is past the point at which he decides how he will shape the actual world and act, or refrain from acting, in it (as this has already been determined by the direction of his will and is based on his prevolitional knowledge). It is through his perfect knowledge of CCFs (Middle Knowledge) that God can decide which possible world is most in accord with his desires. His decision as to what times he will intervene/act in the actual world is also based upon this knowledge.

5.2.5: The Moments Reconsidered

The idea that is central to Molinism is that God's pre-volitional knowledge and his desire that his creatures be free ensures that the agent's freedom is retained, even when God has moved to post-volitional knowledge of the actual world. If God's first two Moments of divine knowledge logically precede the direction of his will, then it is claimed that there is no hard-determining consequences of his knowledge on the free actions of the agent – for it was known that they would be free logically prior to God's decision to create a world in which they would become manifest. God has knowledge of particular facts that are beyond his control and yet the way in which he exercises his will ensures that everything in the created world is under his control (in the sense that nothing that occurs in the actual world that God does not want, or permit, to occur).

Let us briefly return to our example involving Jones. Through Natural Knowledge God knows that there is a set of possible worlds at which Jones mows his lawn in S at t, and that there is a set of possible worlds at which he refrains from doing so. Through his Middle Knowledge (specifically his knowledge of CCFs) he knows (for example) that *if* instantiated in S (a particular possible complete state of affairs) at t, Jones *would* freely choose to mow his lawn (X). He also knows what type of world would result from such an occurrence. This knowledge allows God to decide whether or not he wants a world to obtain at which Jones does freely mow his lawn.[230] If he decides that the resultant world is not to his preference, then he will never create Jones, or will never place him in S at t, or so forth. He will not however actualise S and act such that Jones must X or must *not-X* – for to do so would be in conflict with his greater desire that Jones be free.

---

230 See Pike (1993), pp. 150-152.

The Molinist believes that there is a substantive sense in which God controls whether or not Jones will mow his lawn in the actual world at t (because it is up to God whether or not a possible world in which Jones finds himself in S at t, and in which he freely chooses to mow his lawn, is actualised). However, the Molinist argues that there is also a substantive sense in which Jones retains his Regulative Control over what he will do, even if God does create a world in which he finds himself in S at t. This is because it was not up to God to decide whether or not he would freely X if instantiated in S at t. God can decide whether or not to place Jones in S at t, but he cannot determine exactly what Jones would freely do if instantiated in this state of affairs, because Jones has libertarian freedom over his effective second order desires and his corresponding actions. God is only interested in weakly actualising a particular state of affairs in which Jones does X at t.

Therefore, it can be argued that God's Free Knowledge (foreknowledge) of the outcome of the agent's free choices does not necessitate the agent's actions. God does not need to observe what is occurring, or will occur, in the actual world in order to know what will obtain. This is because the conjunction of his prevolitional knowledge and the creative act (the direction of his will) is sufficient for him to know all of the events that will ever occur in the actual world (Free Knowledge).[231] There are no truths about what will constitute the actual world until God directs his will through the creative act.

This account is different to that of the Ockhamist, as it is not argued that the agent can perform an act (X) in virtue of which God would have at all previous times have believed that he would X. It is not argued that he has the power to counterfactually affect the past at all. It is rather that God knows through his post-volitional knowledge what an agent will freely do in the actual world, and he can know this through the conjunction of his prevolitional knowledge and the direction of his will.

Can one not argue that even if God's knowledge is atemporal, it still has temporal effects? Consider the following:

> If God atemporally knows that Jones will mow his lawn at $t2$, it is true in the actual temporal world that at $t1$ God knew that Jones would mow his lawn at $t2$.

This being the case, are we not led back into the same problems that confronted the Ockhamist, and are we not therefore going to be left with the conclusion that fatalism is more intuitively plausible? I believe that it can be argued that this is not the case. The reason is that the confusion inherent in this argument is the result of the difficulties of understanding an atemporal being's relation to the temporal world. To be atemporal is not to exist without changing in the temporal universe – it is rather to exist beyond the parameters of the temporal continuum.

---

231 See Flint (1998), pp. 44-45.

It is tempting to say that God believes that *S* will occur at all moments in time, however, it can also be argued that God believes *S* at no moment *in* time – because God does not, and has never, existed in time. I think that the fact that we lack an adequate semantics to reflect the effects of an atemporal God's knowledge on the temporal world leads to such confusion. However, if it is true to say that an atemporal God believed at no temporal instant but at a 'moment' outside of time what the agent does at a particular time, then we can side-step many of the objections that were levelled against Ockhamism. It must be admitted, however, that these ideas are very hard to come to terms with because of the fact, as I have already stated, that we lack an adequate semantics.

5.3: Are There Limits to the Possible Worlds that God can Actualise?

5.3.0: Introduction to Section 5.3

In this Section I attempt to deal with the question of what possible worlds God can actualise, given the fact that he desires his creatures to be free. It is essential to the idea of compatibility of freedom and moral responsibility and God's timeless knowledge that there is a limit to the possible worlds that God can choose to actualise. This is one of the strengths of Molinism. If it is true that God is resolved to only actualise a world in which all agent's are morally responsible and have the capacity to act freely, then this strengthens their compatibilist argument. In this section I will subject this idea to critical scrutiny. How is this issue relevant to the question of divine foreknowledge and morally responsible agency? If God can create a world in which he determines what CCFs are true it can be argued that he controls all aspects of what he foreknows, and that this may detract from the agent's moral responsibility and/or capacity to do otherwise. We will see that is by providing an account of what worlds it is possible for God to actualise, given that he wants his creatures to be free, that the Molinist can argue that the agent has Regulative Control over his actions (and the second order desire that give rise to them). 5.3.1: Can God Actualise Any World That He Chooses?

From the above discussion one could already have begun to suspect that if God wants his creatures to be free and morally responsible he cannot just actualise any possible world that he desires. I will be taking it for granted that God cannot actualise states of affairs that are logically impossible. Furthermore, it should be noted that when God actualises a particular possible world he does not actualise every state of affairs that constitutes it. For example, God actualises possible world *W*, it is true in *W* that God exists (metaphysical necessity), but God does not actualise the state of affairs that includes his own existence (God does not actualise himself nor does he actualise the properties that he has).[232] God also did not create numbers, logic, propositions and so forth (as he knows of these things prevolitionally). Necessary states of affairs, such as 1 + 1 equalling 2, also do not owe their existence to God. With regard to anything that God did not create, he also did not actualise the state of affairs that consists in the existence of those things. God cannot actualise a world that is not dependent on him for its continued existence or in which metaphysically necessary truths are not valid.

When we think of God actualising a possible world W we should think of him as actualising every contingent state of affairs that constitutes W. It is only true to say that God could have actualised a particular possible world W if, and only if, for every contingent state of affairs S included in W, there is a 'moment' at which it is within his power to actualise S (this may involve weak actualisation).[233]

What about the particular actions of the agent? If the agent's actions are contingent, then they are not determined/necessitated by causal laws and/or antecedent conditions. If the agent has Regulative Control over his doing, and his refraining from doing, X in S at t, then his actions are contingent. Thus, God cannot hard-determine the fact that the agent will freely perform a particular action in a particular state of affairs at a particular time (as this would violate the very idea of libertarian freedom). We have seen how the Molinist has dealt with this concern by appealing to God's prevolitional Middle Knowledge of CCFs. However, the question we must now ask is: do these CCFs limit the states of affairs and hence possible worlds that God can weakly actualise? Obviously, God cannot hard-determine an agent such that he must 'freely' do X if in S, if the word 'freely' is to satisfy the libertarian characterisation of the term.

From this fact the Molinist can reason that, if a proposition that frames a CCF states that if instantiated in S an agent would freely X, there is no moment at which God could actualise a possible world in which the agent freely does some other action *not-X* in S. To make a claim to the contrary appears to deny the truth of CCFs (and implicitly do deny that the agent has Regulative Control rather than just Guidance Control) – and this is obviously a line of thought that the Molinist does not want to pursue. Therefore, the Molinist must accept that there is a whole spectrum of states of affairs that God cannot weakly actualise. This obviously limits the total set of possible worlds that he could have actualised through the direction of the divine will.

However, the Molinist is happy to agree with this picture. But he does not believe that the fact that God cannot actualise every possible world (because some of those worlds are in conflict with his desire that his creatures to be free) detracts

---

232   Plantinga (1973), pp. 540-541.
233   Ibid, p. 541.

from the providential control that he has over the actual world. Although there is a limited set of possible worlds that God can actualise due to the counterfactuals of creaturely freedom, it is within the control of God as to which of these worlds he will actualise. Thus, even though God cannot actualise worlds other than those at which CCFs are true (if he wishes to conserve creaturely freedom), he can choose to actualise any particular possible world that does not conflict with them. Suppose that agent A would freely choose to X if instantiated in S at t, God is free to actualise any possible world at which A freely does X in S at t (and any world at which A does not find himself in S at t, any world where A does not exist, and so forth), but is not free to actualise any possible world in which he does *not-X* in S at t (unless he wants to deny this agent libertarian freedom and hence moral responsibility with regard to X).

It may be the case that God would have, for some reason, preferred if the agent would freely *not-X* if instantiated in S, but, nevertheless, he cannot create a world in which the agent does *not-X* in S without compromising the agent's Regulative Control. Because God cannot decide how a creature would freely act, the very patterns of free action that he would most desire from a creature may not be obtainable.[234] However, he can actualise the world that he most desires, given the counterfactuals of creaturely freedom. Thus, God can actualise the world that he most desires in which the agents that he creates have libertarian freedom over their actions. Possible worlds at which the agent's actions are in harmony with CCFs I will call feasible worlds (*f-worlds*). They are feasible in the sense that, given that God wants the agent to be free, they can be actualised without compromising that freedom.

Gaskin notes that, once God has directed the divine will and actualised a particular *f-world* 'He can do nothing to alter these truths [CCFs], but simply must adjust His providential planning to accord with them.'[235] Thus, the Molinist can contend that God only foreknows what particular agents will freely do in the world that he has chosen to actualise, and that this is sufficient for morally responsible agency.

5.3.2: God and Counterfactual Power

In his defence of Molinism, Flint argues against a position that he calls 'Maverick Molinism'.[236] The Maverick Molinist, as characterised by Flint, believes that 'whichever truth-value a counterfactual… has, there nevertheless were things God had the power to do such that, had he done them, that counterfactual would

---

234   Plantinga, (1974a), Ch. 9.
235   Gaskin (1993), p. 413.
236   See Flint (1998), p. 65ff.

have had the opposite truth-value'.²³⁷ Thus, the Maverick Molinist does not, in a particular sense (see below), agree with Flint's contention that CCFs are not under God's control.

According to the Molinist account I have already outlined, true CCFs are insulated from the activity of God. Flint speaks of counterfactuals in the future tense – thus, he claims that all CCFs will be true irrespective of what God proceeds to do. This is because, as we have seen above, it can be claimed that God cannot change the truth-values of the CCFs in question.

Flint accuses:

> Some who are otherwise favourably disposed toward Molinism might be tempted to challenge the alleged prevolitional status of such truths. That is, they may want to say that a Molinist can hold that, whichever truth-value [a CCF]… has, there nevertheless were things God had the power to do such that, had he done them, that counterfactual would have had the opposite truth-value.²³⁸

However, it will not be my intention to undermine the prevolitional status of God's knowledge of CCFs. The argument that I intend to provide does not claim that the truth-values of CCFs are not established at the time of God's prevolitional knowledge. I will temporarily grant the Molinist assumption that this is the case. I will rather argue that this prevolitional knowledge must take into account states of affairs that God would actualise at different possible worlds, in order to be able to fully account for the complete state of affairs that CCFs specify in their antecedent – and that all such actualisation would be reliant on the direction of the divine will.

Let us suppose that some contingent counterfactual $A \to B$ is false. It is perfectly possible that if the state of affairs described in some contingent proposition C were true, then $A \to B$ would have been true. Now let us suppose that the truth of proposition C is within God's power to actualise. Through Middle Knowledge God would therefore know that if he were to actualise the state of affairs described in C that $A \to B$ would be true. For example, let us suppose that God knows that were Eve alone in the Garden of Eden (part of a complete state of affairs S) she would freely refrain from eating the forbidden fruit (X). However, through Middle Knowledge, he would also know that if she were in the Garden of Eden and was tempted by the devil (part of the complete state of affairs $S1$) she would freely eat the forbidden fruit ($-X$). God desires to actualise a world at which she eats the forbidden fruit and therefore he instantiates her in $S1$. He therefore foreknows that Eve will freely $-X$ in $S1$. However, one may now ask does God not play too great a role in deciding what CCF he foreknows will occur? Does this allow for morally responsible agency?

---

237 Ibid, p. 65.
238 Ibid.

The Molinist does not necessarily have a problem with this conception, as it still allows for the contingency of the actions that the agent freely performs, allows for God's prevolitional knowledge of CCFs and allows the agent Regulative Control (although one could argue that it does so only in a diminished sense – I will address this concern below). However, it is possible that someone who insists that there is such a thing as a more robust sense of moral responsibility will find this account less than satisfactory. It may appear as though 'the deck is stacked against us'. If it is true that for any CCF there is a proposition, the truth of which would ensure that a false CCF would have been true (even if there is a minimal deviation in the antecedent), and God has the power to actualise the state of affairs that constitutes that proposition, then it may appear as though it is in the most significant sense up to God and not up to the agent as to how he will 'freely' act. What I mean is that for any action that we perform God could have changed the world such the total state of affairs specified in the antecedent of any false counterfactual would have been minimally different in order to allow the consequent to be true. Thus, it can be argued that God decides what 'free'[239] actions he foreknows the agent will perform, and that the control that he exercises over what the agent will 'freely' do is too great to allow for morally responsible agency.

Kvanvig gives us the following example involving one of his meals.[240] Suppose it is contingently true that if he were offered the choice between asparagus and beans for dinner, he would not choose beans. However, suppose that a proliferation of special pests had blunted the growth of beans but allowed asparagus to flourish. This would have led to much more asparagus consumption in his youth, and to an preference for the unusual taste of beans over asparagus (the explanation of the preference of the former over the latter is due to the rarity of beans in his diet). So suppose that this is an example in which the counterfactual embedded in the consequent is false, even though $C \to (A \to B)$ is true. All that is needed for God to make the counterfactual embedded in the consequent true is for him to actualise the state of affairs corresponding with C. Thus, we can claim that in a particular qualified sense[241] it is God who has power over the truth-value of $A \to B$, even if the truth-value in question is known prevolitionally. God does not have to act such that he changes the truth-value of $A \to B$ – rather, he knows prevolitionally that if he were to actualise the state of affairs described in C that the truth value of $A \to B$ would have been different. This of course takes into account the fact that the total state of affairs that comprises the antecedent would be minimally different in both scenarios. However, it is the idea of God having this type of control that may leave one uneasy. This is because

---

239   From here onwards, when I place the world 'free' in inverted commas, I mean to make apparent that the use of the term in the given context is dubious or mistaken.
240   Kvanvig (2002).
241   What I mean is that God can minimally change the antecedent of a false CCF in order to make it true.

it may appear that God controls what it is that he foreknows that the agent will do in the actual world – and it could be argued that this would undermine morally responsible agency.[242]

Consider the following:

If Jones were instantiated in S, he would freely mow his lawn.

If Jones were instantiated in S1, he would freely refrain from mowing his lawn.

Now let us suppose that the only difference between S and S1 is that at the possible world which comprises S1 God has acted (directed his will) such that some proposition C is true, and in virtue of this fact it is true Jones will freely refrain from mowing his lawn. There is only a minimal deviation between the two worlds – they are identical in all other respects. Therefore, there is a sense in which God is in control of whether Jones will 'freely' mow his lawn or not. It appears on this model that it is possible for God to actualise as many states of affairs as are necessary to ensure that Jones 'freely' acts in the way that God desires, and for him to know prevolitionally of those worlds in which Jones would do so. Thus, God cannot change the fact that Jones would freely X if instantiated in S, but he knows of worlds at which he acts such that there is a minimal deviation from S such that Jones will freely refrain from doing X. Thus, it can be accused that God is in control of what he prevolitionally foreknows and that this fact undermines moral responsibility.

The problem that one may find with the above model is that it is in some ways reminiscent of a rat in a maze. Let us suppose that there are initially two exits from this maze – R and S. Let us suppose that a scientist likes the general shape of the maze but is determined that the rat should only use exit R. The rat may 'freely' choose to turn right or left, but if it makes a turn that the scientist does not like he will change a wall so that it is steered back towards R. Thus, the fact that the rat will 'freely' exit via R is foreknown by the scientist, because he knows how he will act if the rat takes a turn that is not in accordance with his desires. Eventually the rat exits via R – and even though he 'freely' chose every turn that he took, we could argue that he was not free with respect to his exiting via R.

Although this is not a perfect analogy it still serves to illustrate a point. If we think of God as the scientist and the agent as the rat in question, and imagine that God somehow knows which turns the agent will freely take in every possible maze, and knows of one particular maze in which the agent will eventually exit via R without his having to move a single wall – then can we really say that the agent freely chose to exit via R when he is placed in this maze. One may think

---

242 However, it is my belief that such a notion of such control is embedded in the very idea of divine providence – if God does not in some sense have control over the free and contingent actions of the agent then in what sense can he ensure that they are in accord with his providential plan?

that there is something unsettlingly counterintuitive to this idea.

However, the Molinist can respond that as long as the agent has not been interfered with there is no reason to suppose that he did not freely choose the exit in question. Furthermore, he might object that in my example there was no way that the agent could have exited via S. However, God would prevolitionally know of a maze in which the agent would freely choose every turn that would lead him to R, without the way to S being in anyway obstructed or more difficult to egress.

I would now like to suggest another counter-argument that could be offered by the Molinist. It is true that in our everyday experience we constantly find ourselves in situations which minimally result from our activity. Let us suppose that we are like Jones and are deciding whether or not we will mow our lawn at $t2$. Now let us further suppose that it is true that if it does not rain we will freely choose to mow our lawn, and let us also suppose that if it does rain we will freely choose to refrain from mowing our lawn. It would have to be admitted that we can exercise no control over whether or not it will be raining at $t2$. The fact of whether or not it will rain is a result of certain natural processes. Now, if it is raining it is still within our power to mow our lawn – the fact of the rain is not sufficient to deprive us of the capacity to mow it. It is our free choice to act in a particular fashion that makes it true that we will not mow our lawn at $t2$ if it rains – we are not hard-determined by any other factors to so refrain from acting. The same is true of our choice to mow our lawn at $t2$ if it is not raining.

The question that I would now like to ask is what difference it would make if God was in control over whether or not it rains at the specified time, rather than natural processes over which Jones has no power to affect? My answer is that it would make no substantive difference whatsoever to the freedom of his choice. In order to be capable of exercising Regulative Control over his effective second-order desires, irrespective of the state of affairs in which the agent finds himself placed, it is not necessary that the agent have any control over the state of affairs in question. It is further not necessary that no one else have control over that state of affairs. It is the agent's free response to his environment, or his ability to act freely in a given environment, that is essential to his moral responsibility. This is a point that I wish to emphasise - my characterisation of moral responsibility requires that the agent be capable of exercising Regulative Control over his second-order desires and that he be able to act in accordance with those desires, irrespective of the state of affairs that constitutes the world at the time of acting. God may actualise the states of affairs in which the agent finds himself placed, but (in the Molinist conception) he does not strongly actualise the way in which the free agent responds to those states of affairs. The most that God can do is weakly actualise states of affairs which involve the agent acting freely. This, however, is not necessarily in conflict with Criterion (xii) of morally responsible agency. There is a sense in which God decides what it is that he foreknows to be true – this is obviously required if a divine atemporal being is to be capable of exercising providential control over the world that he actualises. However, this does not negatively affect the agent's moral responsibility as long as God does not hard-determine what the agent does in any particular circumstance. It is my claim that the Molinist model allows the agent to freely respond to the states of affairs in which he finds himself, irrespective of whether God has actualised those states of affairs and foreknown that they would occur.

5.4: Difficulties for the Molinist

5.4.0: Introduction to Section 5.4

In this Section I introduce the greatest difficulties that the Molinist will have to address if he is to successfully uphold his position.

5.4.1: Molinism and the Law of Conditional Excluded Middle

One line of objection to the Molinist idea of foreknowledge argues that it relies on the truth of the Law of Conditional Excluded Middle (LCEM) with respect to CCFs, and that this law can be undermined.[243] LCEM says that, for any two propositions with the same (true) antecedent and opposing consequents, one must be true (either $p \rightarrow q$ or $p \rightarrow \sim q$).[244]

Consider the following:

1. If David were to remain in Keilah, Saul would (freely) lay siege to it.

2. If David were to remain in Keilah, Saul would (freely) not lay siege to it.

According to LCEM, if it were true that David remains in Keilah, either the consequent of 1 or the consequent of 2 must be true.[245] Furthermore, it can be claimed that in order for God to have knowledge of which is true (prior to the direction of the divine will) LCEM would have to be valid. If this is the case, the claim that God can have knowledge of counterfactuals would be seriously undermined if LCEM is shown to be false. We will now see that the application of LCEM is not without its problems.

---

243   For discussions of this law see for example Chandler (1967), Cooper (1978) and Priest (1983).
244   For a discussion of this issue see van Inwagen (1997), p. 227.
245   A similar example and the Law of Conditional Excluded Middle is discussed in Adams (1977), pp. 110-111.

Consider the following counterfactual example given by Lewis:

1. If Verdi and Bizet were compatriots, Bizet would be Italian.
2. If Verdi and Bizet were compatriots, Bizet would not be Italian.

The difficulty presented here is that it is distinctly unclear as to which consequent would be true, and yet it appears as though, under LCEM, one of them would have to be true (if it were true that Verdi and Bizet were compatriots). It looks as though both statements could be true, if Bizet were Italian then it would be true that he and Verdi would be compatriots, however, it is equally true that if Verdi was French, and Verdi and Bizet were compatriots that Bizet would not be Italian. With this in mind, it appears as though there are definite cases in which LCEM does not apply to counterfactual states of affairs.

However, there is no reason to suppose that the Molinist needs to endorse the idea that LCEM is unqualifiedly true. The failure of the above application of LCEM is not definitive for CCFs. The Molinist can respond that while it is true that a particular class of counterfactuals are not subject to LCEM that CCFs do not fall within this class – and, therefore, the objection is irrelevant to them. In the above case there are two possible changes that could be made in order for the propositions in question to be true (as noted above). However, let us now reconsider the following CCFs:

1. If David were to remain in Keilah, Saul would (freely) lay siege to it.
2. If David were to remain in Keilah, Saul would (freely) not lay siege to it.

This case differs significantly from Lewis's example, because in the above propositions there is only one relevant variable – either David does freely lay siege to Keilah, or he does not. The fact that LCEM is found wanting when applied to a particular class of counterfactuals, does not mean that it is not valid when applied to CCFs (it should also be noted that CCFs have fully specified antecedents). In the case of David, it can be argued that if the antecedent is true then either the consequent of 1 or the consequent of 2 must be true. This obviously cannot be said of Lewis's counterfactuals. In all CCFs the Molinist can claim that there is only one variable and consequently LCEM does not fail when applied to them.

Therefore, it can be argued that God does have foreknowledge of what the agent 'would freely do if instantiated in S' – and that therefore he can further claim that divine foreknowledge is compatible with libertarian free will. It appears as though the opponent of Molinism will have to find an alternative way of undermining the Molinist thesis.[246]

---

[246] Ibid, esp. pp. 110-111 is concerned about the grounds on which it can be claimed that either 1 or 2 is true. However, this is a concern that I will address in the following section.

5.4.2: The Grounding Objection

The grounding objection attempts to undermine the Molinist's account by claiming that there are no true CCFs. It is alleged that the Molinist can offer no sufficiently convincing argument to show how the truths of CCFs are grounded – and that they must be grounded if they are to be true.[247] The Grounding Objector argues that if it cannot be shown that there is some grounds upon which the truth of the assertion that a particular agent would *certainly* freely do a particular action if placed in a specific circumstance is justified, then it is more prudent to believe that what the agent would do is indeterminate in the sense of being a matter of probability – something that it is likely he will do (to a certain extent) or something that he is unlikely to do. Furthermore, it is argued that if the truth of CCFs cannot be shown to have a grounding then there is no convincing reason to suppose that God can know them to be true. If God cannot have prevolitional knowledge of true CCFs then the whole Molinist project is based on a fallacy - Middle Knowledge cannot be appealed to by the Molinist. This would obviously have a serious affect on the possibility that morally responsible agency is compatible with the knowledge of an omniscient God.

I will now ask who, or what, if anything, grounds the truth of CCFs? The truths of CCFs cannot be grounded in the choices or actions of God because this would hard-determine the particular actions of the agent (God himself would make them true and not the creaturely essences to which they pertain). For example, if God's will makes it true that Jones would mow his lawn if instantated in S, then Jones does not have the power to do other than mow his lawn in S. If this is the case then the counterfactual in question is not a CCF (as it does not allow for libertarian freedom/Regulative Control). Furthermore, any such attempt to ground the truth of CCFs in God would run contrary to the Molinist account of Middle Knowledge (CCFs are part of God's prevolitional knowledge and are supposed to be true independent of him).

However, it appears as though they also cannot be grounded in the individual to which they refer for several reasons. CCFs are true prior to the creation of any particular agent to which they refer. Furthermore, the CCFs known through Middle Knowledge refer to non-actual states of affairs (as they are known prevolitionally) and therefore the events to which they refer have not happened. Also, the assumed psychological state of the individual cannot serve as a sufficient grounding because the actions in question must be indeterminate, if they are to satisfy the libertarian characterisation of freedom (the experiences and psychological dispositions of the individual cannot be sufficient to hard-determine his particular actions). As Adams asserts, if one is really free with

---

247 O' Connor (1992) suggests, following his own refutation of the truth of counterfactuals, that we should simply drop the issue of their truth. See p. 162.

respect to what one does then one 'may act out of character, or change his intentions, or fail to act on them.'[248] Flint, who is a supporter of the Molinist thesis, believes that the grounding objection is perhaps the most serious obstacle to accepting the validity of Molinism.[249]

In order to comprehensively articulate and argue the grounding objection, it is necessary to provide an appropriate account of the relationship between truth and reality and then apply it to CCFs. By the end of this chapter I hope to have achieved this.

The Molinist has several very persuasive arguments in his arsenal with which to counter the grounding objector's arguments. First amongst these is the fact that the idea of CCFs has plausibility for most people who hear it.[250] Indeed, it cannot be questioned that the vast majority of people often ruminate 'What would have happened if ..?' Although it may appear impossible to definitively answer many of these questions, they are valuable when considering future actions, or in assessing the moral worth of what we have done. It also appears as though we are occasionally quite confident about the truth of certain CCFs. As Adams notes:

> There does not normally seem to be any uncertainty at all about what a butcher, for example, would have done if I had asked him to sell me a pound of ground beef, although we suppose he would have had free will in the matter. We say he certainly would have sold me the meat, if he had it to sell.[251]

Assuming the truth of CCFs is often part of what constitutes rational conduct and planning. It is very difficult to imagine how we could plan for the future if we did not make use of the idea of CCFs.

Those who propose the grounding objection insist that there are insufficient metaphysical grounds for the truth of CCFs, irrespective of what many see as their intuitive plausibility. Many grounding objectors are committed to a theory of the relationship between truth and reality that assumes a particular view of truth as correspondence.

Hasker asks, '[w]hat, if anything, is the ground of the truth of counterfactuals of freedom?' or '[w]hat makes counterfactuals true?'[252] Hasker asserts that in order for it to be true that a conditional state of affairs would obtain, it must be

---

248 Adams, R. M (1987), p. 113.
249 Flint (1998), 122.
250 Ibid, p. 77.
251 Adams, R. M. (1987), p. 88. Adams finds this example perplexing but ultimately asserts that the best that one can assert is that the butcher would probably have sold him the meat, since this is all that can be truly grounded by the character and psychological dispositions of the butcher.
252 Hasker (1989), see esp. pp. 29-52.

grounded in some present categorical state of affairs. Thus, according to him, truths about what 'would be the case if ...' must be have a grounding in what already are categorical facts about the actual world. Hasker surmises that the truth of counterfactuals is 'grounded in the natures, causal powers, inherent tendencies, and the like, of the natural entities described in them.'[253]

This theory is obviously in conflict with the Molinist model – the Molinist believes that the truth or falsity of CCFs cannot be grounded in categorical facts about what is already the case, because he holds that they are true logically prior to the existence of the actual world. If Hasker is correct about counterfactuals, then it appears as though there is no way that knowledge of counterfactuals could contribute to God's decision to create any particular world. This obviously would have the consequence of making it impossible for God to know what an agent would freely do if instantiated in any specified circumstance before any particular world is actualised by him. Hence, God would have to act solely on his Free Knowledge – and I have already discussed why this would result in the agent being hard-determined with respect to his actions. Furthermore, if the only true counterfactuals are those causally grounded in antecedent conditions then there cannot be true CCFs, as the agent would be determined by these antecedent conditions such that he would only have the power to act in accordance with them (the best that one can hope for is that the agent would have Guidance Control over his specific actions in any particular state of affairs).

However, I believe that Hasker's assertion that the truth of counterfactuals is 'grounded in the natures, causal powers, inherent tendencies, and the like, of the natural entities described in them,' makes an unnecessarily strong claim that the Molinist would justifiably refuse to subscribe to. Craig notes that 'one can entertain counterfactuals about what the world would have been like were different laws of nature or boundary conditions to obtain.'[254]

In considering the truth of counterfactuals I will rely on an idea that has become known as the theory of 'truth-makers'.[255] This idea involves the claim that in order for a proposition to be true there must be (or, depending on the characterisation of the theory, have been, will be or would be) truth-makers (facts/states of affairs) in virtue of which the proposition in question is true. The truth-maker suffices to establish the truth-value of a proposition that reflects the state of affairs that it encompasses, or which is excluded by it.[256] One who denies that there are such truth-makers for CCFs I will call a sophisticated grounding objector. A sophisticated grounding objector is, therefore, an antirealist in

---

253 Ibid.
254 Craig (1992), pp. 57-78.
255 See Mulligan, Simons and Smith (1984). See also Fox (1987) and Hochberg (1992).
256 Simons, P. (1998), p. 119.

relation to CCFs.

When we consider counterfactuals that pertain to possible futures that will in fact never be actual, we can begin to see how a problem may arise due to the fact that there appears to be a lack of truth-makers to ground their truth. Consider the following CCF: 'If I had an aeroplane, I would (freely) let you fly it next Tuesday'. Let us assume that I do not own an aeroplane and that I will not come to own one before next Tuesday. Thus, there will never be an actual state of affairs in which I will (freely) let you fly my aeroplane next Tuesday. It can therefore be argued that the question of what I would do next Tuesday (if I had an aeroplane) is indeterminate, as nothing ever occurs that determines it, and that any definite assertion concerning what I would (freely) do is false (at most it is a matter of probability). If this is correct then there is no truth that can be known about what I would do.

With regard to propositions concerning future occurrences (for example, 'James will go to work tomorrow') there will at some future time be a truth-maker in virtue of which the propositions will prove true or will prove false (they will either correspond, or fail to correspond, with future states of affairs).[257] However, in the case of CCFs no such truth-maker will ever become manifest. Therefore, it can be argued that there is nothing in virtue of which they are ever true.[258] Thus, predictions/claims about what the agent will do will have truth-makers at the time to which they correspond, in the actual world; however, it can be argued that there will never be truth-makers that suffice to ground propositions expressing CCFs which involve states of affairs that never occur in the actual world - as they pertain to purely conditional states of affairs that are never actualised.

5.4.3: Counterfactuals, Truth-Makers and Brute Facts

It should be noted that there is not always a causal relationship between a truth-bearer and a concrete (actual) object. For example, in the case of the following negative existential proposition this becomes apparent, 'Unicorns do not exist' (in the sense of not being real creatures). Obviously the fact that unicorns do not exist is not the *cause* of anything, nor is there any concrete object that causes

---

257   One can also be an anti-realist with respect to contingent future occurrences. If one is such, then one will claim that any proposition that relates to a future time is indeterminate until that time occurs – and, thereby, one can argue that such propositions are neither true or false, at the time at which they are framed (i.e. before their object obtains, or fails to do so). Such propositions can be thought of as predictions or beliefs that have a varying degree of likelihood of corresponding with future states of affairs (they may prove to be correct predictions) but which are not, strictly speaking, statements that express truth or falsity.
258   Adams is a proponent of this view. Adams, R. M. (1991), p. 345.

the proposition to be true, but there is still a truth-maker that is sufficient for the truth of the proposition in question (the state of affairs that constitutes the actual world does not include the existence of unicorns, and in virtue of this fact the proposition proves true. Thus, the state of affairs that comprises the actual world serves as a truth-maker, even though it does not *cause* the proposition in question to be true). The problem that results is that it may initially appear as though this understanding of truth-makers serves to undermine the grounding objection as construed by many of its proponents:

> Counterfactuals of freedom . . . are supposed to be contingent truths that are not caused to be true by God. Who or what does cause them to be true?[259]

> . . . metaphysically contingent propositions . . . require causal grounding in order to be true. That is, they must be caused to be true by some agent or agents, since it is not of their nature to be true.[260]

When we refer to a 'truth-maker' we should not take it that the fact that 'maker' is involved in the title gives warrant for us to infer that a causal relationship is at play between the truth-maker and the truth-bearer.[261] As already noted, the relationship can be understood as one of correspondence.

Many truth-maker theorists reject the idea of truth-maker maximalism. This is the idea that every true proposition has a truth-maker (in the sense that not every true meaningful proposition corresponds with, has corresponded with, or will correspond with a state of affairs in virtue of which it is true).[262]

Consider the following:

> It is wrong to torture innocent people for pleasure.

This proposition may be argued to be true, even though it could not correspond with an actual state of affairs that would serve as a truth-maker.[263] Indeed, given the fact that CCFs are *counter*factual in nature it appears as though they might be prime candidates for belonging to the class of propositions that do not have truth-makers.

However, the denial that CCFs have truth-makers leaves us in a rather

---

259   Adams, R. M. (1985), p. 232. See also Hasker (1986), p. 547.
260   Freddoso (1988), p. 70. The claim forwarded here is contentious and I will consider it again.
261   See Bigelow (1988), p. 125, Simons (1992), p. 159 and Armstrong (1997), p. 115.
262   For a discussion of this and related issues see, Milne, P. (2005), Rodriguez-Pereyra, G. (2005) and Lopez de Sa, D. and Zardini, E. (2006).
263   I appreciate that asserting that such a statement is true is not an uncontroversial position – however, it is only my intention to introduce it as a possibility. Such statements, if true, would be universally true – and not true in virtue of particular states of affairs.

difficult position. It appears as though if CCFs have no truth-makers they are simply brute facts about what an agent's creaturely essence would 'freely' do in particular circumstances. Brute facts are facts that don't depend on other facts to be true, but also are not self-explanatory. However, many modern Molinists believe that this is an unsatisfactory way of viewing the matter and attempt to offer alternative approaches to grounding God's knowledge of CCFs.

5.4.4: Lewis and Flint on Counterfactuals

In order to best understand the approaches that are available to him, I will now return to Lewis to consider his account of counterfactuals and their truth conditions[264]:

> $(P \square \rightarrow Q)$ is true iff the closest possible world (i.e. the closest to the actual world) in which the antecedent, P, is true, is a world in which the consequent, Q, is also true (or, in other words, $(P \square \rightarrow Q)$ is true iff the closest P-world is a Q-world).

'Closest' worlds are nearest to the real world in the sense that they are more similar. The closest P-world is the world in which P is true and which also has the greatest similarity to the actual world. We can therefore summarise Lewis's contention as follows: A counterfactual $(P \square \rightarrow Q)$ (if P were true then Q would have been true) is true if the world most similar to the actual world in which P is true is also a world in which Q is true. The greatest difficulty with this account is the fact that it requires a judgement regarding which possible world is most similar to the actual world – and it is not always easy to definitively state which world this is. Often questions of similarity are thought to be inherently contextual or indexical (remember the points made about inherent vagueness in the previous chapter). One is tempted to ask for a clarification of the respects in which the similarity is to be measured. When comparing any two distinct things as complex as worlds there may be numerous similarities and numerous differences. However, on Lewis's account we appear to be asked to think in terms of overall similarity.[265]

---

264 The account that I am attributing to Lewis has been simplified in particular ways. This has been done in order to allow ease of understanding and explanation. I have referred to the closest possible world as though there is only one world that might fit this criterion. In fact there might be multiple possible worlds that are equally close to the actual world. However, even if there are more than one *P-world* that should not make the counterfactual come out false, providing that each of these worlds is also a *Q-world*. Lewis offers the following insight, which also helps to solve the problem of the possibility of an infinitely regressive series of *P-worlds* that are also *Q-worlds* each of which is closer to the actual world than its predecessor: $(P \square \rightarrow Q)$ will be true iff there is a possible world, *w*, which is both a *P-world* and a *Q-world*, and that any *P-world* that is as close or closer to the actual world *w* is also a *w-world*.
265 The following account draws on Edgington (1992) and (2001).

Let us take Fine's example, which is discussed by Lewis:

> If Nixon had pressed the button in 1974, there would have been a nuclear holocaust.[266]

However, this appears to suggest that if Nixon had in fact pressed the button that the world that turned out to be actual would have been very different. It would appear as though in the world that is most like the actual world nothing that significantly changed the course of future events would have happened.

Lewis offers a solution to such problems by providing an account of what factors should be considered in judging the closeness of possible worlds. He proposes that the closest *A-worlds* (worlds most similar to the actual world) are those with pasts identical to the actual world up to immediately before the antecedent time, where they deviate minimally such that the antecedent is true.[267] After Edgington, I will call this point of deviation the 'fork'.[268] Thus, the closest *A-worlds* are those worlds in which there is, in the specified sense, a minimal deviation from the actual world.[269] Lewis states that following the fork, 'It is of little or no importance to secure approximate similarity of particular fact, even in matters that concern us greatly'.[270] Lewis believes that after the fork it is just the laws of nature that need to be identical.

I will now consider the account of CCFs offered by Flint (who gives us one of the most insightful and comprehensive accounts offered by a Molinist). Flint uses (as do the majority of the defenders of the truth of CCFs) Lewis's possible worlds semantics for counterfactuals. He agrees with Lewis that there are no occurrences in the actual world that ground CCFs, but argues that they are grounded in other possible worlds (thus the possible states of affairs that constitute other possible worlds suffice as truth-makers for counterfactual propositions). So, once again, the claim is that a counterfactual's truth is determined by the closest possible world(s) in which the antecedent is true. Let us return to our example of the counterfactual involving the aeroplane. In theory, if we could look at the possible world(s) which is most similar to the actual world (in the sense articulated above) but in which there is a minimal deviation such that I do own an aeroplane, then we could observe whether it is true that I would (freely) allow you to fly it next Tuesday. If in that world I do allow you to fly it, then the counterfactual is true, and if I do not then it is false.

However, it is at this juncture that we encounter perhaps the most serious flaw in this account. If it is true that I have libertarian freedom regarding my

---

266 See Fine (1975).
267 Lewis (1979).
268 Edgington, (nd).
269 Lewis (1979), Reprinted in Lewis (1986), pp. 32-66.
270 Ibid, p. 48.

choice to let you fly, or not to let you fly, my aeroplane, then there are possible worlds where I let you fly it and possible worlds where I do not. How can it be conclusively known which is closer to the actual world? One might respond that if I know that you are able to fly my aeroplane that I will let you do so – because that is just the sort of person that I am and any world that does not reflect this fact should not be thought of as the nearest possible world. Yet this is not reflective of the fact that an agent may simply act out of character at any time if he has Regulative Control. Things may be further illuminated by considering a different, and in some ways simpler, example.

Consider the following conditional proposition: 'If John were instantiated in S at t, he would freely choose to eat Frosties'. Let us now assume that there are possible worlds, at which John is in S at t. He goes to the larder and finds that he has a box of Frosties and a box of Sugar Puffs. In these worlds, as in the actual world, he likes both types of cereal. On an equal number of occasions he has chosen to eat each. How can we say with certainty therefore that he would freely choose to eat Frosties if instantiated in S, if this is a contingent indeterminate act that is within his Regulative Control? Can one not assert that there are nearby possible worlds ($W1$) in which he freely chooses to eat Frosties and nearby possible worlds ($W2$) in which he freely chooses to eat Sugar Puffs. It appears as though there is no way in which to decide whether $W1$ worlds or $W2$ worlds are more similar to the actual world.

When considering objections of this sort, Flint outlines Plantinga's suggestion that the similarity of worlds is, in part, determined by which counterfactuals are shared as true.[271] The idea is that if it is true that I would allow you to fly my aeroplane next Tuesday (if I had one) then all of the worlds in which I would do so become closer to the actual world – since they also affirm the counterfactual. Any world in which I do not let you do so moves further from the actual world and the semantics of similarity verify the former counterfactual as true.[272] This, however, appears to beg the question, as the argument of the antirealist is precisely that the counterfactuals in question are not true – because with regard to counterfactuals there is no fully determinate world!

This argument cannot serve to show how counterfactuals are grounded. This is because one cannot claim that the similarity of worlds serves to ground the truth of CCFs, if the similarity in question is determined by which CCFs are true.[273]

Freddoso attempts a different approach. He suggests that CCFs are grounded in a particular type of correspondence.[274] He claims that:

---

271   Fint (1998), pp. 135-136. However, it should be noted that Flint does not believe that Plantinga's suggestion is particularly convincing.
272   See Wyma (2001), p. 7.
273   See O' Connor (1992), pp. 149-150.
274   The following argument is based on Freddoso (1988), esp. pp. 72-74.

> ...it seems reasonable to claim that there are now adequate metaphysical grounds for the truth of a conditional future contingent Ft(p) on H [a hypothetical situation] if there *would* be adequate metaphysical grounds at t for the truth of the present tense proposition p on the condition that H should obtain at t.[275]

Thus, the substantive claim is that a CCF is true if it is the case that if its antecedent should obtain its consequent would also obtain. Furthermore, Freddoso points out that the consequent of any conditional may remain true even if its antecedent never obtains.[276]

However, I think that I would have to agree with O' Connor that this line of reasoning really does not alleviate the problems associated with grounding objection.[277] To say that a CCF now has grounds because it would have grounds if its antecedent should obtain is merely to push the problem of grounding back one step further. What would ground the claim that the CCF would be true should its antecedent obtain? Obviously, the problem still remains in a form that is just as troublesome.

I will now attempt to illustrate the difficulties in any attempt to offer sufficient grounds for the truth of CCFs in possible worlds. Let us take our example of the cereal above, and suppose that there are possible futures ($F1$) in which John freely eats Frosties in S at t (let us suppose that S obtains and that t corresponds to tomorrow morning) and possible futures ($F2$) in which he freely eats Sugar Puffs in S at t. If this is the case then we can conclude that neither is privileged in the sense of being closer to the world as it currently stands. Therefore, it is impossible to know whether the counterfactual 'If in S at t, John will (freely) eat Frosties' or the counterfactual 'If in S at t, John will (freely) eat Sugar Puffs' is true on the basis of appeal to what is true in the actual world, or what is true in the closest possible world(s). One might respond that the one in which John actually does proceed to eat the Frosties is privileged because it will prove to be the actual world. However, the antirealist's whole point is that the future in question cannot be known to be true because there is nothing in the present world that grounds it (it does not now have, and never had, a truth-maker in virtue of which it will prove either correct or incorrect as a prediction, is indeterminate until John actually eats one of the brands of cereal in S at t (there will be a truth-maker at t but it is indeterminate until John actually forms the effective second order to act in a particular way and acts in accordance with it)!

However, the Molinist can argue that it is logically possible that there are no possible worlds at which John *freely* chooses to eat Sugar Puffs. If this were the case then all *f-worlds* would be worlds at which he eats Frosties. However, I do not believe that this is reflective of our intuitive beliefs. This is because one

---

275 Ibid, p. 72.
276 Ibid, p. 73.
277 O' Connor (1992), pp. 155-156.

can reply that there is also the logical possibility that there are *W1-type* worlds and *W2-type* worlds in which he freely acts and that this is intuitively more plausible given the assumption of libertarian free will. Let us suppose that God has actualised a possible world in which John finds himself in *S*. If it is true that there are possible worlds at which John freely does *X* in *S*, and possible worlds at which he freely does *Y* in *S*, then how can God know whether the actual world will prove to be a *W1-type* world or a *W2-type* world? Possible world-types *W1* and *W2* are not restricted because of how John would freely act in *S* (as either action would be free). If John is free and can exercise Regulative Control in *S*, then it can be argued that God's actualising *S* does not mean that he can in any meaningful sense exercise control over John's doing *X*, or his doing *Y*, in *S*. If the preceding argument is correct, God could not even know what it is that John will proceed to do until the time to which *S* is indexed occurs (because the propositions 'If in *S*, John would freely *X*' or the proposition 'If in *S*, John would freely *Y*' are not true as they have no truth-makers – rather 'If in *S*, John would have the power to freely *X* and the power to freely *Y*' is true – and this is not of much use for providential control. Furthermore, the latter proposition would form part of God's Natural Knowledge rather than part of his Middle Knowledge). Therefore, God could not have knowledge of what John would freely do in *S* prior to his instantiating John in *S* and John actually proceeding to act. This obviously would once again result in difficulties in explaining how an atemporal being could have timeless knowledge of temporal events, if his knowledge of the CCFs that correspond with those events is prevolitional.

The Molinist account appeals heavily to our intuitive belief that there are such things as true counterfactuals. However, consider the following two propositions:

1. If John were hungry at *t1* and found Frosties and Sugar Puffs in the larder (part of what constitutes the complete state of affairs *S*) and liked to eat both, but could only choose to eat one of the two, he would eat Frosties.

2. If John were hungry at *t1* and found Frosties and Sugar Puffs in the larder and liked to eat both, but could only choose to eat one of the two, he would not eat Frosties.

It may appear dubious to claim that one of the above two propositions is true before the occurrence of *t1*. It may also appear dubious to claim that God could prevolitionally know what it is that John would freely choose to do in *S*. I have already proposed a way in which the Molinist can maintain that LCEM applies to CCFs. However, it appears very difficult to provide an adequate account of exactly what would ground God's knowledge of which of the above two propositions would prove to be a CCF, even if LCEM is valid (there is a difference between the claim that something is true, and the claim that someone can know it to be true – this is an issue that I will return to). This is perhaps one of the greatest flaws in the Molinist account.

Furthermore, it can be argued that any Molinist arguments involving the idea that counterfactuals are true in virtue of closest possible world(s) will inevitably lead to a vicious circle. This is because, as we have seen, this thesis relies on the argument that whatever counterfactuals are true is dependent upon what possible world has been actualised (counterfactuals are true if they are true in the closest possible world(s) to the actual world). However, the coherency of Molinism relies on the fact that counterfactuals must be true logically prior to God's decision to actualise any particular possible world. Thus, for the argument that counterfactuals are true in virtue of the closest possible world(s) to work, it must be true that there is an actual world (which determines the relation of closeness that obtains between it and all other possible worlds) logically prior to God's knowledge of the truth of the counterfactuals in question. This however, results in the untenable position that God must have actualised a particular possible world before his decision to actualise a particular possible world. Following this line of argument it can be asserted that a vicious circle is established. However, I think that such reasoning stems from a fundamental misconception. I will attempt to show this in the next subsection.

5.4.5: Lewis on Actuality

Lewis is an advocate of possible world realism – what this means is he believes that 'actuality' is modally indexical.[278] Thus, from the perspective of each agent located at each possible world, that world is 'actual'. Thus, if I declare in the world in which I exist that 'I comprise part of the actual world' my statement is valid. However, if my doppelganger declares in the world at which he exists 'I am part of what comprises the actual world' his statement too is valid – even though it is uttered at, and in relation to, another world. The Lewisian form of possible world realism also holds that worlds are spatio-temporally and causally isolated from each other.[279]

Now I would like to propose a response to the above vicious circle argument. In assuming that it would have to be necessary for a particular possible world to be actual in order to establish its relationship of closeness to other possible worlds, the proponent of the previous argument is failing to notice an insight that can be gleaned from Lewis's possible world realism. Why can we not simply argue that God knows that if a particular possible world were actual it would have a relationship of closeness to other possible worlds that would ground the truth of particular CCFs in that world. This does not seem to stretch the imagination or the limits of plausibility too far. There is also no need to assume that this knowledge would have to be post-volitional, as it would be true necessarily

---

278 Lewis (1973), p. 85.
279 Lewis (1986), p. 78.

true that if a particular world were actual it would have definite relationships of closeness with other possible worlds. Thus, God would not have to actualise a particular possible world in order for him to know how close other particular possible worlds would be *if a specific possible world were actual*. However, I do not think that this sufficiently alleviates the problems of deciding whether if instantiated in S, John would freely act such that 3 or 4 is true – and thus does not successfully counter the argument that CCFs do not have a grounding in possible worlds.

5.4.6: Subjunctives of Freedom and Agency

It is my belief that the reason why the Molinist cannot provide grounds for the truth of subjunctives of freedom in the way demanded by the grounding objector is rooted in the very nature of free agency. There is nothing that could make it true that 'If in S Jones would freely X' other than the fact that if in S Jones would exercise his Regulative Control such that he forms the second-order desire to X and acts in accordance with that desire. Why is this the case?

Consider the following proposition about the past– 'Yesterday Jones freely chose to X at t'. What grounds the truth of this proposition? It is my claim that the only thing that grounds this proposition is the fact that Jones exercised his Regulative Control in a particular fashion. One can say that the proposition now has a truth-maker in virtue of the fact that there existed a state of affairs in virtue of which the proposition was proven true. I think that the truth of this is self-evident – however, part of what constituted that state of affairs was Jones exercising his Regulative Control in the way that he saw fit. The only reason that the proposition 'Yesterday Jones freely refrained from doing X at t' did not prove true was because of the way in which Jones exercised his capacity to do otherwise. Jones is the cause of his choice - there can be no other sufficient grounds for his doing X if he has Regulative Control.

The claim that the agent has Regulative Control also implies the claim that there is such a thing as agent causation. If one demands grounds for the truth of how the agent will exercise his Regulative Control beyond the agent as a cause, then one has missed the whole point of what it means to have libertarian freedom. Similarly, if we look for reasons outside of Jones's free exercise of his Regulative Control for the counterfactual 'If in S at t Jones would freely X' then we have missed what it means for him to have freedom with respect to his doing X in S. There could be no further sufficient ground for the truth of the fact that Jones would X if in S if it is assumed that Jones has Regulative Control over his particular actions. However, this leaves the Molinist with the problem of how it is a creaturely essence, and not the instantiated agent, that makes CCFs and SFs true.

5.5: CCFs, Creaturely Essences and Brute Facts

Molina holds 'that the certainty of that Middle Knowledge comes from the depth and the perfection of the divine intellect, by which [God] knows certainly what is itself uncertain.'[280] This notion has become known as the idea of 'supercomprehension'. The idea is that God's intellect so vastly surpasses all created free wills that it understands more about them than would be merely necessary to comprehend them.[281] However, Saurez is critical of this view as he contends that when one comprehends something one knows all that there is to be known about it, and it is ridiculous to claim that anyone, even God, could know more than that.[282] The idea is that even if there is there is nothing objectively to be known about how the agent would freely act in particular specified circumstances that God's mind is so perfect that he would know it anyway.[283] However, it appears very difficult to see how this could be the case.

Let us now return to the question of uninstantiated creaturely essences. The idea that the essence of the agent logically precedes his existence and allows God to know the truth about how he would freely act, if instantiated in a particular state of affairs, is controversial. It is difficult to imagine how an essence would provide knowledge of how an agent would freely act. /If Jones is free and not determined with respect to whether or not he will mow his lawn, then there cannot be something about his essence that necessitates the fact that he will mow his lawn when he finds himself in S at t. As I have already argued, it is plausible to suppose that there is a possible world in which he freely forms the effective second-order desire to mow his lawn, and a possible world in which he freely efrains from doing so when placed in S at t. However, it is not my intention to undermine the fact that there is a truth about what he will do – it is rather my intention to call into question the assertion that God can prevolitionally know what he would do in virtue of his complete comprehension of Jones's essence. One must remember that is essential to free will that after the creative act of actualising a particular possible world the future must remain open (allow for free action).

I will now consider Kvanvig's explanation of creaturely essences.[284]

> D1: God creates the world at t = df. There is a set of essences $e1...en$ such that God instantiates $e1...en$ at t.

---

280 Molina, *Concordia*, qu. 14, art 13, disp. 53. Translation found in Adams (1977), p. 111.
281 Adams (1977), p. 111.
282 Saurez, *De Scientia Dei Futurorum Contingentium*, Bk 2. Ch. 7, n.6.
283 Adams (1977), p. 111.
284 Kvanvig (1986), esp. pp. 122-126. In the following discussion I will retain his original numbering.

> D2: E is an essence = *df*. E is a property which is necessarily such that (i) it is possible that something exemplify it, and (ii) if is not possible that more than one thing exemplify it.
>
> P1: Necessarily, for every *x*, *x* has an essence.

From Kvanving's definitions it follows that when God creates he makes individuals that exemplify essences.[285] He further claims that 'essences are such that, even before they are instantiated, they reveal what an instantiation of them would be like.'[286] He believes that each free individual essence includes a maximal subjunctive of freedom[287] – he states this as follows:

> P3: Necessarily, for every [creaturely] essence *E*… an essential property of *E* is of the form *being such that some maximal subjunctive of freedom F regarding a free instantiation of E is true*.[288]

How is the notion of a maximal subjunctive of freedom to be understood?

> D7: F is a maximum subjunctive of freedom regarding an instantiation of *E* = *df*. (i) *being such that F is true* is included in *E*; and (ii) where '*S*' = 'an instantiation of *E* which is free', every proposition which is a component of *F* is of the form *if S were in circumstances C at t, S would do A at t*.[289]

The idea that is central to Kvanvig's argument is that any essence whose instantiation could be the object of God's will is necessarily such that it includes a sufficiently complex set of subjunctives of freedom for God to know how that individual would freely act if placed in any particular possible state of affairs.[290] However, one must now ask how a creaturely essence can contain all of the world-indexing properties of an agent – including CCFs and SFs. It should be noted that an essence cannot make a choice, essences simply are, they do not act – only a creature can do so. One can of course argue that a particular essence has the property of reflecting how a possible agent would act if instantiated in a maximally specified state of affairs.

However, if a possible agent's essence logically precedes his existence (if God decides that the agent is to exist at all), then the CCFs that can be known as true through knowledge of that essence are not true in virtue of any occurrences in the actual world – including the agent's actual exercise of his free will (as no world is yet actual). Indeed, it is claimed that a possible agent's creaturely essence reflects

---

285 Ibid, p. 122.
286 Ibid, p. 124.
287 See footnote 241 above.
288 Kvanvig (1986), p. 124.
289 Ibid, p. 125.
290 Ibid, p. 126.

the truth of how he would act in specific states of affairs – even if he is never in fact actualised. Thus, the CCFs known through Middle Knowledge are not counterfactually affected by logically posterior occurrences in the actual world – as they are also reflective of how agents that will never in fact be actual would act. If CCFs are not true in virtue of the contingent occurrences of the actual world (including the actual exercise of Regulative Control) then they are essentially true (in the sense that there is no possible world at which they are not true – it is essentially true that creaturely essence P if instantiated in S would 'freely' X). But, as Hasker objects, 'this is fatal to the theory. No individual chooses, or is responsible for, what is contained in that individual's essence.'[291] I think that this claim has intuitive plausibility. The basic problem is that if it is essentially true that I will 'freely' X in S at t logically prior to my actual existence, then in what sense is it in my power to refrain from doing X in these circumstances?[292] Is there any way that the Molinist can offer a means of waylaying this concern?

If the Molinist wishes to claim that the agent has Regulative Control over his actions, then I think that the only way that this *might* be tenable would be if he also accepts that the CCFs that can be known through a creaturely essence are brute facts. I have already defined brute facts as 'facts that don't depend on other facts to be true, but also are not self-explanatory.' Thus, brute facts are 'basic, primitive, ungrounded facts about the way things are.'[293] One can then argue, as Saurez has, that creaturely essence C, has a property (*habitudo*) which is the property of being a possible agent who in S would freely X, or which is the property of being a possible agent who in S would freely refrain from doing X. However, there is nothing external or internal to C, except the property itself, which determines C to have one property rather than the other. God knows what C will do in S, because he knows which property C has.[294] Having one of these properties is a brute fact about C. However, this once again raises the question – if the instantiated agent is not responsible for his essence having the particular property that it has, how can it be claimed that it is reflective of how he would freely choose to exercise his capacity to do otherwise?

There is also the problem of how it is possible for this property to be reflective of how an actual agent with essence C will exercise his Regulative Control when actually instantiated in S – without determining what the individual will do (if it essentially true that an agent A with a creaturely essence E if instantiated in S will 'freely' X, then there is no possible world at which A freely refrains from X – and this is true before A is even created; in virtue of his essence having particular properties – how then does this fact not determine his action if the properties that his essence has are not counterfactually affected by occurrences in the actual

---

291 Hasker (1989), p. 32.
292 Hasker (1989) voices similar concerns.
293 Flint (1998), p. 137.
294 This account of Saurez position is found in Adams (1977), p. 112.

world?). This account does not actually offer any explanation of this mysterious relation (this is of course because it involves the notion of irreducible brute facts). I think any account that attempts to argue that divine knowledge of a brute fact about a creaturely essence (which logically precedes the actual existence of the agent to which it would correspond) would allow for free will and morally responsible agency is intuitively implausible. Any argument to the contrary will ultimately rely on some explanation that involves assertions that cannot be sufficiently explained. Ultimately, the Molinist account is unsatisfactory because either it must accept that CCFs are ungrounded, and therefore God would have to know them through some mysterious process or capacity (which is not in itself an adequate explanation), or they are grounded in creaturely essences which in some mysterious way are reflective of how the agent would exercise his Regulative Control if instantiated in specific circumstances (which is also not sufficient as an explanation).

5.6: Conclusion to Chapter 5

At the beginning of this chapter I stated that it is my belief that Molinism offers a superior compatibilist account to that of Ockhamism. I have attempted to show how it can evade many of the objections that incompatibilist's have raised against Ockhamism. However, the ultimate problem that I believe the Molinist conception has not offered an adequate response to, is the question of how God can know CCFs to be true, without determining the actual agent or without resorting to some grounding principle or entity that is itself mysterious, insufficient, or irreducible. Therefore, I think that while Molinism shows promise, it does not have the power to convince the sceptic. I doubt very much that the incompatibilist will have found sufficient reasons in the Molinist model to abandon his position. There is a certain 'leap of faith' that is involved in Molinism that many will find unpalatable. Whilst I agree that if CCFs can be known to be true by an atemporal God it is possible that divine knowledge of the agent's actions would allow for morally responsible agency (as the agent would have freedom in an apposite sense over his second-order desires) I am not sufficiently convinced by the Molinist that God could have such prevolitional knowledge.

It is important when assessing the validity of the Molinist thesis that one draws a distinction between what is *true* and what is *knowable*. It is not sufficient for the Molinist to show that propositions regarding the future free actions of particular individuals are true; he must also show how they can be known by an omniscient being. It has been my argument that the Molinist has not been entirely successful in either of these endeavours. Ultimately, I have found that the Molinist account relies on mysterious processes or relations that have little power to convince. Perhaps this is the best that the compatibilist can hope for –

perhaps belief in certain things about God does require a leap of faith. However, as a philosophical thesis, I think that Molinism will either have to find a better means of explaining how God can foreknow the agent's future free actions, or accept that Molinism will never serve to convince anyone who is not already a compatibilist. Any theory whose base assumptions are intuitively questionable will have little power to persuade. Rather than re-iterate what has already been argued in this chapter at this stage, I will do so in the final chapter. In closing, my findings in this chapter lead me to the conclusion that Molinism does not offer a sufficiently persuasive argument for the compatibilism of divine 'foreknowledge' and morally responsible agency, due to its ultimate reliance on questionable principles. If it is true that God has prevolitional knowledge of CCFs then there is no reason to assume that this knowledge would conflict with Criterion (xii) of morally responsible agency. However, the Molinist is incapable of giving an adequate account of how God could have such knowledge.

6

Final Discussion and Conclusions

It is my ultimate contention that it is intuitively implausible that sempiternal divine foreknowledge is compatible with morally responsible agency. It is therefore my conclusion that the concerns which gave rise to this enquiry have not been adequately addressed. I believe that the Molinist account shows the greatest promise of arguing for the compatibility of divine foreknowledge and morally responsible agency, but that it has not yet found a convincing way of arguing for God's prevolitional knowledge of CCFs.

In order to reach these conclusions, I began in Chapter 1 by providing an account of morally responsible agency. This account allowed subsequent reference to the morally responsible agent to be clearly understood. Throughout the course of the first chapter I listed the substantive elements of my claims and findings as eleven criteria that I argued the individual must be able to fulfil if he is to be capable of moral responsibility. I contended that the morally responsible agent must:

(i) Be capable of utilising the essential indexical.

(ii) Exhibit strong first-person phenomena.

(iii) Be capable of a specific type of deliberation that incorporates the ability to imagine other possible perspectives.

(iv) Be capable of recognising that he exists in an objective world and understand when a specific time is being alluded to.

(v) Be capable of having ownership of his actions in an apposite way – this requires being able to act in accordance with a will with which he identifies (which involves the ability to form second-order desires and act in conformity with them).

(vi) Be capable of making judgements based on evaluative comparison (this involves having an evaluation system that embodies a hierarchy of values).

(vii) Be capable of doing that which he judges to be of greatest benefit (given what is accomplishable).

(viii) Be capable of having evaluative and motivational systems that completely coincide.

(ix) Have the capacity to adopt the correct moral standard against which his actions and/or desires should be measured (even if he does not do so intentionally or negligently).

(x) Have the capacity to act in accordance with the moral norms that follow from the moral standard.

(xi) Be capable of forming the second-order desire to be moral and be capable of making it his will.

These eleven criteria provided a foundation from which the discussion of the compatibility of morally responsible agency and divine foreknowledge could proceed.

However, one of the most fundamental components of morally responsible agency had not yet been discussed, and so Chapter 2 was devoted to the issue of the type of control essential to moral responsibility. The fact that the agent must have some form of control over what he does is generally taken as self-evident in accounts of moral responsibility. However, it was necessary to delineate the type of control sufficient for moral responsibility. I found that Regulative Control is essential to moral responsibility. I showed why, in order to have moral responsibility for a specific act, the agent must have Regulative Control over the second-order desire that motivates it, and have the power to act in accordance with that desire, irrespective of the state of affairs that constitutes the world at the time of acting. This involves, in a certain context, the agent having multiple actualisable alternatives available to him at the time of acting. I added this capacity for Regulative Control as the twelfth and final criterion of morally responsible agency.

In Chapter 3 I made it clear that I would be assuming a traditional conception of God. I then briefly introduced the divine characteristics that are relevant to the question of the compatibility of divine foreknowledge and morally responsible agency. These were omnipotence, eternality, immutability, omniscience, infallibility and providential control. I also assumed that God had each of these attributes essentially – that is to say he would have these characteristics in every world at which he exists.

I proceeded to consider Pike's claim that, given the existence of God, in order to prove that the agent has the power to do otherwise (in any meaningful way) one would have to show that he has the ability to exercise one of three powers: (i) the power to act at $t2$ in such a way that God would have existed and would have held a false belief at $t1$ (ii) the power at $t2$ to act in such a way that God would have existed but would not have held the belief he held at $t1$ (iii) the power at $t2$ to act in such a way that God would not have existed at $t1$. To be capable of moral responsibility the agent requires the ability to do otherwise with respect to his identification with particular second-order desires. Therefore, I found that the morally responsible agent would have to be in possession of one of these powers if God exists.

I found that the agent could not have the first power (i) as this would involve bringing about a logical falsity. In examining the third possibility (iii) I considered the idea that by understanding the term 'God' as a non-rigid designator it might be possible to argue that a particular entity 'Yahweh', who fulfilled the criteria for being God at a particular time, could cease to do so in virtue of the agent's exercise of his power to do otherwise. However, I agreed with Pike's assertion that it would be more intuitively plausible to understand that the divine attributes are essentially held by the individual who is God. In other words, if Yahweh is God he is essentially God and is therefore essentially omniscient and infallible. The proposed strategy therefore failed to be convincing.

I proceeded to introduce Pike's Proposition 2 and found that the denial of possibility (ii) would rely on a particular understanding of the past and the way that certain facts are fixed at particular times. Pike argues that because God's foreknowledge is a feature of the past, and because it is impossible for the agent to change the past, the agent's actions are fatalistically necessitated by that foreknowledge. However, the validity of this claim is not as self-evident as one might be tempted to assume. Therefore, it was prudent to investigate the truth of this claim and the alternatives that are offered by the compatibilist.

An account that denies the complete fixity of all past facts is central to Ockhamism. Chapter 4 was devoted to investigating the coherency of the Ockhamist position on the power to do otherwise and moral responsibility. I began by making clear exactly what I mean by an Ockhamist. I then delineated the different ways in which the idea of necessity can be understood in relation to divine foreknowledge. I proceeded to introduce the idea of 'accidental necessity' and attempted to provide an understanding of it that would prove sufficient for later arguments. Next, I outlined the Ockhamist claim that the agent has the power to counterfactually affect certain aspects of the past.

In order to critically engage with this idea I offered different characterisations of the difference between hard and soft facts – initially focussing on those provided by Adams and Hoffman and Rosenkrantz. I found Adams account lacking as under its criteria every fact would ultimately prove to be soft. I found Hoffman and Rosenkrantz's model more internally coherent. I proceeded to explain why God's past beliefs about the agent's future contingent actions would prove to be soft facts according to their understanding. However, I then claimed that just because a model is internally coherent, that does not mean that it is intuitively plausible or that it should be embraced.

I next considered Fischer's contention that even if God's beliefs about the agent's future free actions are soft facts about the past that they are nevertheless soft facts that have hard 'components'. I delineated what is involved in what he calls 'hard-core soft facts' and 'hard-type soft facts'. I then explained why an understanding of these ideas allows one to argue that the agent does not have the power to perform an action in virtue of which God's past beliefs would be counterfactually affected. I also outlined a way in which the Ockhamist can attempt to counter such an argument. The validity of the Ockhamist thesis was shown to be ultimately reliant on the tenability of this counter-argument.

I proceeded to consider Hasker's objections to the Ockhamist account. He believes that if we allow *de re* considerations into the distinction between hard and soft facts that every fact will turn out to be soft. He also insists that the Ockhamist must allow some *de re* considerations if his account is to be coherent. I considered some objections to Hasker's thesis. However, I found that he was correct in his contention that at least some *de re* considerations must be allowed by the Ockhamist, and I further claimed that such an allowance, as proposed by the Ockhamist, was arbitrary.

It is my belief that accidental necessity does attach to propositions that express God's beliefs about the future. To show that this is the case I provided extensive examples involving divine revelation and a discussion of occurrent knowledge. By doing so, I attempted to strengthen the arguments and insights of Fischer and Hasker. I finally argued that the idea that the agent has the power to counterfactually affect God's past beliefs is implausible. I concluded that the Ockhamist account is ultimately unconvincing, as it has difficulty in offering an adequate definition of its own terms. I also claimed that Ockhamism is merely a negative compatibilist solution and is not reflective of our intuitive understanding of the concepts that it employs. Due to the many shortcomings that are inherent in the Ockhamist thesis I ultimately found that the idea of theological fatalism was more convincing with regard to the foreknowledge of a sempiternal God.

In Chapter 5, I considered the Molinist approach to reconciling God's knowledge of future occurrences with the agent having moral responsibility for his actions. I introduced the Molinist idea that, by insisting that God's anterior knowledge of future events has four logical Moments, it is possible to assert that the agent is free in a way that allows for moral responsibility. I explained what is involved in each of these Moments. The Molinist argument is that God knows (through Middle Knowledge) what an agent would freely do in a particular state of affairs before choosing to make that state of affairs actual. He then proceeds to make that state of affairs obtain, but, because his knowledge of the free actions of the agent is logically anterior to his actual decision to make any world actual (it is prevolitional), this preserves the agent's free will and hence his moral responsibility.

I then discussed what worlds God is free to actualise, given that he is constrained by the fact that he wants his creatures to be free. My reason for doing so was that it is essential that God cannot choose what he foreknows the agent will 'freely' do if the agent is to have morally responsible agency. The fact that the agent will freely X if in S must be insulated from God's activity if he is to be capable of fulfilling Criterion (xii) of morally responsible agency. It must therefore be the case that God will only actualise a possible world where the agent's effective second-order desires are free.

I proceeded to examine the possibility that God plays a role in deciding what CCFs he prevolitionally knows to be true (because the fully specified antecedent of any particular CCF will involve facts about divine activities that would contribute to the state of affairs in which the agent would find himself instantiated) and that this would negate the possibility of morally responsible agency. I argued that even if God has control over what states of affairs the agent finds himself in, this does not mean that he is not responsible for his free response to those states of affairs.

Next, I discussed the various objections to the Molinist thesis. I found that the 'grounding objection' was perhaps the greatest obstacle to accepting the validity of Molinism. Having critically evaluated several modern Molinist arguments, I found that it was not possible to ground the truth of CCFs in possible worlds. This was principally because there is no sufficiently justified way to tell which is the closest possible world (or set of worlds) when considering an agent's free choices.

I found that the Molinist is incapable of offering an adequate explanation of how God's knowledge of CCFs could be grounded. It is my contention that if CCFs are true, and if God has prevolitional knowledge of them, then it is possible to argue that divine knowledge of the agent's future actions would still allow for morally responsible agency, but there is no sufficiently convincing argument to the effect that God does have such knowledge.

It is my ultimate finding that sempiternal divine foreknowledge of the agent's actions does not allow for morally responsible agency. It is also my finding that atemporal divine prevolitional knowledge of CCFs/SFs involving those actions would allow for morally responsible agency, but that arguments which claim God has such knowledge rely on questionable foundations/principles, and therefore lack the power to convince.

References

Aaronovitch, H. (1979). Rational Motivation. *Philosophy and Phenomenological Research*, 40, 173-193.

Adams, M. M. (1967). Is the Existence of God a "Hard Fact"? *The Philosphical Review*, 76, 492-503.

------ (1977). Middle Knowledge and the Problem of Evil. *American Philosophical Quarterly*, 14, 109-117.

------ (1985). Plantinga on the Problem of Evil. In Tomberlin, J. and van Inwagen, P. (eds) (1985). *Alvin Plantinga: Profiles (Vol. 5)*. Dordrecht, Reidel.

------ (1983). Divine Necessity. *The Journal of Philosophy*, 80, 741-752.

------ (1987). Middle Knowledge and the Problem of Evil. In Adams, R. M. *The Virtue of Faith and Other Essays in Philosophical Theology*. New York, Oxford University Press.

------ (1988). Symposium Papers, Comments, and an Abstract: Presumption and the Necessary Existence of God. *Noûs*, 22, 19-32.

------ (1991). An Anti-Molinist Argument. *Philosophy of Religion*, 5, 343-353.

Alston, W. (1985). Divine Foreknowledge and Alternative Conceptions of Human Freedom. *International Journal for Philosophy of Religion*, 18, 19-32.

Anderson, J. F. (1956). *On the Truth of the Catholic Faith*, Bk. II. New York, Hanover House.

Anon, (n.d.). Luis de Molina. *The Catholic Encyclopedia* [online]. Available from: http://www.newadvent.org/cathen/10436a.htm. [Accessed 01-03-06]

Anscombe, G. E. M. (1958). *Intention*. Oxford, Blackwell.

Aquinas, St. T. ([c. 1265-73] 1917). *Summa Theologica* (trans. Fathers of the English Dominican Province), London, R. & T. Washborne.

Aristotle ([c. 350 BCE] 1985). *Nichomachean Ethics* (trans. Erwin, Terence). Indianapolis, Hackett Publishing.

Armstrong, D. M. (1997). *A World of States of Affairs, Cambridge Studies in Philosophy*. Cambridge, Cambridge University Press.

Augustine, St. ([387-395] 1964). *On Free Choice of the Will* (trans. Benjamin, A. S. and Hackstaff, L. H.). New York, Bobbs-Merrill.

------ ([397] 1998). *The Confessions.* (trans. Chadwick, H.) New York, Oxford University Press.

Baker, L. R. (2000). *Persons and Bodies: A Constitution View.* Cambridge, Cambridge University Press.

Bishop, J. (1983). Agent-Causation. *Mind,* 92, 61-79.

Boethius ([c. 522] 1897). *The Consolations of Philosophy* (trans. James, H. R). London, Routledge.

Bradley, F. H. (1888). On Pleasure, Pain, Desire and Volition. *Mind,* 13, 1-36.

Braine, D. (1988). *The Reality of Time and the Existence of God: The Project of Proving God's Exisetence.* Oxford, Clarendon Press.

Broome, J. (1991). Desire, Belief and Expectation. *Mind,* 100, 265-267.

Cargile, J. (1967). On Omnipotence. *Noûs,* 1, 201-205.

Cargile, J. (1996). Some Comments on Fatalism. *The Philosophical Quarterly,* 46, 1-11.

Casteneda, H-N. (1967). Omniscience and Indexical Reference. *The Journal of Philosophy,* 64, 203-210.

Chandler, H. S. (1967). Excluded Middle. *The Journal of Philosophy,* 64, 807-814.

Chisholm, R. (1967). Identity through Possible Worlds: Some Questions. *Noûs,* 1, 1-8.

Cooper, N. (1978). The Law of Excluded Middle. *Mind,* 87, 161-180.

Copp, D. (1995). *Morality, Normativity and Society.* New York, Oxford University Press.

Craig, W. L. (1992). Hasker on Divine Knowledge. *Philosophical Studies,* 67, 89-110.

------ (2000). Omniscience, Tensed Facts, and Divine Eternity. *Faith and Philosophy,* 17, 225-241.

Creel, R. E. (1986). *Divine Impassibility.* Cambridge, Cambridge University Press.

------ (1999). Immutability and Impassibility. In Quinn, P. and Taliaferro, C. (eds.) (1999). *A Companion to Philosophy of Religion.* Oxford, Blackwell.

Davidson, D. (1980). *Essays on Actions and Events.* Oxford, Clarendon Press.

Dennett, D. (1986). *Elbow Room.* Oxford, Clarendon Press.

Edgington D. (nd) (accessed 13-06-06). www.nyu.edu/gsas/dept/philo/courses/content/papers/edgington.pdf.

------ (1992). Validity, Uncertainty and Vagueness. *Analysis*, 52, 193-204.

------ (2001). The Philosphical Problem of Vagueness. *Legal Theory*, 7, 371-378.

Eshleman, A. (2004). Moral Responsibility. In *The Stanford Encyclopedia of Philosophy* [online]. Available from: http://plato.stanford.edu/entries/moral-responsibility. [Accessed 10-01-06]

Fine, K. (1975). Critical Notice of David Lewis, Counterfactuals. *Mind*, 84, 451-458.

Fischer, J. M. (1982). Responsibility and Control. *The Journal of Philosophy*, 79, 24-40.

------ (1983). Freedom and Foreknowledge. *The Philosophical Review*, 92, 67-79.

------ (1986). Hard-Type Soft Facts. *The Philosophical Review*, 95, 591-601.

------ (1989). *God, Freedom and Foreknowledge*. Stanford, Stanford University Press.

------ (1991). Snapshot Ockhamism. *Philosophical Perspectives*, 5, 355-371.

Fischer, J. M. & Ravizza, M. (1991). Responsibility and Inevitability. *Ethics*, 101, 258-278.

------ (1998). *Responsibility and Control: A Theory of Moral Responsibility*. Cambridge, Cambridge University Press.

Flint, T. P. (1998). *Divine Providence: The Molinist Account*. Ithaca, Cornell University Press.

Flint, T. P. and Freddoso, A. J. (1983). Maximal Power. In Freddoso, A. J. (ed.) (1983). *The Existence and Nature of God*. Notre Dame, University of Notre Dame Press.

Fox, J. F. (1987). Truthmaker. Australasian Journal of Philosophy, 65, 188-207.

Frankfurt, H. G. (1969). Alternate Possibilities and Moral Responsibility. *The Journal of Philosophy*, 66, 829-839.

------ (1971). Freedom the Will and the Concept of a Person. *The Journal of Philosophy*, 68, 5-20.

------ (1975). Three Concepts of Free Action. *Proceedings of the Aristotelian Society*, 51, 95-125.

Freddoso, A. J. (1983). Accidental Necessity and Logical Determinism. *The Journal of Philosophy*, 80, 257-278.

------ (1988). *Luis de Molina On Divine Foreknowledge (Part IV of the Concordia)*. Ithaca, Cornell University Press.

------ (1998). 'Molina' and 'Molinism'. In Craig, E. (ed.) (1998), *Routledge Encyclopedia of Philosophy*. London, Routledge, 461-467.

Gale, R. M. (1991). *On the Nature and Existence of God*. Cambridge, Cambridge University Press.

Gaskin, R. (1993). Conditionals of Freedom and Middle Knowledge. *The Philosophical Quarterly*, 43, 412-430.

------ (1994a). Fatalism, Foreknowledge, and the Reality of the Future. *Modern Schoolman*, 71, 83-113.

------ (1994b). Molina on Divine Foreknowledge and the Principle of Bivalence. *American Philosophical Quarterly*, 32, 551-571.

------ (1998). Fatalism, Bivalence and the Past. *The Philosophical Quarterly*. 48, 83-88

Geach, P. T. (1977). *Providence and Evil*. Cambridege, Cambridge University Press.

Geiger, J. R. (1925). Concerning the 'Good Man' and the Moral Standard. *The Journal of Philosophy*, 22, 634-637.

Gibbard, A. (1985). Moral Judgment and the Acceptance of Norms. *Ethics*, 96, 5-21.

Glannon, W. (1995). Responsibility and the Principle of Possible Action. *The Journal of Philosophy*, 92, 261-274.

Goldman, A. I (1986). *Epistemology and Cognition*. Cambridge, Harvard University Press.

Greenspan, P. (1978). Behaviour Control and Freedom of Action. *Philosophical Review*, 87, 225-240.

Haack, S. (1974). On a Theological Argument for Fatalism. *Philosophical Quarterly*, 24, 156-159.

------ (1975). On "On Theological Fatalism Again" Again. *Philosophical Quarterly*, 25, 159-161.

Haji, I. (2003). Flickers of Freedom, Obligation and Responsibility. *American*

Philosophical Quarterly, 40, 287-302.

Hasker, W. (1985). Foreknowledge and Necessity. *Faith and Philosophy*, 2, 121-157.

------ (1986). A Refutation of Middle Knowledge. *Noûs*, 20, 545-557.

------ (1987). *The Hardness of the Past: A Reply to Reichenbach.* Faith and Philosophy, 4, 337-342.

------ (1988). Hard Facts and Theological Fatalism. *Noûs*, 22, 419-436.

------ (1989). *God, Time and Knowledge.* Ithaca, Cornell University Press.

Helm, P. (1974). On Theological Fatalism Again. *The Philosophical Quarterly*, 24, 360-362.

------ (1975). Fatalism Once More. *The Philosophical Quarterly*, 25, 355-356.

------ (1988). *Eternal God.* New York: Oxford University Press.

------ (2000). A Different Defence of Divine Eternity. In Davies, B. (ed.) (2000). *Philosophy of Religion A Guide and Anthology.* New York, Oxford University Press.

Hick, J. (1960). God As Necessary Being. *The Journal of Philosophy*, 57, 725-734.

Hochberg, H. (1992). Truth Makers, Truth Predicates and Truth Types. In Mulligan, K. (ed.) (1992). *Language, Truth and Ontology.* Dordrecht, Kluwer Academic Publications, 87-117.

Hoffman, J (1979). Pike on Possible Worlds, Divine Foreknowledge, and Human Freedom. *The Philosophical Review*, 88, 433-442.

Hoffman, J. and Rosenkrantz, G (1980). What An Omnipotent Agent Can Do. *International Journal for Philosophy of Religion*, 11, 1-19.

------ (1984). Hard and Soft Facts. *The Philosophical Review*, 93, 419-434.

------ (1999). Omnipotence. In Quinn, P. and Taliaferro, C. (eds.) (1999). *A Companion to Philosophy of Religion.* Oxford, Blackwell.

Honderich, T. (1996). Compatibilism, Incompatibilism, and the Smart Aleck. *Philosophy and Phenomenological Research*, 56, 855-862.

Hughes, C. T. (1997). Belief, Foreknowledge, and Theological Fatalism. *Faith and Philosophy*, 14, 378-387.

Hume, D. ([1739] 2000). *A Treatise on Human Nature* (ed. Fate N. D.). Oxford, Oxford University Press.

Hunt, D. (1998). What Is the Problem of Theological Fatalism? *International Philosophical Quarterly*, 38, 17-30.

Jack, H. (1965). A Recent Attempt to Prove God's Existence. *Mind*, 25, 575-579.

Kane, R. (1989). Two Kinds of Incompatibilism. *Philosophy and Phenomenological Research*, 50, 219-254.

------ (1998). *The Significance of Free Will*. New York, Oxford University Press.

Kenny, A. (1968). Intention and Purpose in Law. In Summers, R. S. (ed.) (1968). *Essays in Legal Philosophy*. Oxford, Basil Blackwell.

------ (1979). *The God of the Philosophers*. Oxford, Clarendon Press.

Koivisto, W. A. (1955). Moral Judgments and Value Conflict. *Philosophy of Science*, 22, 54-57.

Kordig, C. R. (1981). A Deontic Argument for God's Existence. *Noûs*, 15, 176-183.

Kretzmann, N. (1966). Omniscience and Immutability. *The Journal of Philosophy*, 63, 409-421.

Kvanvig, J. L. (1986). *The Possibility of an All-Knowing God*. New York, St. Martin's Press.

------ (2002). On Behalf of Maverick Molinism. *Faith and Philosophy*, 19, 348-357.

Lamb, J. W. (1977). On a Proof of Incompatibilism. *The Philosophical Review*, 86, 20-35.

Leftow, B. (1991a). *Time and Eternity*. Ithaca, Cornell University Press.

------ (1999). Eternity. In Quinn, P. and Taliaferro, C. (eds.) (1999). *A Companion to Philosophy of Religion*. Oxford, Blackwell.

Lewis, D. (1973). *Counterfactuals*. Cambridge, Harvard University Press.

------ (1979). Counterfactuals and Time's Arrow. *Noûs*, 13, 455-476.

------ (1986). *Philosophical Papers, Vol. 2*. New York, Oxford University Press.

Lopez de Sa, D. and Zardini, E. (2006). Does This Sentence Have No Truth-Maker? *Analysis*, 66, 154-157.

MacDonald, Scott (ed.) (1991). *Being and Goodness*. Ithaca, Cornell University Press.

MacKay, A. N. (1982). The Incredibility of Rejecting Belief-Desire-Actions Explanations. *PSA*, 2, 117-126.

Mackie, J. L. (1982). *The Miracle of Theism: Arguments for and against the existence of God*. Oxford, Clarendon Press.

Mannheim, K. (1946). *Ideology and Utopia*. New York, Harcourt Brace.

Martin, C. B. (1964). *Religious Belief?* Ithaca, Cornell University Press.

McArthur, R. P. (1977). Timelessness and Theological Fatalism. *Logique et Analyse*, 20, 475-490.

McLean, F. and Aspell, P. (1997). *Ancient Western Philosophy: The Hellenic Emergence*. USA, Council for Research in Values and Philosophy.

McKenna, M. (2001). Source Incompatibilism, Ultimacy, and the Transfer of Non-Responsibility. *American Philosophical Quarterly*, 38, 37-51.

Mele, A. R. (1990). Irresistible Desires. *Noûs*, 4, 455-472.

Miller, A. R. (1982). Intention and Practical Reasoning. *Mind*, 91, 106-108.

Milne, P. (2005). Not Every Truth Has A Truthmaker. *Analysis*, 65, 221-224.

Morris, T. V. (1984). Properties, Modalities and God. *Philosophical Review*, 93, 35-56.

------ (1987c). Perfect Being Theology. *Noûs*, 21, 19-30.

Morris, T. V. (ed.) (1987). *The Concept of God*. New York, Oxford University Press.

Morris, T. V. (2000). A Modern Discussion of Divine Omnipotence. In Davies, B. (ed.) (2000). *Philosophy of Religion A Guide and Anthology*. New York, Oxford University Press.

Morris, T. V. and Menzel, C. (1987). Absolute Creation. In Morris, T. V. (ed.) (1987). *Anselmian Explorations*. Notre Dame, Notre Dame.

Mulligan, S., Simons, P. and Smith, B. (1984). Truth Makers. *Philosophy and Phenomenological Research*, 44, 287-321.

Murphy, M. C. (1999). The Simple Desire-Fulfillment Theory. *Noûs*, 33, 247-272.

Myrdal, G. (1944). *The American Dilemma*. New York, Harper & Sons.

Nagel, T. (1979). *Mortal Questions*. London, Cambridge University Press.

Nathan, N. M. L. (1984). A New Incompatibilism. *Mind*, 93, 39-55.

Neely, W. (1974). Freedom and Desire. *The Philosophical Review*, 83, 32-54.

Nolt, J. E (1986). 'What are Possible Worlds?'. *Mind*, 95, 432-445.

O' Connor, T. (1992). The Impossibility of Middle Knowledge. *Philosophical Studies*, 66, 139-166.

Ockham, W. ([1321-1324] 1969). *Predestination, God's Foreknowledge and Future Contingents* (trans. Adams, M and Kretzmann, N). New York, Appleton-Century-Crofts.

Otsuka, M. (1998). Incompatibilism and the Avoidability of Blame. *Ethics*, 108, 685-701.

Padgett, A. G. (1992). *God, Eternity and the Nature of Time*. New York, St. Martin's Press.

Parfitt, D. (1984). *Reasons and Persons*. New York, Oxford University Press.

Penelhum, T. (1960). Divine Necessity. *Mind*, 69, 175-186.

Perry, J. (1993). *Problem of the Essential Indexical and Other Essays*. New York, Oxford University Press.

Perszyk, K. J. (2000). Molinism and Compatibilism. *International Journal for Philosophy of Religion*, 48, 11-33.

Pettit, P. and Smith, M. (1996). Freedom in Belief and Desire. *The Journal of Philosophy*, 93, 429-499.

Pike, N. (1965). Divine Omniscience and Voluntary Action. *Philosophical Review*, 74, 27-46.

------ (1966). Of God and Freedom: A Rejoinder. *Philosophical Review*, 75, 369-379.

----- (1969). Omnipotence and God's Ability to Sin. *American Philosophical Quarterly*, 6, 208-216.

------ (1970). *God and Timelessness*. New York, Schocken Books.

------ (1977). Divine Foreknowledge, Human Freedom and Possible Worlds. *Philosophical Review*, 86, 209-216.

------ (1984). Fischer on Freedom and Foreknowledge. *Philosophical Review*, 93, 599-614.

------ (1993). A Latter-Day Look at the Foreknowledge Problem. *Philosophy of Religion*, 33, 129-164.

Plantinga, A. (1973). God and Possible Worlds. *The Journal of Philosophy*, 70, 339-352.

------ (1974a). *God, Freedom and Evil*. New York, Harper & Row.

------ (1974b). *The Nature of Necessity*. Oxford, Clarendon Press.

------ (1980). *Does God Have a Nature?* Milwaukee, Marquette University Press.

------ (1985). Reply to Adams. In Tomberlin, J. and van Inwagen, P. (eds). *Alvin Plantinga: Profiles (Vol. 5)*. Dordrecht, Reidel, 371-382.

------ (1987). On Ockham's Way Out. In Morris, T. V. (ed.) (1987). *The Concept of God*. New York, Oxford University Press.

Platts, M. (1986). Desire and Action. *Noûs*, 20, 143-155.

Pohle J. (1911). 'Molina' and 'Molinism'. In *The Catholic* Encyclopedia. New York, Robert Appleton Company, pp. 436-441.

Price, H. (1989). Defending Desire-As-Belief. *Mind*, 98, 119-127.

Priest, G. (1983). The Logical Paradoxes and the Law of Excluded Middle. *The Philosophical Quarterly*, 33, 160-165.

Prior, A. N. (1962a). Possible Worlds. *The Philosophical Quarterly*, 12, 36-43.

------ (1962b). The Formalities of Omniscience. *Philosophy*, 37, 114-129.

Putnam, H (1975). The Meaning of 'Meaning'. In Putnam, H (ed.) (1975). *Mind, Language and Reality*, London, Cambridge University Press.

Quinn, P. and Taliaferro, C. (eds.) (1997). *A Companion to Philosophy of Religion*. Oxford, Blackwell.

Railton, P. (1986). Facts and Values. *Philosophical Topics*, 14, 5-31.

Rainer, A. C. A. (1949). Necessity and God: A Reply to Prof. Findlay. *Mind*, 58, 75-77.

Reichenbach, B. (1987). Hasker on Omniscience. *Faith and Philosophy*, 4, 86-92.

------ (1988). Fatalism and Freedom. *International Philosophical Quarterly*, 28, 271-285.

Reid, T. ([1785] 1941). *Essays on the Intellectual Powers of Man* (ed. Woozley A. D). London, Macmillan.

Rescher, N. (1999). How Many Possible Worlds Are There? *Philosophy and Phenomenological Research*, 59, 403-420.

Robinson, M. D. (2004a). Divine Guidance and an Accidentally Necessary Future: A Response to Hunt. *Religious Studies*, 40, 493-498.

Rodriguez-Pereyra, G. (2005). Why Truthmakers. In Beebee, H and Dodd, J (eds) (2005). *Truthmakers: The Contemporary Debate*. Oxford, Oxford University Press,17-31.

Rowe, W. (1991). Responsibility, Agent Causation, and Freedom. *Ethics*, 101, 237-257.

Sarot, M. (1992). *God, Possibility and Corporeality*. Netherlands, Kok Pharos.

Saunders, J. T. (1966). Of God and Freedom. *Philosophical Review*, 75, 219-225.

Saurez, F. ([1620] 1963). *De Divina Gratia*. In Berton, C. (ed.). *Opera Omnia, vols 7-11*. Brussells: Culture et Civilisation.

Schiffer, S. (1976). A Paradox of Desire. *American Philosophical Quarterly*, 13, 195-203.

Schueler, G. F. (1995). *Desire: It's Role in Practical Reason and the Explanation of Action*. Masachusetts, MIT Press.

Sharp, F. C. (1921). Is There a Universally Valid Moral Standard? *International Journal of Ethics*, 32, 72-99.

Simons, P. (1992). Logical Atomism and Its Ontological Refinement: A Defense. In Mulligan, K. (ed.) (1992). *Language, Truth and Ontology*. Dordrecht, Kluwer Academic Publications.

------ (1998). *How the World Can Make Propositions True: A Celebration of Logical Atomism*. In Omyla, M (ed.) (1998). *Sklonnosci Metafizyczna*. Warsaw, Uniwersytet Warszawski, 113-135.

Song, I. (2002). *Divine Foreknowledge and Necessity*. New York, University Press of America.

Speak, D. (2002). Fanning the Flickers of Freedom. *American Philosophical Quarterly*, 39, 91-105.

Stalnaker, R. C. (1976). Possible Worlds. *Noûs*, 10, 65-75.

Stampe, D. W (1987). The Authority of Desire. *The Philosophical Review*, 96, 335-381.

Stillwell, S (1985). Confirmation, Paradoxes, and Possible Worlds. *The British Journal for the Philosophy of Science*, 36, 19-52.

Strawson, P. (1982). Freedom and Resentment. In Watson, G (ed.) (1982). *Free Will*. Oxford, Oxford University Press.

Stump, E. and Kretzmann, N. (1981). Eternity. *The Journal of Philosophy*, 78, 429-458.

------ (1992). Eternity, Awareness and Action. *Faith and Philosophy*, 9, 463-482.

(2000). A Modern Defence of Divine Eternity. In Davies, B. (ed.) (2000). *Philosophy of Religion A Guide and Anthology*. New York, Oxford University Press.

Swinburne, R. (1993). *The Coherence of Theism* (revised ed.). Oxford, Clarendon Press.

Talbott, T. (1993). Theological Fatalism and Modal Confusion. *International Journal for Philosophy of Religion*, 33, 65-88.

Taylor, R. (1962). Fatalism. *The Philosophical Review*, 71, 6-66.

------ (1963). A Note on Fatalism. *The Philosophical Review*, 72, 497-499.

Van Inwagen, P. (1978). Ability and Responsibility. *The Philosophical Review*, 87, 201-225.

------ (1983). *An Essay on Free Will*. Oxford, Clarendon Press.

------ (1997). Against Middle Knowledge. In French, P. A. et al (eds) (1997). *Midwest Studies in Philosophy, Volume 21*. Notre Dame, University of Notre Dame Press.

Watson, G. (1982a). 'Free Agency'. In Watson, G (ed.) (1982). *Free Will*. Oxford, Oxford University Press.

Watson, G. (ed.) (1982b). *Free Will*. Oxford, Oxford University Press.

White, D. A. (2000). Divine Immutability, Properties and Time. *Sophia*, 39, 70-78.

Whitehead, A. N. (1978). *Process and Reality, An Essay in Cosmology*. New York, The Free Press.

Wienandy, T. (1984). *Does God Change?* Still River, MA, St. Bedes Publications.

Wierenga, E. R. (1989). *The Nature of God*. Ithaca, Cornell University Press.

Wolterstorff, N. (1982). God Everlasting. In Cahn, S. M. and Shatz, D. (1982). *Contemporary Philosophy of Religion*. New York, Oxford University Press.

Wyma, K. (2001), Christian Scholarship ...for What? http://64.2333.183.104/search?q=cache:8jJKrsOeuakJ:www.calvin.edu/academic/philosophy/virtual_library/articles/wyma_keith_d/divine_modeling_counterfactuals_of_freedom_and_the_grounding_objection.pdf+freddoso+counterfactuals&hl=en&gl=uk&ct=clnk&cd=2

Yates, J. (1990). *The Timelessness of God*. Lanham, University Press of America.

, L. T. (1991). *The Dilemma of Freedom and Foreknowledge*. New York,

Oxford University Press.

Zemach, E. M., and Widerker, D. (1987). Facts, Freedom and Foreknowledge. *Religious Studies*, 23, 19-28.

Zimmerman, M. J. (1988). *An Essay on Moral Responsibility*. New Jersey, Rowman & Little.

Index

A

Accidental Necessity 13, 80, 84, 172
Adam 4, 6, 56
Adamic 4, 6, 56
Adams 5
Agency 11, 12, 1, 9, 16, 22, 35, 157, 179
Alston 84, 169
Alternative Possibilities 12, 38
Anscombe 23, 169
Aquinas 3, 4, 23, 62, 65, 79, 169, 181
Aristotle 2, 169, 181
Atemporal 1, 105, 126, 135, 136, 137, 143, 155, 161, 167
Augustine 3, 4, 59, 169, 181

B

Baker 12, 13, 170, 181
Benefit 11, 22, 24
Bivalence 172
Blameworthy 2, 3, 55, 57
Boethius 59, 60, 170
Bradley 18, 170
Broome 20, 170
Brute Facts 1, 149, 158

C

Casteneda 170
Causal responsibility 11
Compatibilism 36, 46, 94, 122, 162
Compatibilist 1, 39, 43, 48, 50, 51, 97, 108, 123, 124, 133, 137, 161, 162, 165, 166
Contingent 4, 5, 6, 7, 79, 80, 81, 82, 84, 85, 87, 88, 89, 92, 96, 97, 104, 105, 111, 114, 124, 127, 128, 129, 130, 131, 133, 134, 138, 140, 142, 149, 150, 153, 154, 160, 165
Control 12, 35, 36, 37, 38, 39, 41, 43, 44, 45, 48, 49, 51, 52, 53, 54, 55, 56, 57, 58, 61, 62, 67, 71, 72, 73, 75, 76, 80, 81, 82, 84, 85, 88, 92, 98, 112, 114, 124, 126, 127, 128, 130, 131, 136, 137, 138, 139, 141, 143, 146, 148, 153, 155, 157, 160, 161, 164, 171, 172, 181, 182, 184
Control Condition 12, 35, 36, 37, 51, 52, 57
Counterfactual 14, 1, 109, 116, 130, 139

Counterfactual Fixity 14, 116
Counterfactual Power 14, 1, 109, 139
Counterfactuals 1, 117, 149, 150, 151, 171, 174
Craig 60, 65, 106, 148, 170, 172
Creaturely Essences 1, 158

D

Davidson 22, 23, 170, 182
Dennett 38, 39, 170
Desire 11, 16, 17, 18, 22, 24, 29, 41, 170, 174, 175, 176, 177, 178, 182, 183
Determinism 3, 36, 39, 40, 42, 43, 48, 50, 55, 61

E

Edgington 151, 152, 171
Effective desire 17, 23, 128
Essential Indexical 11, 10, 176, 182
Eternity 170, 173, 174, 176, 178, 179
Evaluation 11, 22, 27, 29

F

Fallible 5
Fatalism; fatalist 2, 3, 7, 60, 76, 114, 124, 165
First-order desire 18, 19, 20, 21, 23, 25, 26, 27, 28, 31
First-person entity 12
First person phenomena 12
Fischer 14, 35, 36, 38, 45, 51, 52, 53, 71, 72, 73, 75, 89, 94, 95, 96, 97, 98, 99, 100, 101, 102, 116, 122, 123, 165, 166, 171, 176
Flint 1, 64, 127, 130, 131, 132, 134, 136, 139, 140, 147, 151, 152, 153, 160, 171
Foreknowledge 1, 3, 1, 2, 3, 4, 5, 6, 7, 58, 59, 61, 62, 64, 65, 67, 69, 71, 73, 75, 76, 77, 78, 79, 80, 82, 83, 84, 92, 93, 94, 95, 96, 102, 105, 113, 114, 115, 116, 121, 122, 123, 124, 125, 126, 134, 136, 137, 144, 145, 162, 163, 164, 165, 166, 167
Forking Paths 37, 44
Four Moments 14, 126
Frankfurt 12, 17, 18, 35, 39, 40, 44, 45, 47, 48, 49, 50, 51, 53, 54, 56, 171, 182
Frankfurt 12, 17, 18, 35, 39, 40, 44, 45, 47, 48, 49, 50, 51, 53, 54, 56, 171
Freddoso 64, 81, 94, 125, 127, 134, 150, 153, 154, 171, 172
Free Knowledge 1, 6, 133, 134, 135, 136, 148

G

Gaskin 60, 127, 128, 133, 139, 172
Glannon 36, 49, 52, 172
Grounding Objection 1, 146

H

Hard Facts 13, 14, 5, 85, 86, 89, 92, 93, 98, 100, 169, 171, 173
Hard-Type Soft Facts 14, 98, 100, 171
Hasker 14, 60, 102, 103, 104, 105, 106, 107, 108, 122, 123, 147, 148, 150, 160, 166, 170, 173, 177
Helm 60, 65, 173
Hick 65, 173
Hoffman 14, 64, 86, 89, 90, 91, 92, 93, 94, 95, 98, 102, 103, 104, 110, 122, 165, 173
Hume 25, 26, 173

I

Incompatibilism 173, 174, 175, 176
Incompatibilist 1, 2, 7, 35, 36, 37, 38, 39, 43, 51, 52, 68, 75, 77, 78, 82, 85, 93, 94, 96, 97, 100, 102, 109, 112, 114, 119, 122, 123, 161
Infallible 1, 2, 3, 4, 7, 59, 64, 67, 69, 70, 71, 76, 77, 106, 121, 124, 125, 127, 165
Intuition 14, 93
Irresistible Desire 41
Irresistible Threat Contexts 12, 50

J

Judgement 14, 20, 22, 24, 27, 31, 32, 54, 59, 104, 151

K

Kane 36, 50, 174
Kenny 22, 64, 174, 183
Kretzmann 65, 66, 174, 176, 178

L

Law of Conditional Excluded Middle 1, 144
Lewis 14, 1, 109, 116, 117, 118, 119, 120, 123, 124, 145, 151, 152, 156, 171, 174
Libertarian 44, 46, 59, 61, 65, 94, 116, 119, 123, 125, 126, 130, 136, 138, 139, 145, 146, 152, 155, 157

M

MacKay 20
Middle Knowledge 14, 7, 128, 129, 130, 131, 135, 138, 140, 146, 155, 158, 160, 166, 169, 172, 173, 176, 179
Miller 22, 175
Molina 6, 7, 127, 158, 169, 172, 177
Molinism 14, 1, 2, 125, 126, 132, 135, 137, 139, 140, 144, 145, 147, 156, 161, 162, 167, 172, 174, 176, 177

Molinist 100
Moral Categories 2, 9
Morally Reactive Attitudes 2, 39
Morally Responsible Agency 1, 6, 9, 13, 14, 15, 16, 22, 24, 29, 32, 33, 35, 38, 42, 47, 48, 54, 57, 58, 60, 61, 62, 65, 66, 76, 77, 112, 124, 126, 128, 131, 137, 139, 140, 141, 142, 143, 146, 161, 162, 163, 164, 166, 167
Moral Responsibility 1, 1, 2, 3, 4, 5, 7, 9, 10, 11, 12, 13, 15, 16, 18, 21, 22, 28, 29, 31, 32, 33, 35, 36, 37, 38, 39, 41, 42, 43, 44, 45, 46, 47, 48, 50, 51, 52, 57, 58, 59, 60, 75, 128, 137, 139, 141, 142, 143, 144, 163, 164, 165, 166
Moral Standard 172, 178
Motivation 3, 22, 30

N

Nagel 14, 175, 183
Natural Knowledge 14, 127, 128, 129, 131, 135, 155
Necessity 13, 78, 80, 84, 169, 172, 173, 176, 177, 178, 181, 183

O

Ockhamism 13, 2, 62, 77, 102, 109, 119, 122, 123, 125, 127, 137, 161, 165, 166, 171; Ockhamist 13, 1, 5, 6, 63, 67, 76, 77, 78, 80, 83, 85, 88, 92, 93, 94, 95, 97, 99, 102, 108, 109, 110, 111, 112, 113, 116, 119, 120, 121, 122, 123, 124, 126, 127, 136, 165, 166
O' Connor 146, 153, 154, 176
Omnipotence 170, 173, 175, 176
Omniscience 5, 67, 170, 174, 176, 177
Ownership 11, 16, 17

P

Parfitt 23, 176
Penelhum 65, 176
Perry 10, 11, 13, 176, 184
Pike 13, 5, 63, 65, 66, 67, 68, 69, 70, 71, 72, 73, 74, 75, 77, 78, 80, 82, 83, 84, 85, 86, 121, 122, 127, 135, 164, 165, 173, 176
Plantinga 63, 64, 81, 82, 83, 84, 85, 98, 107, 133, 138, 139, 153, 169, 176, 177
Platts 18, 21, 177
Possible Worlds 1, 137, 170, 173, 175, 176, 177, 178, 184
Power to do Otherwise 13, 59, 67
praiseworthy 2, 54, 57
Principle of Moral Responsibility 12, 37, 38
Principle of Possible Action 12, 52, 172
Principle of Responsibility 12, 39, 57
providence 6, 59, 67, 125, 126, 128, 142, 171, 172
Putnam 97, 177

Q

Quinn 170, 173, 174, 177

R

Railton 19, 177
Ravizza 35, 36, 38, 45, 51, 52, 53, 171
Regulative Control 12, 35, 36, 37, 38, 39, 43, 44, 45, 48, 49, 51, 52, 53, 54, 55, 56, 57, 58, 61, 62, 67, 71, 72, 73, 75, 76, 80, 81, 82, 84, 85, 88, 92, 98, 112, 114, 124, 126, 127, 128, 130, 131, 136, 137, 138, 139, 141, 143, 146, 153, 155, 157, 160, 161, 164
Rosenkrantz 14, 64, 86, 89, 90, 91, 92, 93, 94, 95, 98, 102, 103, 104, 110, 122, 165, 173

S

Saunders 5, 84, 85, 86, 96, 120, 121, 178, 184
Schiffer 18, 178
Soft Facts 13, 14, 85, 92, 93, 98, 100, 171, 173
Stampe 18, 19, 178
Stoics 3
Strawson 11, 178, 184
Stump 65, 66, 178
Subjunctives 1, 157
Swinburne 64, 65, 66, 71, 179

T

Theological fatalism 3, 4, 60, 61, 69, 75, 76, 102, 105, 115, 119, 124, 166
Thomas 4, 6, 56
Truth-Makers 1, 149

V

Vagueness 171
Value 11, 24, 174
van Inwagen 35, 52, 53, 144, 169, 177

W

Watson 24, 25, 26, 27, 28, 178, 179

Z

Zagzebski 14, 94, 95, 109, 116, 118, 119, 120, 121, 179

www.ingramcontent.com/pod-product-compliance
Lightning Source LLC
Chambersburg PA
CBHW060953230426
43665CB00015B/2185